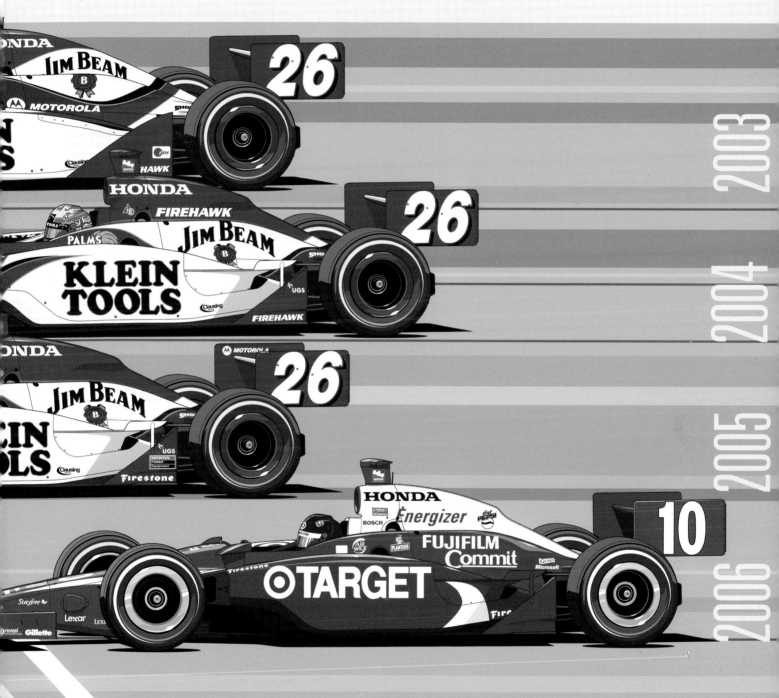

2003

2004

2005

2006

ILLUSTRATION: PAUL LAGUETTE

2005

WINNER:
IndyCar Championship

WINNER:
89th Indianapolis 500
Andretti-Green Racing
Average speed: 157.6mph

"It was such a proud moment for me, the proudest of my life"

HONDA

2011

WINNER:
95th Indianapolis 500
Bryan Herta Autosport
Average speed: 170.2mph

"This win is for my family and my mother back home. It has been an incredible day"

HONDA

This is a Lionheart Books LLC publication

This edition published in 2016

Lionheart Books LLC

9600 Koger Blvd

Suite 105

St. Petersburg

FL 33702

United States

info@lionheartbook.com

Photographs © as credited throughout

Text © Lionheart Books, LLC

Produced by ANH, UK on behalf of Lionheart Books, LLC

A catalogue record for this book is available from the British Library

ISBN 978-0-9926421-9-8

Print and production managed by KEP Print Ltd, UK

+44 (0) 1827 280880

LIONHEART
REMEMBERING DAN WHELDON

by Andy Hallbery & Jeff Olson

The family Wheldon and the famous Borg Warner Trophy. Susie carrying Oliver and Dan holding Sebastian

Welcome

Putting this book together has shown just how much love there is for Dan, and what he meant to so many people throughout his life. I've heard stories from people who knew, or worked with Dan when he was just starting out as a kid in karting, and I know there are some stories in here that his family in the UK may not have known.

I want to thank everyone we contacted, not just for their contributions to the book, but for the way it has helped in building Dan's legacy. One of the key things when we started this project was not just to honor and continue Dan's memory, but for our children, Sebastian and Oliver, to have something that shows what people thought about their father. For them to learn about him when he was younger and to see how much respect there was for him throughout his career.

Since Dan's passing I have been touched by the response from fans worldwide, and I know his family has too. Seeing people at races still proudly wearing Dan T-shirts and hats, or coming up to tell me Dan was their favorite, or about the first time they met him – it's obvious he touched a great many people's lives, and still does.

Part of the proceeds of this book will go to benefit the Alzheimer's Association, a cause Dan was excited to be part of and was looking forward to working with. Additionally, I founded The Dan Wheldon Foundation in 2014 to serve as a means to carry on his charitable work and continue giving back. Thank you for your support in carrying on this part of his legacy.

Susie, Sebastian and Oliver Wheldon

St. Petersburg, Fla., May 2016

LIONHEART
Remembering Dan Wheldon

by Andy Hallbery & Jeff Olson

"Dan always gave his best and never gave up;
no matter what, he found a way to win" Clive Wheldon

LIONHEART Remembering Dan Wheldon

DURING THE COURSE of piecing together Dan's life for a book – assembling the images, voices and stories that surrounded and followed him – this sentiment recurred often:

Dan would love to know a book is being written about him.

In my mind, another sentiment often followed: And he would want it to be perfect.

With that in mind, Andy Hallbery and I set off on a journey to gather family, friends and competitors for their stories and images about a man whose unusual story and remarkable accomplishments touched so many lives. The project was important to us; we both knew and worked with Dan for years, so we understood the gravity of getting this absolutely right.

This is *Lionheart – Remembering Dan Wheldon*. We hope we got it right.

After discussing it at length, we decided on the format you're holding – a large, high-quality, hardcover photo book. We felt that Dan's story should be told by those who knew him best: family, friends, fellow racers, journalists who covered his career, and people who knew him beyond the walls and fences of racetracks. We also decided that his persona – Lionheart – must be part of the title and the central theme of the book.

Another key element of the project, we felt, was that it be a charitable enterprise. With that in mind, a portion of the proceeds beyond production costs go to two entities close to

Dan – Alzheimer's Association and the Dan Wheldon Foundation. Dan's mother, Sue, died of Alzheimer's in 2014, and Dan had been committed to the association ever since learning of her diagnosis. The Foundation was founded to carry on Dan's charitable work and continue giving back.

A further goal for us was to create a legacy in print for Dan's sons, Sebastian and Oliver, to learn more about their father and the respect he had earned and the regard in which he was held. Fitting, then, that the beneficiaries of the telling of Dan's life story entail the full cycle – beginning and end; past, present and future.

Four people were critical to the book's development in the early days. First, Holly Wheldon, Dan's sister, listened to the plan, immediately took a liking to it, and helped immensely in moving it forward. We decided early that the project belonged to Holly and Susie, Dan's wife, so we wanted them to have full access and final approval on the content and subjects.

Second, the project couldn't have been completed without Susie's blessing and invaluable contributions. Andy and I met with Susie at the Dan Wheldon Memorial ProAm Karting Challenge in September 2015 at New Castle, Ind., and her enthusiasm for and devotion to the book kept us going throughout.

Third, T.E. McHale, the motorsports manager of American Honda, listened to our pitch and decided in the early days – as Andy and I were trying to decide which companies/sponsors in racing

Authors Andy Hallbery and Jeff Olson had tremendous support for the book, not least from Tony Kanaan, Scott Dixon, Dario Franchitti and Bryan Herta

would be willing to help us fund the project – that Honda would be the sole backer. After all, Dan was a Honda guy throughout, so it made sense that Honda would help tell his life story.

Fourth, Dario Franchitti was instrumental in the formation of the book. He was there – as were T.E., Holly and others – at the first meeting in the Honda motor coach at St. Petersburg, Fla., in March 2015, when the foundation of the book was built. He was also there when young Daniel was tearing up the kart tracks in England and a firm friend throughout his life. Dario has been supportive and encouraging throughout, as have his former teammates and Dan's close racing friends, Scott Dixon, Tony Kanaan and Bryan Herta.

We owe gratitude to so many other people who helped piece the book together, as well. The brilliant images you'll see in the pages that follow – some of the best work from the finest motorsports photographers in the world – were donated. Likewise, all of the subjects in the book donated their time to create their chapters.

Special thanks also go to Johanna Husband and Dyanne Gilliam, who helped sort, edit and proofread the words you'll read, and Steve Moore, whose designs jump off the pages.

Dan's career covered the spectrum. He began in karts, racing at tracks near his home in Emberton, England, against a future Formula 1 World Champion, Jenson Button; a sports car world champion, Anthony Davidson; and even fellow IndyCar winner, Justin Wilson. He worked his way through the national single-seater system and was always a winner and contender.

From there, he landed in the United States, carefully working up to a two-race IndyCar audition in 2002 with Panther Racing that led to a full-time ride with Michael Andretti's team. Dan won the Indianapolis 500 in 2005, followed it with the IndyCar Series championship that year, and won 14 other IndyCar races before he found himself in the unlikely position of unemployment in 2011.

At that point, he embarked on the most impressive and unlikely chapter of his career. In a one-off effort with a team that combined the efforts of Herta and Sam Schmidt, Dan claimed his second Indy 500 victory in 2011. It was, as Herta explains, Dan's finest moment as a professional racer.

This book is the story of a unique soul and the effect he had on others. Gifted with a natural ability to drive a racecar, Dan worked relentlessly to make himself better. At the same time, he made the people around him feel important. If you knew Dan, you understood this. If you didn't know Dan, he would have wanted you to feel as important as those who already did.

The heart of a lion is loyal, reliable, strong and trustworthy. The heart of a lion never stops beating. It is with us now, and always.

Jeff Olson, May 2016

Part #1 MY SHINING SON

Young Daniel's dad took his boy's natural ability, added dedication, and made a winner

by CLIVE WHELDON

■ KART RACER, SUCCESSFUL BUSINESSMAN

DAN CONNECTION
Father, mentor

Daniel always wanted to have a go when I was racing, and I remember Reg Deavin suggesting we make a 60cc kart for him to drive during the intervals. He was only four or five, and that's what we did. It didn't take long before that wasn't quick enough, so Reg made another one with a 100cc engine on it and that's how he started his karting career.

People used to watch him during the lunch break. Bruno Ferrari of All Kart asked if he could sponsor Daniel. Bruno was well known in karting, and Reg's company, Deavinson, was a bit upset because they also wanted to do it – and they'd made him the kart. All Kart was a good kart in Italy and that's where the Cadet class

was basically formed, and Bruno was a lovely guy. It was an ideal solution to race with them and I knew Bruno was enthusiastic in making sure we always had the best engines and so on.

Then I had a big accident at Kimbolton and I had my leg in plaster up in the air for weeks. I decided it was time to hang up my helmet, and rather than trying to run two people I concentrated on Dan. I got more fun out of it to be honest. I was everything, the trucker, chef, and mechanic...

That's when it really started getting serious. I had this trailer. It was all kitted out with lights and everything inside; tire racks, engine racks, and an awning that went right around.

We had a thorough routine, too. Monday night was cleaning the motor home out from the weekend before. Dan would do all of the cupboards and give it a general clean. Tuesday was our night off. Wednesday we used to go to Simon Wright Karts or down to Bruno's, and make sure the engines were all right, pick up any tires or anything else we needed. Thursday night we put everything back in the motor home ready for the weekend. Friday we were off racing

The first kart (far left) set the tone for trophies, hard work and preparation in the awning with Bruno Ferrari, and headlines in the local newspaper

Dan's desperate to win!

● KART-KRAZY: Daniel Wheldon is All-England Junior Champion.
Two weeks ago

THE WHELDON COLLECTION

again. That was a normal week and weekend – every weekend.

We were lucky with Dan's school, Bedford School for boys. It is quite strict and one of the best, but from day one the headmaster supported him. There were Saturday morning lessons, so if we were racing locally, I would go with the motor home, get everything ready, and then borrow a car to pick him up from school.

He'd miss the first couple of practices but would get there for the afternoon. If we were racing farther away, the school would make sure they gave him extra homework on a Friday night, so while we were traveling down the motorway he would do that. The school is very sporty so also got involved. We'd take the kart and do little things around the playground and they would do write-ups. They were proud of his achievements.

In the kart, he learned quickly. Before he could race we used to do all our testing at Rye House. I had a marker cone at the track for his braking point. As he went around he wouldn't see me but I'd move it forward a small bit each lap until he realized there was no way he was going to get around the corner! He would end up spinning until he confronted me one day and asked, "What's happening Dad?" and I told him...

It's true that I was very hard with Dan. One time I had him up against the motor home. He had been unbeaten for two years in Cadet racing – a record no one has broken. At Rye House one day

we had a big lead, then all of a sudden he was slowing and I thought the engine was going off. Tom Sisley went past him and suddenly Dan was right behind him to the finish. I asked what had happened. He said "Oh, Dad, I let him win." That's when I strung him up against the side. I said, "Do you think I put all this effort in for you to come to a track and let someone win because he hasn't won before?" He never did that again.

The Cadet racing was the best. In those days you had 20-30 drivers. Most of the Dads got along. There was John Button with Jenson, Keith Wilson with Justin; lots of good guys.

"You could see that focus once he dropped that helmet on, that's when Dan was at his best"

15

Cadet karting mixed with school days, with Tom Sisley, who was gifted a win by Dan. That wouldn't happen again. Senior karting (opposite page) saw great success too

Wheldon seals Van Diemen drive

Daniel Wheldon has been confirmed as the lead factory Duckhams Van Diemen driver in the 1998 Slick 50 Formula Ford championship.

The 19-year-old will remain in the series for a second season, having finished fourth with Andy Welch Racing in a tumultuous first year, and begins this year as clear favourite for the title.

'Wheldon is a good little driver,' said Van Diemen boss Ralph Firman, 'and I have every confidence in him. He has a few rough edges, which we will iron out of him, but he has an enormous amount of talent.'

Wheldon has been linked to the team for several weeks, and was relieved to finally clinch the deal: 'I didn't want to leave the series with unfinished business.

'Van Diemen is the best team and my engineer Mickey Galter is one of the best in the business, not just Formula Ford,' said Wheldon.

Wheldon joins Australian Marcos Ambrose in the team, while Ricardo van der Ende is close to a deal.

We did Cadets from nine to 12 years old and he won three consecutive championships. If you watched Dan against the other kids, he had a great brain for it. He was so fast; he would carry so much speed through the corners. You could see that focus once he dropped that helmet on, that's when Dan was at his best. You could see the concentration in his eyes. He was a lovely kid but when the helmet was on there was only one thing he wanted to do: win.

Dan took it very seriously. He was also really technical, he could do it all himself. That was the clever thing. When you're unbeaten, you have to try and stay unbeaten. His own preparation – like everyone tells you – was immaculate. Everything had to be laid out properly. He did all the stickers on his own, and in a lot more detail when he started racing the bigger karts in Europe. When we left from home in the mornings when he was 8 years old, he was dressed in his overalls ready to go. He packed his bag himself, his helmet, shoes, all of it... He would take care of all that.

Dan and I kept notes on everything. We had the files in the motor home, so when we went to a track we'd know our best engines. In the school holidays, I used to say "Right Dan, today we're going to test carburetors" and we'd just spend all day testing carburetors. We were so prepared for every race we went to. When we took the kart off the trailer, we had it set up so that we pretty well knew we were going to be quick out of the box. Then it was just fine-tuning.

> ## "When we left home in the mornings when he was 8 years old, he was dressed in his overalls, ready to go"

Our engines were always what mattered. I didn't have a dyno at home but I used to run them on the stands before we'd leave. Bruno would still say put it on the kart, start it up and make sure that it was crisp. I could tell by the tone, just opening it up.

Dan had so many great wins in karts, it's hard to pick one as my personal favorite. I wasn't there or I would've said the Ayrton Senna Memorial Cup Japan when he won it driving with Terry Fullerton. It

was like the World Championship, Giorgio Pantano and all of them were there. That was a big win.

One event that I was at is funny too. We'd just started racing in Europe, and there was an English guy in charge of the tires at Bridgestone. If you weren't well known, you got the crappy tires. In the heats, Dan would be right at the front, leading, then all of a sudden he'd drop back because the tires were going off.

The guy from Bridgestone came to me and said, "You're in the plumbing game, aren't you? I'd like a bathroom." I said, "I'll tell you what I'd like... I'd like some of those tires." So I did a deal for the pre-final and final for yellow spot tires.

We put those on, and we'd already qualified 10th or something, but all of a sudden we were near the back – then they came in. Dan came through the field, with some unbelievable overtaking. Pantano was leading and we passed him with five or six laps to go and won. It was an absolutely amazing race to watch.

In the final, it was pretty close from pole for the first couple of laps, and then Dan started to pull away from Pantano and won. My Bridgestone guy came from South West England and I had to go and do his bloody bathroom suite. But that was the deal. He had his bathroom suite, and we got the tires. After that, thanks to his boss who was there to see us win that day, we got the tires anyway! It's what you had to do to get on.

The karting days were good to us, looking back there's loads of great memories. We had two rooms full of trophies – nearly 400 of them! Every weekend we'd come back with one. I started getting rid of mine to start with, to make room for his. I chucked most of his karting trophies out, when he started racing – he was still alive at the time. It proves you never know what might happen.

I only kept the special memory ones, like the British championship and the Cadets, which was quite big. I remember the first time they presented that one; he couldn't hold it because he was so small!

I put everything I had into Dan's racing in karts. Ashley, the next oldest to Dan, decided he wanted to have a go, too. We were at Rye House one day and Dan was in Junior Britain. I had the Cadet kart with me. I was working with Dan, and Ashley goes out in Dan's Cadet kart. I heard this crash, and saw this kart go up in the air above the motor home, and I thought, "I recognize that helmet...." I went over, and Ashley was laid out on the track. That was the end of Ashley's career in karting!

Austen would have been really good, too, but I was at the stage where I couldn't do it again. I'd done it. I'd done it every weekend, during the school holidays, every day we were testing.... Dan was going into cars and I had to take a backwards step. You have to let them get on with it.

They were great days, great memories. ∎

YOUNG, GIFTED AND QUICK

Even as a cheeky young karter Dan Wheldon quite obviously had what it took to win races

by SIMON WRIGHT

■ FOUNDER SWRD KART TEAM

DAN CONNECTION
Multiple junior championship-winning
SWRD kart team owner

Dan won the British championship with us in his second year. He was very professional as a young lad. He had done his cadet racing with Bruno Ferrari, before going into juniors. He was being groomed by his dad, Clive, to get him up to speed, but you didn't need to see the results or the data; he was one of the fastest, most naturally gifted drivers we've ever had – and that includes people like Jenson Button, David Coulthard and numerous other professionals. He was naturally very, very fast.

Racing came first but, away from that, he was very much a live wire, incredibly mischievous. Practical jokes were his thing, and quite a lot of them were aimed at me, or his Dad.

Clive used to come over on a Wednesday night to mess around with the kart a bit himself, and to bring the engines back for checking and servicing. Normally, somebody would go and get a takeout curry during the evening because we'd all be hungry. It was a 20-minute round trip there and back. I remember one occasion when Dan and my son, James, who raced in the same category at the time, decided to ask our mechanic Nick Chandler to drive them to go and pick up dinner as we were still working. Unfortunately, Nick had no idea where the curry place was and Dan instigated a "sight-seeing trip", which took in excess of an hour and a half. By the time they got back, everyone was very stressed about where they'd gotten off to, certainly Clive was.

There are some funny little memories as families. Mine got on well with them all, and went on numerous holidays, where, it seemed, Dan's job was to wind up Clive or me. It could drive you to distraction. One time, in the Canary Islands, he wound me up so much that I chased him down the beach trying to get ahold of the little sod to chuck him in the sea. I ended up kicking a rock in the sand and busting a couple of toes, and spent the rest of the holiday on crutches. He found that highly amusing....

Dan wasn't too bothered about the actual mechanics of his kart, but right from an early age it was drummed into him by Clive, the mechanics and myself about his feedback; without good feedback, we couldn't adjust it. He was very good at telling you what was happening. He wasn't that bothered with the nuts and bolts of it all. He wasn't a good loser; he just wanted to be fast. He wanted to win.

One race sticks out in my mind. It wasn't a win, but it was pretty impressive. It was horrendously wet for the final of a British championship race, and the rain was getting heavier, so there was

> ## "He was one of the fastest, most naturally gifted drivers we've ever had — and that includes people like Jenson Button, David Coulthard and more"

Racing SWRD-prepared karts, DW was the man to beat on the British karting scene. With partner in crime and mechanic Nick (rear of kart), ready for action

particular vehicle. So, they pulled Nick over. Obviously, he had no idea, because it was one of Clive's vans that we had borrowed. Then they were asked for their passports. Nick got his out with no problems. Dan got his passport out... and he'd gotten my son's. They'd managed to pick up each other's passports by mistake.

So, they had a hell of a job trying to explain why this young kid was with the wrong passport, in a van not owned by the driver with the wrong tax, and coming back from overseas...

When he was racing with us, Dan would always help look after the younger guys in the team. They looked up to him for all he'd achieved in cadets and juniors in the UK and abroad, so if he said this or that, they would do it. He was a pretty independent guy but if he could help anybody in the team, he certainly did.

I've worked with a lot of young drivers who've gone on to great careers, and Dan was no exception. I am very proud of his achievements. ∎

standing water on the track. I remember Dan coming down the straight flat-out in third place, and he hit a puddle that had built up, did a couple of 360 spins, kept it in a straight line and still finished third. That was quite an achievement.

We had some adventures, too – stuff you'd have trouble getting away with today. We'd been running in Genk, Belgium. Nick and Dan had driven over from the UK in a van, and when they were coming back through customs, the police/customs guard noticed that the road tax license on the van wasn't the right one for that

Dan flew in his first year out of karting, fighting hard in Formula Vauxhall Junior

FROM KID TO CONTENDER

Cub writer who followed the transition from karts to cars

by MATT JAMES

■ REPORTER & DEPUTY EDITOR, 1995-NOW

DAN CONNECTION
UK Motoring News/Motorsport News reporter, Formula Vauxhall Junior & Formula Ford

Even then a copious note-taker

first met Dan at Silverstone at the end of 1995 when he was 17. He was winning in karting and this was his first time in a racecar. The sponsor of some of the UK's karting championships also sponsored Formula Ford, so they took a Swift SC95 to Silverstone to let a bunch of karters have a shot at it, and give them a chance to get used to a car. Dan was there, Jenson Button was also one of them, Gary Paffett, Michael Simpson the world champion, Bobby Game... lots of good people.

They'd invited me along as a reporter and I immediately hit it off with Dan. The drivers were told: "This is definitely not timed, it's not against the clock, we just want to give you the experience of what driving a car's like when you graduate."

Dan had seen that I was with the officials. "They are timing it, aren't they?" he asked. He was right, they were. "You'll let me know what the times are...?" I couldn't, they wouldn't let me. So, he devised a system where I'd write it on my notebook, and then hold my notebook behind my back and he would stand directly behind me so he could see the times that everyone was doing! He went out and was a tenth quicker than anybody else.

That kind of cemented our friendship from the start. That day he was asking more questions than anybody else but in a mischievous sort of way. The others were a little bit...not shy, but a bit out of their comfort zone. Dan went straight to the instructors asking them, "What's this, what's that and how do I do this?" He was really quite inquisitive from the start but in a humorous way.

I did the Formula Vauxhall Junior beat for MN the next year, where Dan was racing. Dan lost that championship – all he needed to do in the last round was finish in the top three or four. He should easily have done it but he just couldn't keep himself from trying to overtake Luciano Burti into Paddock Hill Bend and they both went off. It was one of those times where Dan didn't need to do it but he was just so het up and hot headed that he messed it up.

The rivalry with Burti was ongoing. They had some monster battles. It wasn't only him, though. I remember at Silverstone in Formula Ford, in 1997, he'd been banging wheels all the way through the race with his teammate Aluizio Coelho.

Dan actually won the race at the end, but he was furious when he got out of the car. Strangy [Simon Strang of rival magazine *Autosport*] and I were covering the race. We went to speak with him afterward, and he turned around and said, "If he f***ing does that again I'm gonna f***ing put him off!" We looked at each other, and then had a quick word with him.

"Dan, you do realize you're talking to journalists, right? That's probably not the smartest thing to say. We won't print that, let's just leave that quote out." "Ah, yeah, alright." It was all part of the learning process. That was part of his determination; a part of what was evident throughout the rest of his career.

"That day he was asking more questions than anybody else but in a mischievous sort of way"

Dan should have won the Formula Ford Festival in 1998. He was in his second year of Formula Ford. For him, it was like "You've got to win now, you're in the works Van Diemen."

That whole year his car wasn't the best. It wasn't Dan's fault. You can only ride a donkey as quick as it'll go, you know. But it was the coveted works drive – the same one that launched Ayrton Senna's and many other drivers' careers. I also think Dan was a little bit put out because that was the year Jenson Button arrived for his first year in Formula Ford. He came with such fanfare as European Super A karting champion. Formula 1 photographer Keith Sutton had already been spreading the word through F1. In Formula Ford, the Jenson bandwagon had started rolling even quicker. It didn't help that Dan knew Jenson had the money and support to carry on.

Dan, at that stage, must have been thinking that drive was basically his last chance to get a springboard – and Jenson came along and rode the coach and horses through Dan's plans.

Exuding camera confidence even as a kid

They did get along, they did talk but I think there was a little bit of animosity from Dan's side, a little bit of jealousy, perhaps. It was the first time I've been in a Formula Ford paddock and had to speak to a manager in order to speak to a driver. "Can I speak to Jenson?" "Yes, you can." I could just walk into Dan's garage at any time and he'd be fine. There were he and Clive, and that's all the crew he had. You know he deserved to have more support than he had.

I didn't realize how critical the money situation was in 1998, because they kept that quiet. It's only afterward I found out he had absolutely nothing, and it was crisis point. At the time, we were just young boys knocking around having a laugh and going to racetracks. Going out on a Friday night and just having a laugh. That sort of money stuff you didn't really think about. We just thought, "We are all here, so let's have fun."

By the end of the year, Dan and Van Diemen had really worked on the car, and it all came together. Dan should have won but he was trying to play a clever game, trying to back up people into Jenson, and he got taken out.

He hadn't learned at that point what it was to win. He knew how to race quickly and win races but he didn't know how to win a championship, or The Big One. It was just Dan being a little bit naïve. I was pleased he'd gotten out of that by the time he got to America.

> ## "'Matt, Matt, Matt! I am going to get on the front page for this aren't I?' I said, 'Yeah, Dan, of course you are.' 'Sweeeeeeeeet Man!'"

He never got upset about anything I wrote, and I did criticize him a few times because he'd messed up. He would obviously read it, but he took it on the chin and he wouldn't have a go at me about it. I don't know if that's because we were friends or because he agreed with what I was saying.

I kept in touch with Dan in America. I phoned him after his first year there in U.S. Ford 2000, and he was staying in all these random towns in $20 motels. I asked if he was enjoying it. He said: "Yeah, mate, but you know I'm still not making money out of it. The only reason they're $20 is that you get woken up by gun shots in the middle of the night!" It sounded like a proper adventure.

After his first Indy 500 win, I was impressed that I managed to get ahold of him because by then I hadn't seen him for a few years, and everybody wanted to speak with him; TV, newspapers, he was doing media tours. I sent an e-mail to his PR, that just said, "Tell him it's me." Literally, within half an hour, he phoned me back. Not his PR person, *he* phoned me back right away saying "Hey, great to hear from you. How's British F3?" He hadn't forgotten us.

It was the same after his second Indy win. We spoke for about half an hour, I've still got the recording. At the end of it, in the faux American accent he had adopted, he said, "Matt, Matt, Matt! I am going to get on the front page for this aren't I?" I said, "Yeah, Dan, of course you are." "Sweeeeeeeeeet Man!"

I regret I never went to see him because every time we spoke, he'd say, "Man you've got to come and see what I've got now. Don't worry I'll look after you and everything." He was very proud of what he'd gotten, and he'd still have been a good guy to hang around with, I'm sure of that. I'm glad we had that good long chat after his 500 win in 2011.

I had been working at races in the UK that October day. It was late at night when I got home, and I went to bed and listened to the radio. It was the lead item on the news. *The lead item.* I couldn't believe it. It just wasn't right. So, I phoned my boss to ask what happened. All I can remember him saying was, "Mate, we didn't know how to tell you."

I had to write a two-page appreciation, and within three hours I'd written two and a half thousand words. It seemed like the easiest thing in the world to write, as well. I could have written five, six, seven thousand words...

It was cathartic doing it but I also felt that the British public didn't really know who Dan was. They hadn't been in that little episode – those three years when I got to know him when he was a kid – so they wouldn't really have known who the guy was. Therefore, it was important for me to write it and kind of tell people. I said the good and the bad stuff – it wasn't all flowery praise! I said he was a determined little bugger and he could be a bit of a shit-bag at times, but it just felt easy to write. I still miss him. ∎

DW was twice a finalist in the prestigious McLaren/Autosport BRDC Award; despite scoring wins, the prized works Van Diemen wasn't the Formula Ford car to have in 1998

THE WONDER YEARS

Adversaries from an early age, Jenson Button recalls lessons learned from racer and rival

Snetterton, UK, 1998, scene
of a memorable battle where
Dan fended off Jenson with a
lesson in defensive driving

by JENSON BUTTON

■ FORMULA 1 DRIVER, McLAREN-HONDA, 15 WINS
FORMULA 1 WORLD CHAMPION, 2009

DAN CONNECTION
Rival in karting from cadets through to Formula Ford

CHRIS WALKER

an was a year older than me, which meant a lot in those days. I arrived in karting and he already had the number one plate on. It was like, "Oh my God, the British champion". I remember he was so tiny, even though he was a year older than me.

Then, he was always the guy to beat – *always* the guy to beat.

In karting, we had some really good battles in Cadets and then he moved up to Juniors the year before me. When I moved up, we were racing again. There were so many good drivers in karting then, like Justin Wilson and Anthony Davidson, but Dan is the guy I always remember as the one I knew I had to beat if I was going to go anywhere.

He was the first kid in Cadets who won the championship, and I thought, "Wow, this kid is very special." We'd only just started but that carried through into other Formula as well. So, in that sense, yeah, he definitely shaped my career. Not in terms of driving though, we always had different styles of driving. I think when you choose a style or find something that works for you, you don't really change it that much. But there were certain things... I remember going into one weekend in juniors and I blew up all my engines somehow that race weekend. Dad had been tuning them at the time; that was in Junior 100 Britain. It was because I was overlapping throttle and the brake so everything was getting very hot. Dad was saying, "You're doing this, you don't realize you're doing it, but you've got to sort it out." He told me to go and watch Dan. So I did. I used to go and watch Dan at Hoddesdon, his home circuit. At Kimbolton, I remember watching him into Turn One to see how he was braking and handling the throttle. So, yeah, I suppose I did learn from him but I still kept my individual style. He always pushed me to my limit when we were racing. We had some great battles.

Cocky? Totally! Yeah, he was massively cocky when I was growing up with him. He was a proper Londoner. He was small then as well, he was so much smaller but he came across as so confident in his ability. He was a miniature version of his dad at that moment of time. When you got to know him though, he was a lovely guy – a great

Don't be put off by the cheeky smile, once the helmet was on Dan's focus was solely on winning. His competition on the track was a high standard

character and great personality. You can see why a lot of people got along with him and they have great stories of spending time with him.

When he started karting in Europe I thought, "Oh my god, he's gone to Europe and he's racing against the best in the world and he's doing really well with Fullerton karts." So, again, I followed him out there a year later and started racing in Europe too.

After that, there were a couple of years where he'd moved to single-seaters in the UK and I stayed in karts and won the European championships in Super A. I came back to the UK and there he was again – in Formula Ford! He'd had a year of experience and was now racing for the works Duckhams Van Diemen team. It was like, "Oh noooo!" I wanted to win this in my first year and I'm up against Dan. Again, I felt that there was so much talent in the years that I was racing in junior single-seaters, but Dan was always the one who stood out because he was such an intelligent driver as well. When you beat him you knew you'd done an exceptional job.

I remember quite a few races with Dan but one that stands out was at Snetterton in Formula Ford in 1998. He was leading, I was behind him, and we were out in front. In karting, you couldn't – or

It was a talented intake in cadet
karts with Anthony Davidson (in
kart), Jenson Button (standing)
and Dan Wheldon (on tire)

"Dan was always the one
who stood out because he
was such an intelligent
driver as well. When you
beat him you knew you'd
done an exceptional job"

you weren't allowed to – move. You weren't allowed to weave or you got black-flagged. But in Formula Ford you could do what you wanted and it was such a shock to me! I mean he was moving all over the place, but he was just doing it *perfectly*. Every time I nudged alongside he'd just move across. I was so frustrated after the race, and so angry. He kept weaving on the straights so I couldn't get past him, but it definitely taught me a lot about racing in single-seaters, and where to put your car. We all love the challenge of overtaking but when I think in terms of how to protect myself and how to keep people behind, he was the master at it. I learned a lot that day about ways of stopping people from getting past – you always need it your career. You're not always at the top of your game, but when you find yourself in a good position, then you need to be able to defend.

I won the Formula Ford Festival that year, which is the World Championship Formula Ford. I tried to overtake Marcos Ambrose for the lead into the second-to-last corner, a lap from the end. It was a late lunge, because I had to come from a long way back as he was blocking every lap. He left room, I went up the inside, we touched and he spun off. Then, on the last corner, Dan was behind me and he nudged me and I ran wide. I beat him by about a foot to win the Formula Ford Festival, and that was the final time we raced together.

That was the case through so much of my career: To try and do as good as Dan or try to do better than Dan. He'd started racing in Europe one year before me in karting, so when I went there the next year I had to do as good as him, if not better. It was always like that and in a way it took away the pressure, I think, of the need to do well. So, yeah, Dan was a massive part of my career. He really was. Then I moved up to Formula 3 in the UK and he went to America.

> **"Through so much of my career the aim was to try to beat Dan, or be as good as him. I forgot the aim was Formula 1. At that moment in time the aim was to beat Dan Wheldon"**

We didn't see each other much after that. Dan did come to Indianapolis a couple of times when I was racing there in F1, and we'd meet up and have a coffee together and a chat. We reminisced about a lot of the fun times we had as well because it wasn't all racing; we weren't *always* rivals. We had fun away from the circuit, in a group of drivers, on a Sunday night after a Formula Ford race, or the Festival or something.

But that was it really. I remember 2003 when I had my accident in Monaco, the weekend before Dan had a big shunt in Indy and two weeks after Anthony (Davidson) had a big shunt at Le Mans, ending up in the hospital. We were main competitors in karting and it was like… "Oh my God, what is going on?" But for Dan and I, the same thing happened in terms of success; he won the Indy 500 and I won Monaco. We both reached our dreams, I think, as children and we both achieved so much in motorsport, just different sides of the pond, if you like.

Basically, we had all of our early careers together, we followed a similar path through karting and open-wheel racing up until that point, and we always had great battles. We weren't the closest of

Dan and Jenson (above) sharing the podium after their final race together, the 1998 Formula Ford Festival. Eyes on the prize in karting (left) as the man to beat

friends but I think that was because we were so competitive. I spent a night at his house once when we were karting but that was it. As I say, we weren't best friends, but we did have a lot of respect for each other.

We would speak but you could tell there was something there between us where we knew we couldn't be close friends because we were so competitive. It felt like we were main rivals, and I sort of forgot why I was there. I forgot the aim was Formula 1, because the aim wasn't Formula 1 at that moment in time, the aim was to beat Dan Wheldon.

He was one of the best drivers – for me, he was the best driver when I was growing up – and you had to beat him or be as good as him, if you were going to go anywhere. It's a shame that we didn't see him in Formula 1 but he seemed very happy with his career choice in the end, and what he achieved. Jeez! He obviously should've been very happy with what he achieved. Winning the Indy 500 twice was a great accomplishment. ■

OLD SPARRING PARTNERS

In 1998 Dan Wheldon entered the world of Marcos Ambrose and left an indelible mark

by MARCOS AMBROSE

■ TWO TIME AUSTRALIAN V8 SUPERCAR CHAMPION, NASCAR RACE WINNER

DAN CONNECTION
Van Diemen Formula Ford teammate, 1998

I hadn't really seen anyone like Dan before as a teammate nor did I want to be involved with him either. I came from Australia where we are all fairly laid-back, knock-about easy characters, you know? Dan came in from the Vauxhall Junior series after having done very well in that, and then had gone to Formula Ford ready to prove a point. The year I came, in 1998, he was meant to be the gun. He was very shrewd, he really worked the team well, pretty sneaky, keeping things to himself, trying to get any advantage he could....

So, early on, it was a pretty tetchy relationship to be honest. Once we'd worked each other out and found that respect works both ways, we actually became pretty good mates. We went out a few times, he came over and stayed at my place a few times.

Certainly he was a cagey operator, very determined, and pretty sly to get what he wanted. But he worked really well, worked all the angles. I look back at it now, and he was just amazing to do what he did at such a young age. You could see he had that "tiger eye" look in him. I naturally learned from that and started to adapt my style because he was handing it to me early on. I managed to pick up my form, too, and by the end of the year we were running pretty much nose to nose.

Jenson [Button] came in and stole the show that year. It was his first year in, and I know it was a tough pill for Dan to swallow. They'd been racing karts together a lot. Dan was a year or so in front of him on the stairway to professional racing. Jenson came in and put a whacking on us really, won a lot of races and the title that year. The Mygale that he had was the car to have. Dan and I were caught behind early on. We did catch them by the end but it was too late. It was an amazing year really, and it wasn't

Ambrose and Wheldon, in the works Van Diemens, came up against Jenson Button in UK Formula Ford

> **"I look back at it now, and he was just amazing to do what he did at such a young age. You could see he had that 'tiger eye' look in him"**

just Jenson and Dan. It was Nicolas Kiesa and Craig Murray and a whole bunch of guys. It was a very, very competitive year.

Our career paths changed, of course. I went back to Australia and we drifted apart, but I followed his career pretty closely and he had a great run.

I would have loved to see him when my career took me to America, too, but I didn't. NASCAR is all consuming and once I got into my world that was it. Dan was over in IndyCar so we never crossed paths again.

When I look back at that year I had with Dan there in Formula Ford, it was a "trying" year between us early on, a bit of friction, but once we'd worked each other out we had some good times. He generally wished me well, and I felt the same for him. I watched him closely after that in what he did, and he did it all very well.

It was terrible what happened to Dan. He was a great racer, one of the true racers I've come across. He was absolutely focused, dedicated, fully committed to it, loved it. He was a really sharp operator. ■

GROOT-BRITANNIE

NG-KONG

ITALIE

Team "Groot-Britannie" with Kolby and future F3 champion Marc Hynes; Dan and Kristian light up with 2001 Atlantic champion Hoover Orsi

SMELLS LIKE TEEN SPIRIT

Karting rivals with racing dreams, they grew up together as best friends — and suffered some of the growing pains too

by KRISTIAN KOLBY

■ FORMER INDY LIGHTS RACER

DAN CONNECTION
Childhood friend and fellow karter

My first impression of Dan wasn't necessarily of someone I thought I'd grow to like, never mind become best friends with. I started karting over in Denmark, and then my family moved to the U.K. when I was 12 years old. I did some local club meetings in Cheshire, where we lived, but I vividly remember one of my first national events was at a place called Shenington.

I hadn't been involved in the U.K. karting scene, so had no idea of the hierarchy in terms of who was good. I did the first practice session, just minding my own business, passing a few karts and getting a feel for the place.

When I went out for the second session, I got fired into the tires so bloody hard. I got back to the pits and said to my dad, "What just happened? This kid just knocked me off and, no question, it was on purpose." As I was getting out of the kart, this little kid (and he was really little) came over and said, "That was for overtaking me earlier." So, basically, my first meeting with Dan was, you know,

contentious. I dared to overtake him and his response was to send me into a tire wall as hard as possible!

As we grew up, though, and I got more involved in the scene, I became good friends with him and his family. We did a lot of races together, both in the U.K. and abroad.

Something that always sticks in my mind was when we did the European championship in Italy. We were about 14 then and part of a group representing England. We all had various problems during the knock-out-style rounds, where you had to finish in the top 20 out of hundreds of kids in order to qualify. Dan's engine seized in his heat, so he was already out. I'd had some issues in my heat, but I was making my way through the field and I remember on the side of the track, the person jumping up and down, cheering the loudest, was Dan. He didn't need to do that, but in terms of cementing a friendship it was pretty special. I never really told him how much that stayed with me, but seeing someone who is, in essence, a competitor cheering for you, that meant the world to me.

We became incredibly close friends and we were tight outside of racing, too. We spoke to each other most days and every weekend, when we weren't off racing together, we'd be staying at one another's houses. He had a little moped that we'd run around on as 16-year olds, mainly to the chip shop in Olney for Dan's beloved beef curry. He even arranged for me to be at his house when he got his GCSE

Kolby dug out his race gear to team up with the Wheldon brothers for the annual Dan Wheldon Memorial karting challenge in England, 2016

JAKOB EBREY

> ## "It was true friendship between two kids. We got drunk for the first time, went on typical kid's holidays, wrecked our family's homes and chased girls together"

exam results! He was adamant that I go down to his house and go with him to collect them. When I asked why he replied, "Because my dad is gonna kill me!" He knew he'd failed but, in his mind, if I was there, his dad would go slightly less mental at him. He didn't.... It wasn't that big of a surprise, as any free time we had was spent messing around on go-karts or chasing girls. School was very, very low on the priority list.

Dan was incredibly focused at the circuit; he had that hunger in his eyes, even from a young age. He was very conscious of doing things professionally; doing and saying the right things. He made it on absolute, sheer determination. Then, obviously, grasped the opportunity when it was there, but he was always going to. He was a good guy but he was quite ruthless, too.

I don't think many people got to know Dan that well, which makes me value our friendship even more. There was nothing false, just true friendship between two kids essentially growing up together. We got drunk for the first time, went on typical kid's holidays, wrecked our family's homes and chased girls together.

One time, me, Dan, Mark (a friend from school) and Marino [Franchitti], who we always called Morris, decided to settle into the camper van at my home for the night. We found some bottles of red wine and, well, one thing led to another...I can honestly say I don't remember much. I do remember Dan suddenly collapsing onto the table and I thought he'd passed out, until the inevitable happened. He turned his head and started spewing everywhere, which set off a chain reaction among us all. To make matters worse, Morris had a nosebleed in the middle of it all, so the camper van ended up looking like a scene from a horror movie! It certainly taught us all a valuable lesson, however, as no night is ever worth having to clear up your own bodily fluids with a hangover the morning after!

We were little terrors; typical kids really. But I will always treasure those great memories of growing up with Dan, my best friend. ∎

OLD HEAD, YOUNG SHOULDERS

A championship-costing rookie error was followed by mature understanding

The end of Dan's Formula Vauxhall Junior title hopes in the 1996 season finale

by SIMON STRANG

■ HEAD OF AUTOSPORT SPECIAL PROJECTS

DAN CONNECTION
Race reporter and friend

My first serious conversation with Daniel Wheldon involved him emphatically laying out the terms of our professional relationship and how important it was for me to portray his performances in the correct tone. I was the Formula Vauxhall Junior correspondent for *Autosport* in 1996 and for Dan that carried weight. He was only 17.

Our meetings swiftly became far more convivial. He never lost his love of spinning yarns – like trying to convince me that he was about to sign a pre-contract for Ferrari while racing in Formula Ford.

For many who watched it, nothing else came close to the 1996 FVJ series. A team owner puts it, "We were lucky. It was the best junior championship any of us ever saw – we just didn't know it at the time!" Coming into the last round, four guys could still win it. It was a ruthless, if accurate, proving ground for very young talent.

Wheldon crashed out of the opening race at Donington, which was won by the early season pacesetter, and future Jaguar Formula 1 racer, Luciano Burti after a wheel-banging scrap for the lead with Ulsterman Tim Mullen. Dan bounced back, dominating the second round and, from that point on, was always in contention for victories.

These three, along with Burti's super-consistent teammate Leighton Walker, set the tone for the year. Burti was often the fastest, but Danny and Tim's race craft was superior and, at times, Wheldon was out on his own in terms of skill. When he had the chance to demonstrate this, it delighted him.

With Burti getting caught up in midseason tangles, the points lead swung between Tim and Dan so, going into the finale, Mullen was one point ahead of Dan in the championship, with both Burti and Walker poised if either of these two should not finish....

Through this whole period of Dan's life, he brimmed with a cheeky blend of confidence borne out of the knowledge that he clearly had the ability to back it up. At this time, though, we didn't know how tight he was running on budget. We all thought he was well heeled, enough at least to get him to Formula 3. Looking back now, he was learning faster than those around him because he needed to. He didn't have the time and luxury of a large budget that some of his rivals did. Here was an obvious natural talent. Dan stood out as a driver who you knew would make it if all the stars aligned.

Dan approached the final weekend at Brands, outwardly at least, with maturity. "It's all about the championship, I'm not doing anything daft," he'd told me. He knew all he had to do was follow pole man Burti home, and finish ahead of Mullen. In the first couple of laps, it played out just the way Dan had planned. Burti was leading with Dan in his wheel tracks. but the leader's ever wider entry into corners was tantalizing. Dan went for a gap, which Burti instantly

Twice a finalist in the prestigious McLaren Autosport BRDC Award, young Wheldon was put through his paces in Formula 3 (above) and in fitness tests against future international racers Peter Dumbreck, Darren Turner and Jonny Kane

"'Perhaps I should have stayed in second. It's easy to be wise after'"

moved to counter. Dan's car went momentarily airborne before firing off into the gravel, and Mullen came through to take the title. Dan should have known better, and he was well aware of it. He sat on the bank behind the barrier telling himself so, his hopes gone.

A few weeks later, Dan and I ghosted a column for *Autosport* and his considered approach to this disappointment was strikingly mature. "It would have been such an advantage to have taken the title because it would have looked so impressive," he said. "Perhaps I should have stayed in second, but it is easy to be wise after the event. I don't believe you can plan tactics before a race. You can have a basic plan, and then you react to circumstances."

Maybe that's one of the reasons he was so good on ovals. His IndyCar rival and the 1995 FVJ champion, Justin Wilson, once remarked that it sometimes seemed as if Dan could see the drafts, such was his reactive feel for the smooth and turbulent streams of air on the superspeedways. Justin used to marvel at it and said there was no one out there with as natural a feel for oval racing.

Over the years, I stayed in touch with a lot of the drivers from that period, in particular Justin. But Dan left for America earlier than most, and success and time zones made it naturally harder with all the constraints and pressures that brought. But whenever we did catch up with one another it was just like those FVJ days.

On one occasion, we randomly bumped into one another on the escalators at a shopping mall. Dan was living in the States by then and driving with Andretti Green – his big break. Nevertheless, there he was in Dartford, in southern England, Christmas shopping. "Strangy," he shouted. So surprised were we by this chance meeting that three times we passed each other before we figured one of us should stop and wait at the bottom so he could meet my future wife. He told her he was going to win the Indy 500. That was late 2004.

The last time I saw Dan was the morning after the 2010 Indy 500, where he'd sworn to me he'd have had Dario on the line if the race hadn't finished behind the pace car, because of Mike Conway's shunt. We'd been meaning to catch-up properly all weekend, and just as I went into the drivers' trailer zone he was leaving in a huge shiny black SUV with chrome wheels. He pulled to a stop, jumped out. "Strangy, Strangy... You must meet Sebastian!" and he introduced me to his baby boy.

Now Justin and Dan are both gone, and sadness tinges the memories. It's different, though, for each. With Justin, just as with so many guys from that period, we never saw the stars align the way they truly should have. But at least the world got to appreciate how good Dan really was. ∎

A young Dan (front left) having been judged driver of the day. Judges include Martin Hines (back left), Richard Dean, TV host Steve Johnson, David Coulthard and Barry McGuigan

A TRUE TEAM PLAYER

Making every member of the team he drove for feel special was a real skill. It was a trait throughout DW's career

by RICHARD DEAN

- MANAGING DIRECTOR, UNITED AUTOSPORTS

DAN CONNECTION
DRIVER COACH AND JLR RACING PRINCIPAL, FORMULA VAUXHALL JR, 1995-96

When I started in Formula Ford, I drove for Jim Lee Racing, and Jim helped me get my career going. As I progressed, I always stayed in touch, because he was such a brilliant guy. I was racing in Japan when he fell ill with cancer, and I came back to the UK to do some driver coaching for him. That year, 1995, we ran Justin Wilson in Formula Vauxhall Junior, and then I coached and was team manager for Dan the year after.

I knew of Dan long before then, though. I was asked by Bill Sisley of Buckmore Park to be a judge at the Super One round of the British kart series – it was a big event. Mr Karting, Martin Hines, and David Coulthard were there, with boxing world champion and rallycross driver Barry McGuigan. I was racing in Formula 3000 at the time. We were all asked to pick a driver of the day, and I had to choose from the juniors who were around age 12. I picked Dan Wheldon. He just stood out a mile.

There are drivers who have natural ability, a great style, are flamboyant, and could destroy everybody in the rain. For me, Johnny Herbert was that driver when we were juniors at 13. One of the few you'd come up against, but deep down if somebody forced you to admit to it, you'd have to say, yes, actually, he is better than me. Johnny was one of those.

Dan had that too, but he also had the complete off-track side to him from an early age. He knew the psychological gain, he knew how to out-psyche people. He was polished, presentable, and he knew the political game that he had to play even at such a young age. It was quite a coincidence when we later ended up running him with Team JLR and I was his full time driver coach. But back then, in junior karting, he stood out by a country mile.

I was at every one of his races when he first moved to cars, reporting back to Clive. Dan was 16 when he started with us, so I wasn't just a driver coach; he needed ferrying around too. He was almost a complete driver when we got him…it was one of the easiest driver coaching jobs I've had! It was really only about accelerating his understanding of the circuits and a little on the car. He certainly didn't need to be taught how to race, overtake or even qualify.

The pressure that kids are under nowadays at the top level in karting, like Dan had been, meant he came mentally very tough and well-prepared. When people think, "How's he going to cope with the pressure of cars?" they forget they had been through all of that already in karting. Dan was really prepared for that, I was just showing him the ropes.

I'd like to tell you he was studious and meticulous with notes, and all of that, but… No! I certainly found Dan was cocky – lovably cocky – very, very sure of himself, and quite confident. He used to constantly tell me my girlfriends were only using me so they could get to spend more time with him! He certainly had that little bit of arrogance, in the nicest possible way. In motorsport, arrogance can be a good thing, and he definitely had that.

Dan leading in Formula Vauxhall Junior 1996 (above); JLR truckie Bob Peck shuttles DW to the grid. The pair went to the Isle of Man TT together

As a racer he wasn't a note taker, certainly in his early days. He very much believed he could do it. I'm not at saying he didn't listen. He did listen, and he took it all in, but he was a natural driver and to his rivals he wouldn't want to be seen making notes in a book of tips. He was bright enough anyway. If you told him something once, it wasn't often you'd have to point out that he was doing it wrong again.

Dan had a pretty intense season with us in Vauxhall Junior in 1996. He did the full 15 race weekends, but if I remember rightly we started at the end of the year before, and did close to 40 days testing over an 18-month period, so I really got to know him and got

close to him. When drivers move on after a season, you can't help but follow their progress. Dan was someone you really wanted to do well. The whole team just fell in love with him…

All our young drivers started out with great intentions to come and spend time in our shop up in West Yorkshire, north of England to understand the car and get to know the team… Maybe one or two do early on but there's never really a reason to come, and when they do they're in the way!

Dan would come up and spend a week with us. He'd stay at the mechanics' houses and go out with them to eat, come in and help clean the truck, vacuum the people carrier and so on. You knew he was winning the people over, and by doing that he got the best out of them as well. If he barrel rolled the car while pushing hard and had taken three corners off of it, he knew that every single member of the team – including the truckie and the mechanics on the other cars in the team – would all roll their sleeves up and get it fixed. Not because it was their job or they're being paid for it, but because it was for Dan. That's not saying he was manipulative. The time he

"He'd stay at the mechanics' houses and go out with them to eat, then come in and help clean the truck"

spent with the guys he knew put in the long hours for him on his racecar was genuine. What proves they meant something to him is that he stayed in touch however many years on, was still dropping all of them notes, texts and messages on Facebook, asking how they were and what they were doing, even after winning Indy.

Our truckie, Bob Peck used to race motorcycles and he had a nice collection of classic racing bikes. Bob is a really down-to-earth proper Yorkshireman and would go to the Isle of Man for the TT every year, just to do the parade laps on his bikes. Dan said to him at the time that he'd love to go too. So Bob offered to take him with him – and he went! He jumped in the back of a grubby transit van, took the ferry crossing and had a weekend sleeping in the van with Bob, while helping him work on his classic bikes, all so Bob could do the parade laps. He absolutely loved it. Bob and all the guys here still talk about that – and Dan – with a lot of affection.

Running and working with Dan was genuinely a pleasure, as was getting to know him so well. It's such a shame. I always thought he should have gone a lot further than he did. He definitely had the ability to get to Formula 1. ■

THE PRIDE OF THE LIONHEART

Dan had three younger brothers and a sister. The boys all looked up to the eldest — and got into their fair share of scrapes too

by ASHLEY WHELDON BROTHER #1

WE HAD A GOOD TIME growing up. Dan was three years older than me, and I absolutely loved it when he was karting. I used to go to the races, and stay in the camper van. Karting really was a whole-family thing for us. Dad would get home from work on Friday and we'd jump in the camper and drive off through the night. Dan obviously got the best bed. We'd be on the bunk, or whatever. They are good memories.

We all went to different schools than Dan. He went to Bedford School. He would always come in, go into the dining room and do his homework; he was good like that. As we got older, into our teens, I didn't see that much of him as he got an evening job in the grocery store stacking shelves. We got a 50cc moped (which he and Dad quickly took the engine out of and replaced with a 100cc) and then his purple Corsa road car to get around. And, of course, he had a girlfriend. But most of his time was spent with karting, then racing – preparing for it or away weekends doing it.

Every Friday night, Mum and Dad used to go out for a meal, so we used to play soccer in the house with a soft ball. Our lounge had a door at each end that would be the goals. It would be Austen and I versus Dan and Elliott. We naturally thought we were quite good...

We used to kick or chip the ball over the sofa between the two doors. Dad used to have all these decanters for show on the side, although nobody drank whisky or vodka in the house, only beer and wine.

I have no idea how many times we'd slice a kick and knock these decanters over, and whisky would go on the carpet. We'd be getting bottles of Vanish, scrubbing the carpet, and a hairdryer to dry it all off so Mum and Dad wouldn't know. Dan used to win decanters as prizes a lot in karting, so he'd go up to his cupboard, find a similar one, and we'd fill it up. One of them was filled with Coke for years! Another just sat there with ginger ale in it, and Dad never knew.

We were – and all of us still are – competitive. You could get all the way around our house and, in the summer holidays, we'd set up a track using old kart tires, and have BMX bike races, skidding into corners all day long. Dad would come back and say, "What the hell have you done to my patio?" There were bike skid marks everywhere. So, there we all were again with Turtle Wax shampoo, jet wash, brushes, scraping up all of that!

Dan always looked after us, too. His bachelor party was in Las Vegas, and he flew Austen and me over. Dan was there to pick us up in a limousine. He had a deal with the Bellagio – it was like the film, *Hangover*. It was a giant penthouse suite, and even though the groom wasn't supposed to, Dan paid and looked after us.

It was tough for us all when Mum was diagnosed with Alzheimer's. If you haven't experienced it, you can't describe what it's all about. I don't want to sound horrible about other diseases, but if somebody has cancer, they are still that person. You can still have conversations with them. I know it was really tough for my dad, and Daniel did all he could. He flew Mum over to Boston to see the best people. The doctor here in the UK was great for us, too. He answered all of our questions. Even though he couldn't do anything, he was brilliant in telling us what was going on.

I will forever remember when Dan passed. I could feel that Mum somehow knew what had happened. I remember there were tears in her eyes. We had the TV on at the family home in Emberton, and it was on the news with a picture of my brother. She was looking at

Page boy fashion for Ashley and Dan

"When I was younger I used to tell my brother is better than Schumacher. I was convinced he would be World Champion"

it and said, "Ahhh, bless him." It was weird. I think she knew.... But then she didn't give the reaction of crying, the natural emotion you'd expect. It was hard having to leave Mum at home, because she couldn't travel for the funeral.

It was all so surreal. My wife, Jo, and I both felt that Dan would have been looking down on us laughing, because we never had the private Lear jets and so on. So, being picked up from the house by Virgin Atlantic in private cars and taken into the secret entrance they have at Heathrow for VIP guests, private security, straight to the first class lounge where there was a whole area cordoned off for us to have breakfast, was all very strange. They made sure we were the last to board the plane.

When we landed, there was a private jet waiting for us, sent by Roger Penske. I'd never been on a private jet before. This was the sort of stuff Dan was used to. He would have been laughing at that.

When we touched down in St. Petersburg, Dario and Dixie were there waiting for my dad. They were both wonderful. Scott, when he comes over to the UK with his wife Emma, who is British, always comes and sees us, always comes karting with us. He's such a nice guy. They are so welcoming and helpful to us. Everybody says it, but IndyCar is like a close family. When you do experience it, you realize it's there, it's genuine and they look after each other.

It still frustrates me that Dan didn't get the appreciation and recognition for what he achieved at home in the UK. It is nothing like what he had, and still has, in the States. Most of my memorabilia of Dan is in my head, in the form of memories. I have some bits and pieces: gloves, suit, helmet and stuff. But there are things about Dan that really touch you every now and then.

My wife and I recently bought a house in Derby, England, that needed a lot of work. We called a local electrician, and this guy turns up and we're talking about soccer. I asked if he followed it closely. He said, "No I'm a motorsport man myself..."

I asked if he liked IndyCar. He said, "Oh, I love IndyCar". In the UK, finding people who even know that IndyCar exists is rare, so I went and got my helmet of Dan's. He was a bit shocked... The first thing he said was, "I knew your name was Wheldon, but I didn't put two and two together...I'm so sorry for your loss."

I said to him, "Honestly, I don't mind people talking about my brother." When I was younger I used to tell my friends that my brother is better than Michael Schumacher. I was convinced he would be World Champion...although that might be a bit biased! But for a random 32-year-old electrician to come into my house in Derbyshire, where I've lived for 15 years, and know of my brother and what he achieved? You can't get a better tribute than that. ◾

by AUSTEN WHELDON BROTHER #2

IT'S DIFFICULT TO KNOW what to say about Dan. I have so many memories, some funny, some personal and, of course, a lot that are unprintable! But it's the little stories, triggered by a photo or another random memory, that say the most. I have memories of us playing soccer together, and going fishing with Granddad and then getting bored when we didn't catch anything.

We got on really well as kids, but he used to take the rap for us a lot. We knew Dad wouldn't tell Dan off, so it was perfect, we'd always blame him!

Even as a kid, Dan was very particular and precise about things. When he wasn't there, I would often go into his room and use his aftershave or deodorant. I'd remember exactly how it was when I put it back, but he still always knew someone had been in his room. He was quite a fashionable kid, too. I would get his clothes handed down to me, so I was a fashionable kid two years removed.

I remember Dan would win all sorts of things when he was karting, including a stereo system that Dad still has in the gym. At one event, he won a quad bike that we would all race around the driveway on. We'd make a track from old kart tires and spend hours and hours sliding and skidding this quad around. Then we'd have to spend just as much time cleaning up the skid marks off Dad's driveway.

The trailer we used for karting would be parked in the driveway as well. One winter the cat got stuck on the roof of the house. So Dan got a ladder and put it across from the top of the trailer to the roof, then climbed across to rescue the cat! Absolutely priceless; health and safety would have had nightmares at just the thought.

I didn't get over to see him race in America as much as I wanted to because I was playing my rugby then. So, I mainly followed his IndyCar career on television in the UK.

My favorite times were when he was karting. I loved going to the kart races.

We'd all go away in the motor home; those were the best days. We all knew everyone so we'd play soccer on the track and knock the ball around with Jenson Button and such. I still see some of guys from back then. There were some good guys.

One year I went to every race; I didn't miss any of them. I wasn't allowed to work on the kart though because I once sprayed WD40 on his brakes so he had no brakes in the race! I got into a lot of trouble for that and had to stay away after... I guess I was not the greatest mechanic.

We used to go to a track called Rye House and they had a dog-racing track right alongside, too. Me and Dan went down one night after his races and won absolutely loads of money! That was a really good night.

We always had the best of times and, of course, we were

> "I once sprayed WD40 on his brakes so he had no brakes in the race! I got into a lot of trouble for that and had to stay away"

massively competitive. On vacation, we'd always be racing around in karts or sometimes even hire cars, making our poor parents hyperventilate! Many a Portuguese rental car was returned with panels covered in mud to hide a multitude of bumps and dents...

Dan was a great brother and will always be with me.

I have the Lionheart tattooed right across my back in his memory. It took 10 hours to do in total and I wanted to get it done in one go, not lots of sessions. It's weird because I can't even get a blood test done without passing out usually, but the tattoo didn't bother me at all. I actually fell asleep! ◼

Brotherly love from Dan to Austen; Familiy vacions were always a highlight. Dan in a rare moment of down time between pranks, games and sibling competion

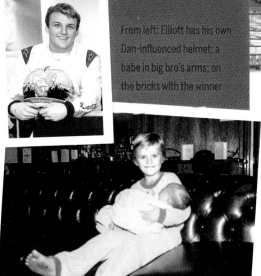

From left: Elliott has his own Dan-influenced helmet; a babe in big bro's arms; on the bricks with the winner

PHIL ABBOTT/LAT/JAKOB EBREY

by ELLIOTT WHELDON BROTHER #3

DAN WAS 10 YEARS older than me but he was always very good to me. He was a great brother and I really couldn't have asked anything more of him. I was a bit of a terror as a kid although, obviously, I turned out OK! But whenever we got into trouble, Dan would always stick up for me, especially if Dad was telling us off.

Growing up, we used to get in to all sorts of mischief, I had so much fun with him. We all loved playing soccer and our house is opposite a church. We would use the lamppost outside as the goal, but people complained about us kicking the ball against the wall. Dad told us that we shouldn't really be playing there and, like most kids, we never listened! Dad had a noisy BMW then, so when we woud hear it coming up the lane, we'd all run inside the house, hot and panting. He'd come in and we'd all be sitting there as good as gold; so he never knew.

Another time, Dan was chasing me upstairs, trying to beat me up or something, as usual. I slipped on the stairs and put my foot straight through the banister, snapping it in half. Mum always helped us, though, so we nailed it back together and used shoe polish to hide it. Dad didn't know anything about it until he had the stairs redone years later!

I loved spending any time I could with Dan. In 2002, he would come back from the U.S. a lot because he was struggling to get a drive. We shared a room and, even though I had school the next day, Dan didn't like being on his own so would wake me up to talk about my day. Those were the best days for me.

I'd go over to visit Dan in America a lot, especially with my mate Jason [Moore]. For Christmas, Dan would buy us tickets to go out and see him. He was so great like that, and we would always have a lot of fun when we were there.

Some of the best memories I have are of us doing the Robo-Pong kart race in Indianapolis together. One year he got a team for me and Jason, who's been karting for years. When we arrived, the guy at the track said he'd looked online and found out all about Jason and his history, but couldn't find anything there about me. I said, "Well I don't do this, I'm a plumber."

So they decided I should get plenty of time practicing in the kart and sent me out on track. Of course, as a family, we Wheldons always went karting together, even on vacation, and we'd usually get thrown out because we were so competitive. I wasn't short on miles, let's just say that. When I came back in to the pits the guy said, "You're the quickest plumber I've ever seen!"

When Dan was in there with us, he would be telling us what to do and stuff. He told us that on the first corner you've got to brake really late. On my next lap I saw him looking, so I braked really late; so late I was on the grass. He just shook his head and went, "Oh God…" That was funny. It was just like the way I remember Dad shaking his head at Dan when he first let him drive his BMW…and he went and did burnouts in it!

I still have the suit and helmet Dan wore at the Robo-Pong kart race, and his helmet designer, Jason Fowler, made me a special one in memory of Dan. I wear it at the DW charity karting events. Dan trusted Jason completely and he always had the best helmet designs; so many great memories just looking at them.

I think my favorite race was the 2011 Indy 500. Being there to see him win was just amazing. We were all up in the hospitality suite. It was the last lap and I saw JR Hildebrand crash. I was the only one who saw it though, so I jumped up with joy and everybody was looking at me puzzled going, "What?" Then they realized what happened and we all rushed down to Victory Lane, it was so good. That was such a special moment.

He really was a brilliant brother. ∎

Part #2 CARS... AND AMERICA

Three years racing cars in the UK promised much, but funds were scarce. Along came the American dream

by CLIVE WHELDON

■ KART RACER, SUCCESSFUL BUSINESSMAN

DAN CONNECTION
Father, mentor

At the end of 1995, Dan was going into cars from karting, and I had to take a step back. You have to let them get on with it. He went with Jim Lee Racing to race in the Vauxhall Junior championship; went to the final round and finished second. That was all so tight, four of them could have won.

Andy Welch was probably not the team we should have gone with for Formula Ford after that first year, and Ralph Firman and Van Diemen was definitely not the team we should have gone with the second year in Ford. We should have gone with Mygale then. But Ralph wanted a championship, and the year we decided to go with

Ralph was the year he was in the hospital, so we were in the car from the year before whereas Mygale had taken a big leap forward. He apologized, but you make your choice, and that's it.

I didn't want to do the Formula Ford Festival with Van Diemen in 1998, and Mygale wanted us to do it with them. To be fair, Ralph said, "Stay with me for the Festival, Clive, I'll engineer Dan myself." He did, and the car was quick. Mygale was still good. Dan got by Jenson [Button] on the last lap, but it was just as a yellow came out, Button left a gap, Dan dived down the inside and took the lead. Dan backed off on the last two corners and let Button back again because he'd seen the waved yellows.

Over the winter, Andy Pycock with Paul Stewart Racing popped up and asked us to do some testing, so we went off to Pembrey. Dan was signed up to do Formula Vauxhall for 1999. I thought, great, the deal would be Vauxhall, Formula 3 with them and then move on. But basically, within a week, it was off. The team [Stewart GP]

Right: A deal with Sir Jackie Stewart's son's team Paul Stewart Racing fell through when it closed to focus on Stewart GP. That led to a championship-winning season in 1999 in USF2000 followed by Toyota Atlantic (left) and Indy Lights (above)

wasn't doing very well in Formula 1 and Jackie [Stewart] was told to concentrate on that and drop all of the junior teams.

Where could we go? All of the subsidized drives had gone. Then Andy, through Ralph Firman, suggested we go and do a test with Baytos in America, because they had just won the Formula 2000 championship. We also had Formula Renault in France, so they were our two options. We decided to go and do the test in America straight away, and in the first test he was quicker than the guy who won the championship. Andy suggested that if Dan liked it, while they were there he and Dan should go and look at apartments for him near where the team was based. They did that, then had the rest of the day off and had the time of their lives on jet skis and whatnot... on my credit card!

Jon Baytos wanted Dan in the team and Formula 2000 was massive in America at the time. Ralph rang and said he would supply a car free of charge and all the spares, so we didn't have to worry about crashes or anything.

This was right before Christmas 1998, and Baytos said he wanted Dan there more or less right away to go testing – January 2, just after Christmas.... It was the saddest day. Off he went with his bags and his helmets over to his new apartment, but Baytos hadn't gotten the new cars from Ralph. That meant no testing. Dan didn't have any friends because he didn't know anyone there. He rang up one night and he was in tears, homesick. He said, "Dad, I want to come home. I'm not doing any testing, and I just want to be in a car." I told him we'd made our bed, and we'd have to stick to it. I told him I'd call Baytos and find out what the hell was going on.

I rang Jon up and said, "If you don't get him out in a car testing, you aren't going to have a driver. He wants to come back to England. He needs to get in that car, test and make sure in his head that he is quick enough to win." I also told him that he'd best get his butt around to Dan's apartment and help the kid – which, to be fair he did – and they ended up being best of friends. That's how his racing started in America. He won the USF2000 championship in his first year, and then he was made.

"Dan didn't know anyone there, had no friends. He rang up one night and he was in tears, homesick"

"When he'd finished, he'd FedEx his race kit from the hotel so he could travel only with hand luggage"

I went over to every Formula 2000 race, and I went to quite a lot of his Atlantic races the next year. I used to fly out on Friday morning, and fly back on Sunday night! People would say to me, "What was Toronto like?" I'd say, "From the airport to the track was great...didn't see much else." In the early days of Formula 2000, Baytos used to put us in some real crap motels. I remember one in Jacksonville, where there were bullet holes in our bedroom window.

I didn't go to that many Indy Lights races because I was so involved in work in England that I couldn't get out there to be with him all the time. When we went from karts to cars in the UK, we had a manager and I stepped back. They paid for his racing in Vauxhall Junior – well, they did in the end. There were lots of late payments. I'd get phone calls from the team, "He can't go in the car, we've got no money." It got to the end of the Formula Ford days, and I was paying all the bills for Ralph Firman. I've never missed a payment.

I decided that when we went to America, they weren't good enough. Julian [Jakobi] approached me. I went to London and met him and he said, "Look, we will look after Dan. I don't want a penny until he starts earning money. But when he starts earning money, we take a percentage. No more, no less."

I thought about it, went back in, and we never looked back. From 2000, Adrian [Sussmann] was put in to look after Daniel and then Mickey [Ryan], too.

Dan always gave Adrian such a hard time, Julian, too. I walked into the bedroom one time and he was on the phone giving Julian a really hard time. He used to give him some shit! But they were always great friends. Adrian took things on the chin, but Dan did make them work for their money.

I'll tell you the funniest thing... Later on Dan had the code for Julian's company FedEx account, so he used to send stuff back and forth, like all the Christmas parcels, everything... He always said, "Don't worry, FedEx it back." When he finished at a track, he'd FedEx his race kit back from the hotel, so he could travel with only hand luggage. He'd FedEx his suitcases and race gear! It was more than $1,500 a month! Julian couldn't understand why the FedEx

In 2000, Dan was runner-up to champion Buddy Rice in Toyota Atlantic (left). Five years later his first Indy 500 win was the reward for making the move to America from Europe

bills were so high! He finally found out and put a stop to that....

When Dan had that year out [in 2002 after Lights] because there was no money, Dan really pushed them: "If you think I'm that good, why can't you raise any money?" In the end, it was the last two races of IndyCar in 2002. I said to Dan, if we don't race these last two races – it doesn't matter how good you are – you'll be history. So, a deal was done for the last two races with Panther Racing.

I went out to the first one, which was at Chicago, and he was

mega. He was up there with them all and he was noticed by Michael Andretti. He did the Texas race, but they put a busted battery in and the radio communication was gone. But he was up there at the front, and that's where it all happened with Michael who made contact with Adrian, and he got the deal for 2003 with Andretti Green.

In the 2005 season, he was unbeatable. He had a really good engineer, Eddie [Ed Jones], and Dan hit it off very well. He won four of the first five races, including Indy, Chip [Ganassi] wanted him

"At that time, BMW also came calling. Basically Dan was wanted in Formula 1"

In December 2011, Dan had been due to receive a prestigious Autosport Award in London to celebrate his Indy 500 win. Clive accepted it from long-time friend, Dario Franchitti

MICHAEL LEVITT/LAT

and, to be fair, Andretti wasn't paying him what he deserved, but they had taken him on, and Dan never moaned about it.

At that time, BMW also came calling. Basically Julian wanted Dan in Formula 1. Everyone thinks about F1 don't they? In his early interviews in karting and in the UK, Dan's dream always was to be Formula 1 World Champion.

The thing with the F1 deal was it was going to be a testing year because they didn't know what was going to happen with Jacques Villeneuve. BMW couldn't guarantee that Dan would be racing in the car the year after because they were governed by the deal Villeneuve had with Sauber. Dan wasn't happy with the fact that if he went testing he didn't want to be stuck not racing after, and he was giving up a great career in America. When you hear that someone's won the Indy 500 – that was huge in America – and he will test but may not be in the car the year after.... Well, then you start to think about trying to get back into a decent team in America if he didn't get in the car. We were up all night. We had Julian and Adrian on the phone, Dan and myself, and the conversations were where we were going to go. He was going to earn good money from BMW Sauber. But a racing driver wants to race.

Dan decided to go to Chip for 2006 and won a lot, but that got a bit strange at the end of 2008. It had been typical Chip, he'd wanted a fresh driver in Kanaan, and Dan found out about it. TK's in it for himself, which is fine, that's racing drivers. But he was not straight with Dan. Meanwhile, Andretti was waiting for Kanaan to sign, and he was hanging it out, waiting to see what Chip's deal was. In the end we worked together, and Michael said to TK, "Right, if you don't sign now, there's no seat." TK signed.

So, Dan was in the UK with us at home and Chip was ringing up, saying, "Come on Dan, I want you to sign." I can't remember Dan's exact words, but it was perfectly put together. In as many words it was, "I don't want to drive for someone who doesn't want me." Chip was taken aback. "You don't want to drive for me, Dan?" Dan said, "No. Not really."

I didn't want him to leave, I wanted him to stay with Chip, and

he and Scott [Dixon] got on really well. But Dan wanted to go with Panther and National Guard. I was against that because it was an unknown, while Chip was winning races. We talked with the guys all night again. We adjourned at midnight for an hour. We had to make a decision by the morning. So I spoke to Dan on my own. He said, "Dad, I don't want to drive for Chip again," and gave me his reasons why, and I understood that. The deal with John Barnes – National Guard, Panther – was he could have anything he wanted, he could have his engineer, testing, everything. At 1 a.m. we decided we were going down that route, and that was that.

Basically when we got to the team, there was no testing. Dan did, I think, just two tests in the simulator in Bicester, and after that it all went downhill. It was the old car, which we didn't know about. In the end, Dan bought a car and was told he was going to get the money back. It was coming toward the end of the season, and they owed him a lot. It was all a mess. It was eventually resolved but that meant Dan had the year off because Barnes didn't want to renew

The summer of 2011 for Dan was spent testing the all-new IndyCar for 2012, a car he helped develop and was looking forward to racing. In his honor it was renamed "DW12"

his contract and, with IndyCar getting harder to sell to sponsors, there were no other decent seats available.

That's when he did the TV work with Versus. He was brilliant at that. They'd never done the "grid walk" in America before. They loved it. TV wanted to keep him, but we knew we were getting the deal with Andretti for 2012, because Adrian was working on that with Michael – and the money, too – to put Dan in the car.

That's what I said to Dan when he was doing the Vegas race.... We always spoke before every race. He had come in on the Saturday night, he and Susie had gotten their tattoos done, they had just come back from dinner and were getting ready for bed. I asked him what was the car like. He said, "It's shit! But the guys are working on it through the night. I'll sort it Dad, don't worry about it."

I said, "You don't have to do this race." But IndyCar had offered this prize to this competition winner if Dan won. He said, "I've got to do it Dad. I met the woman today, they've flown her in, given her the VIP treatment, I can't back out now." He ran a good team, Sam

Schmidt. You saw in the first few laps, that the car was quick. If it wouldn't have been for that gimmick, I think he'd have pulled out, because he'd already signed the deal with Andretti that morning.

You can't stop a driver from doing what he loves doing, no matter how much you want to. You can say your bit, but that's it.

I'm very proud of all that Dan achieved, and the good times and memories we have of us getting there. There are only a few things on display at home now, a helmet and some awards. I keep a corner for Dan, talk to him every morning. There's also a picture on the wall after the Indy 2011 win, which he wrote a message to us on and signed. That is very special. ∎

To Mum + Dad

Our 2nd Indianapolis 500 win, as a family, was a very emotional one. Without the two of you, none of this would be possible. You both are the best parents a son or daughter could ever ask for. I Love You.

Dan #98

NEW TERRITORY

Fresh from Europe and facing a new challenge, Dan Wheldon had to settle into his new home across the Atlantic

by JON BAYTOS

- TEAM OWNER, PRIMUS RACING; OWNER USF2000 SERIES

DAN CONNECTION
Winning USF2000 championship team owner, 1999

MICHAEL LEVITT/LAT

I was managing a team in USF2000, running Van Diemen chassis; I was the U.S. importer, too. In 1998, David Besnard was with us and won the championship. For a couple of years, we would send the USF2000 champion over to Europe to do the Formula Ford Festival as part of the works Van Diemen team.

So, David went over there to join the works guys, Dan Wheldon and Marcos Ambrose. David and Dan were a bit opposite in terms of personality, but they ended up getting along really well. David came back and told me he'd really worked on this young guy to come over.

Ralph Firman, owner of Van Diemen, was intent on getting people to race from over there. We started off trying to convince Ambrose to come over for 1999, and I talked to him and Ralph, but I don't think he was too keen on the ovals. Dan wasn't on the radar for us because he was trying to do something with Paul Stewart Racing. If it was going to be anything, it was going to be Vauxhall Lotus because there just wasn't the cash to do the F3 thing they wanted to do.

That didn't happen, and I got a call from Clive. He immediately started working on me from the cost standpoint! We agreed to get him over here and do a test at Sebring. He came with Paul Stewart's Andy Pycock who was acting as his manager. Ralph Firman just happened to be in town as well, so Ralph and I met up with Andy and Dan down at the Vinoy in downtown St. Pete.

He was incredibly quiet at dinner. I don't know if that's because Ralph was around or maybe it was because it was all new. I drive a "dually" pickup truck, and when we got in to go to Sebring for the

test, he was really impressed – thought it was fantastic. As he said, "You don't see many of those in England – well, any." We drove and as we talked and talked about the truck, he relaxed… As soon as he got to the racetrack his personality came out, that's for sure.

The test went very well, and my partner and engineer at the time, John Hayes, really clicked. We were going over it all, and Pycock is telling me "We're $15,000 apart." Clearly we were going to do a deal but there was this $15,000, and Dan walked up and said to him: "Just give him the $15,000. I'm doing this bloody thing regardless…" And, that was that.

I set up this nice apartment a couple of miles from the workshop, but Dan was obviously struggling. We were really late getting cars and Clive was starting to freak a bit. Dan was at the workshop every day, but we weren't out testing, and he had too much time on his hands. Clive was telling me I had to get him in something to test because he was getting homesick in a big way. Every day he would walk into the workshop and sit in front of my desk, and drive me crazy… just talking. Then he'd go out to the shop and roll around on a stool and talk to everybody while they were trying to work.

> "Every day he would walk into the workshop and sit in front of my desk, and drive me crazy… just talking"

He got friendly with one of my mechanics, John Newberg, and he started getting into the St. Pete scene a little. Things were a bit easier going forward from there.

The first race was on the oval at Phoenix. Dan was pretty cocky about wiping the Americans out, despite the fact that we didn't actually test on an oval because of the lateness of the cars. It was all brand new to him. But Besnard, being the character he was, told him, "It's only two corners, they just happen to be two 135mph corners..." For David, it was super easy, and for some people it is. Dan finished second, amazingly, but said that it was a hell of a lot more difficult than he thought it would be. Looking back, for him to come and say that it was difficult was really something. He would never, ever, say that. He obviously made a mental note of it.

We went to quite a few ovals that year, and the last one was Pikes Peak. He probably should have won Atlanta and Charlotte, but those were really about big pack racing. He got to Pikes Peak and he absolutely dominated – which he really needed to do, because he was behind in points at that stage.

I was down in Turn 1, watching. Dan's commitment and the way he leaned on the rear wheel was so different than it was when he was at Phoenix. His head was way down. Pikes Peak is a lot like Phoenix in that it's not quite flat unless everything is exactly spot-on.

He won the championship and moved to California when he went up to Toyota Atlantic. We remained great friends, and we'd still talk all the time. He came back and worked for me in 2001 up to a bit of '03. I owned the USF2000 series from 2000, and Dan was trying to earn some money, so I employed him as the series driver coach, and he was fantastic at it. Even when he got the Andretti deal, he still did the first part of the year. He was such a money grabber, though; he was constantly hitting me up for a pay raise. He was very precise, even as a coach. He would come in from a corner with his segment times, and they were written like they'd been done on a typewriter!

As for his race-kit, oh, man – that was a sickness! Everything in that race bag had its place, and if anybody messed with that, he would flip. He had these little compartments and partitions so that things wouldn't touch each other. Joking aside, he was always incredible at the preparation side of it all, every aspect of being ready for a race. Back then, it wasn't as easy as it is today for young drivers with YouTube and so on.

I had been so busy in 1998, that by 1999 I really couldn't have cared less. I was burned out and I didn't know if I even wanted to do it again. Dan came along and we had a blast, such a fun time, and it rejuvenated me. All the guys in the team were friends and we went out because they worked hard, played hard and stuck together. Dan was the ringleader, like a giant comic, and it leaves us with great memories. It was a wonderful year. ■

PANTHER ON THE PROWL

Two races at the end of 2002 for Panther Racing intoduced the IndyCar world to a new predator

> "He really was the handsome Prince who had vanquished the infidels, conquered his rivals and returned from the Crusade victorious. 'Lionheart!'"

by MIKE GRIFFIN

- PANTHER RACING CO-OWNER 1997-2014

DAN CONNECTION
Panther Racing 2002, 2009-2010

Dan was a boyish charmer. His smile lit up a huge area all around you. He radiated a positive energetic presence that was magnetic in attracting your attention. He was very self-confident, having raced his way to America by learning to read the car and its behavior with every cell of his body. He learned people in the same way, by trying them, probing them, racing against them. Remembering and cataloging in detail their responses to his "moves." He was constantly "racing."

A very smart man who earned his success with a total commitment to settle for nothing less, and he considered his life an ongoing project. He worked out to strengthen himself physically and mentally, and build endurance. Shoes, clothes, appearance, concentration and focus were his mantra. He was constantly improving himself and his performance.

Great racing drivers develop the ability to focus their entire reality completely on the car, the track and the "chess game." During a pit conversation leaning into the car, you'll see his eyes refocus on a distant point at the end of Pit Road. He has mentally "flipped the switch," shifting focus to the track. An engineer or crewmember might provide more information via radio and it will be heard, noted, processed and added to the database, but, mentally, he is already driving out of the pits.

Dan was perhaps one of the most driven people I've ever known. It was almost as if he was with you, doing whatever you were doing, but he was also watching the sand flowing through his hourglass at the same time. I wondered if he ever just daydreamed: Nature, sunshine, silence...be-here-now kinds of feelings.

Impatient with mundane tasks and with little tolerance for wankers, he often moved as if he were being pursued. He was a perfectionist in nearly everything that he did, but hurried. Preoccupied with what was around the next corner. Not necessarily rude but more interested in the near future than the now. He had little patience with anyone who was not making a 200 percent effort all the time because he was.

In Victory Lane, he came to life, grinning and sparking and bubbling. He could finally let his emotions flow and let go of the concentration, focus, and discipline required to drive a racecar perfectly at the edge. He really was the handsome Prince who had vanquished the infidels, conquered his rivals and returned from the Crusade victorious. "Lionheart!" He lived his life for this moment. He loved it. He was joyous, spraying the cheering crowd with champagne or even better, milk. The joy was contagious. ■

SMOKED 'EM

DAN WHELDON'S VICTORY at the 2005 IndyCar Series season-opener at Homestead-Miami Speedway set the tone for his championship year. Four wins from the first five races allowed the Andretti Green racer plenty of opportunity to use his Honda power to please the crowds with celebratory donuts. He would end the year with six wins, including the Indy 500 crown, and the title of 2005 IRL IndyCar Series champion.

THE DREAM TEAM

Baby sister Holly Wheldon fires the questions at family friend and racing teammate Dario Franchitti

When Dan Wheldon made the move from England to America just after Christmas 1999, his baby

sister, Holly, was only 6 years old. Any memories Holly has of her brother's racing career in karts or

junior formulae in the UK come from family memories and scrapbooks and the odd home video.

One driver (later teammate, rival, fellow winner and champion) witnessed Dan's formative years

in karting, became a firm family friend and has also won the IndyCar title and multiple Indy 500s.

Dario Franchitti was the ideal person for Holly to sit with and download memories of her brother.

There are moments of support, disagreement, respect and above all pride about Dan Wheldon's

journey to his first Indy 500 win in 2005, when Holly had yet to become a teenager.

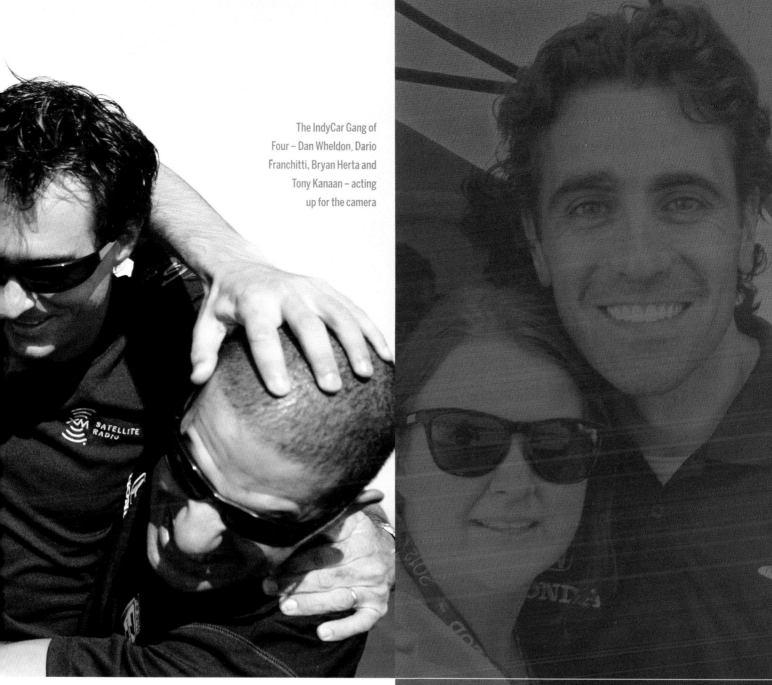

The IndyCar Gang of Four – Dan Wheldon, Dario Franchitti, Bryan Herta and Tony Kanaan – acting up for the camera

DARIO FRANCHITTI

INTERVIEW by HOLLY WHELDON

■ THREE-TIME INDY 500 WINNER, FOUR-TIME INDYCAR CHAMPION

DAN CONNECTION
Lifetime friends; teammates at Andretti Green, 2003-2005

HW: When did you first meet Dan?

DF: My first recollection of Dan was not meeting him, but seeing him. It would have been 1985 maybe? Clive [Dan and Holly's Dad] was still racing. It was testing at Rye House in the UK and he'd have been about 6 or 7, I'd say.

HW: That's about the same age as Sebastian [Dan's son, Holly's nephew] is now.

DF: Yeah, and he was little. In the lunch break, he would go out and run around. It was a proper 100cc kart as far as I remember. It went like hell because he weighed nothing. I stood there, mouth wide open thinking, "Who the hell is that? This kid is really good…" I mean, I was only 11 or 12 and it was just shocking that this little kid could do this. I was driving a Deavinson Sprint and Clive drove a Sprint kart also, so I found out more about him and got to know Clive a little. But I never really spoke to Dan at that point.

A young Dan tops the podium (above); Something borrowed – something blue...(right), DW in Dario's racesuit for his AGR debut at short notice

I always remember Clive used to show up in his transit van from his plumbing business... then he showed up in a 911 turbo one day and I thought, "Wow! Plumbers aren't the same in Scotland as they are in England!" He was still racing then, and winning. There were some good guys back then.

HW: He never won a championship though. We always mock him for that.

DF: He was never doing it seriously. Clive had a business, a job, and a family. He wasn't a professional. But he was very, very good. In 1986, Cadet karting started and my little brother Marino started racing with Dan – they were born something like two weeks apart. That's when I really got to know Dan. Well, I say I got to know him, but he was kind of a mouth on legs. Anyway, I was a teenager and way too cool to hang about with that lot. You've got no time for your little brother's mates at that age!

HW: I remember someone telling me that your parents and my parents would be together, and my mum used to make you sandwiches....

DF: Well my mum wouldn't come to races. She would stay at home and look after business. So Dad would take Marino and me to the track. Your mum was always really kind and if I couldn't find Marino I knew he'd be in your motor home with your mum feeding him loads of food! Our priority was getting the kart to go as fast as we could, so for us there was nobody, no sort of catering... and,

"Dan was just a mouth on legs. He was so cocky and so loud"

yeah, your mum was really very good to us.

Your dad took it very seriously, so there were guys like him, John Button, all these guys who were taking it very seriously. From day one, Clive was like that with Dan.

I remember when he won his first British championship; I think it was at Wombwell. That might have been the day Marino missed a race because he was out playing with his mates! But that was the thing to remember, they were kids. It was bad enough starting at 10 but these kids were 8 years old. Dan was under a lot of pressure because of, again, the level to which Clive took it. He gave Dan a massive opportunity to eventually go racing but he was expected to do well because of the effort that was put in.

There are all these funny stories about your dad taking the

Wheldon (above left) was the new kid in town, testing, 2003; High heels and high jinx for a good cause (above); The result of a hot-headed decision (left) while battling each other for the lead in Japan, 2005

engines home at night to a hotel room and hiding them under the bed. Whether or not that's true, I don't know....

HW: That's definitely true! He told us that he would take the engines home at night and just put them in the hotel room that he was staying at, because he didn't want them to get taken or tampered with....

DF: In those days, Dan was just, like I say, he was a mouth on legs. He was so cocky and so loud – all those things. I was just like "God almighty!" (Laughs) But the thing was he could back it up. He was a bloody good young driver, and he made me laugh.

HW: What happened when you went to cars from karts?

DF: I moved to England in 1991. I was driving for the Leslies in Vauxhall Junior, so I had been commuting from Scotland. In 1992, I lived just outside Milton Keynes with my engineer, and then in 1993 I was there full time in Harrold – the next village up from you in Emberton. I was there two years before I went racing in Germany with Mercedes. At that point, Dan spent a lot of his time racing abroad with Terry Fullerton. I saw Dan a bit during this period, as we were living just a few miles apart and he was hanging out with Marino and Kristian Kolby and I was dating Kristian's sister Kirsten.

I went to America after that and next thing I know, I'm standing on the pit wall at Mid-Ohio and a much more serious, more professional Dan Wheldon comes up to me and says, "Hello, it's been a while," or words to that effect. "Can you help me, I've never

been here before?" He was racing Formula 2000. I said, "If there's anything you need pal, just let me know." From that point until the end of 2005, he never stopped asking questions!

HW: Were you aware of Dan's racing in the UK after you'd gone?

DF: I knew what he'd done in Vauxhall Junior and Formula Ford, again because Marino was a very similar age. I always kept an eye on what was going on. I knew he'd gone out to America, which struck me as a bit of a waste, him having to go so early.

I know why he did it, the same reason a lot of guys do: money. But I always felt that Dan had the talent and potential to be a Formula 1 World Champion. Even when he was a young boy I thought he had something special. Ultimately, he went to IndyCar and had a great career there. But when I saw him there at Mid-Ohio, I thought it was a bit of a shame.

I don't really remember much else of that time, him in Atlantics and Lights. I was in the middle of a championship fight in '99, and was focused on CART. You know what it's like.

HW: I remember going to see him when he was in Atlantics in 2000. I can picture the apartment in my head. I would've been 7 or 8.... So I guess the first time you actually raced him would have been in IndyCar?

DF: Yes, I was still in CART when Dan came on at the end of 2002 for a couple of IRL races. Tony [Kanaan] and I had signed for Andretti Green as the team moved to IRL for 2003. I'd been with them in CART for five years anyway by then. Dan came on to the team as a sort of development driver. Kim Green was a huge Dan fan; from day one he was massively impressed with Dan. Dan did a lot of the winter testing for us in the Indy car.

HW: I remember a story that you called and asked how the new boy was doing. You'd all sent him testing (laughs)...

DF: Yeah! Well, it was the early days of the Honda engine and Dan was trusted to do the work. Which says a lot about how they felt about him because he was basically a rookie.

I don't know if it was always apparent that he was going to take over from Michael [Andretti] after Indy, but I broke my back, and Dan did the race at Motegi in Japan, and then he did Indy, where he ended up upside down.

I wasn't at a lot of the races because I was having surgery getting my back fixed. I came back at the start of '04 and Dan was already a big part of the team. We'd gone from three to four cars because Bryan [Herta] had driven my car when Dan took over full time from Michael, and had done such a good job they wanted to keep him. So Bryan drove the XM car, which was a Honda development car. We used to call Bryan "EB". It stands for Engine Bitch, as he used to do

Celebrating as one when the planets aligned and the Dream Team finished 1-2-3-4; Signing autographs (below) as superstars of Indy!

"That podium is one of those moments that has special meaning now"

all the development work. He got this monster engine they built for Michigan in '05 where he won. He came back after the celebrations; he turned to us and said, "Who's the Bitch now?"

HW: The 2005 season was a good one for Dan. A very good one!

DF: Yes, right from the start he was on it. He won Homestead, St. Pete, Motegi and Indy. He didn't win Phoenix... That was when we had a falling out. We'll come to that in a moment, as it shows how strong we were as a team.

But in Japan – after winning the races at Homestead and St. Pete – by Motegi, he was on a roll. At one of the restarts, Dan got a run and went down the inside wheel to wheel into Turn Three and we went through Turns Three and Four like that. You know those situations where you're just being stubborn? I should've just backed out of it, but I wasn't going to because he'd won a couple of races, and I was going to redress the balance. It was stupid, I got on the marbles and crashed, and he went on and won the race.

HW: So, come on then, why did you two have a falling out at Phoenix?

DF: I was battling Sam Hornish for the lead. Something had happened to Dan, and we came up to put him a lap down. He let Hornish go and then he held me up and I finished second to Hornish. He didn't let me through when he was a lap down. We had a meeting, me, him, Tony and Bryan. We gave it to him with both barrels!

That was how we sorted things like this out, how we worked in the team, the four of us. No team managers or anything like that; we always took care of ourselves. It was like we controlled ourselves because majority always ruled, whoever it was. Whether it was Dan, Tony, Bryan or me, whoever was not doing what they should do we had a chat to clear it up. Sometimes I got in trouble, sometimes it was Tony, sometimes it was Bryan, and sometimes it was Dan.

Phoenix was the first one of our really big meetings. We sat in a hotel room and it was explained to Dan that that was not what teammates do. That's not the way we worked and not the way we were going to work. The team was bigger than any one of us and he wasn't going to do that and we were not going to condone that.

He got really upset. Not combative, just very upset. He was really apologetic and he took it on board. It was serious, there was a lot of emotion in that meeting shall we say! But that was it. Then we had the next race, where we finished one, two, three, and four at St. Pete.

HW: There is a great photo from that St. Pete race of you all hugging after; I've seen a big print of it....

DF: That podium is one of those moments that – looking back – has special meaning now. I do remember how upset I was that day in Florida. We could only get a half tank of fuel at the stops. I remember Kyle [Moyer, strategist] coming on the radio and saying if we've got a full load in this time you've got it won. But we hadn't...

That podium was so special, we were up there and we saw Bryan standing at the side and called him to get up with us too. Looking back now at the whole situation; we'd fallen out at the previous race, had our big team meeting to sort it out, and set boundaries if you like – for all of us – and we scored the perfect result. And we did it in Dan's hometown.

HW: Are there any on-track moments that stick out?

DF: We were in always in good shape at Indy. Tony was fast, I was fast, Dan was fast, and Bryan was too. One moment that reminds me how close we were was also one of the bravest things I've ever seen. Bryan crashed at Turn One during qualifying in 2004, usual story. Went in and boom, backed it in. He went home to California.

He came back the next week and I remember Dan, Tony and myself standing at the data watching, and on his first lap he went through Turn One flat-out. The three of us were amazed. That gives you some idea of the kind of team morale we did have. People would call us the Gang of Four or The Dream Team and all that...but we were genuinely friends. We competed bloody hard. And we helped each other a lot too. Ultimately we were good friends.

The 500 in 2005 is another moment. Dan drove a belter. There was one restart where I thought I could have a shot at him near the end. I knew I had to get by him on a restart or I wasn't going to make it. Dan deserved that one, he really did. ∎

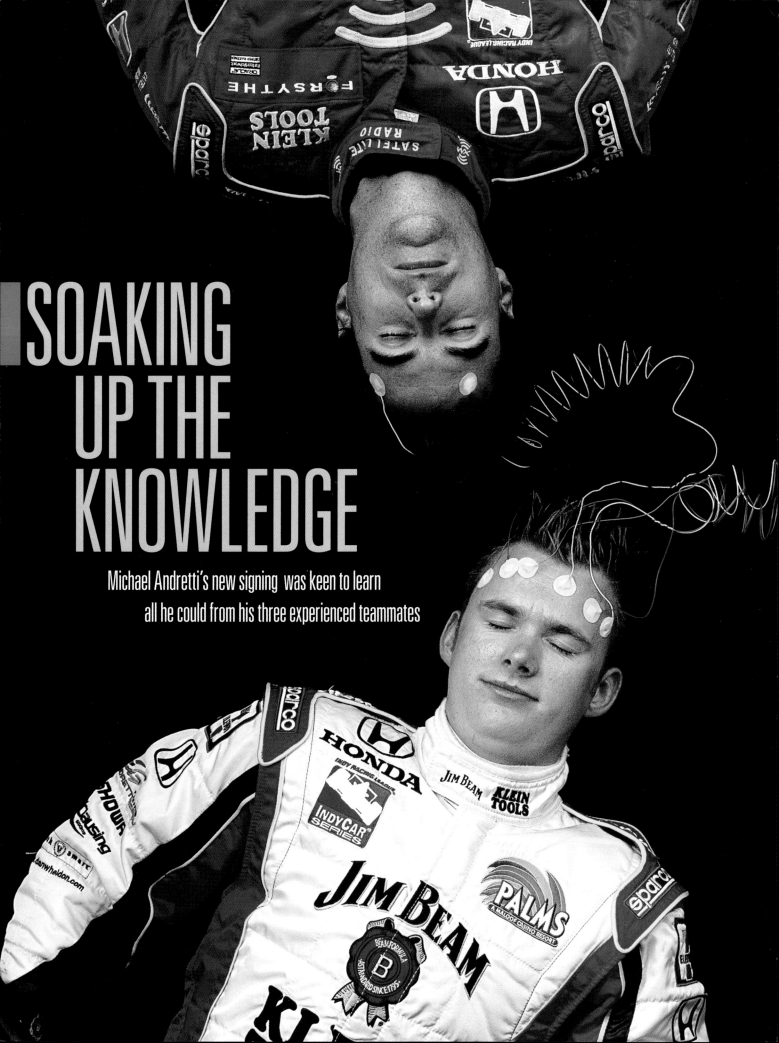

SOAKING UP THE KNOWLEDGE

Michael Andretti's new signing was keen to learn
all he could from his three experienced teammates

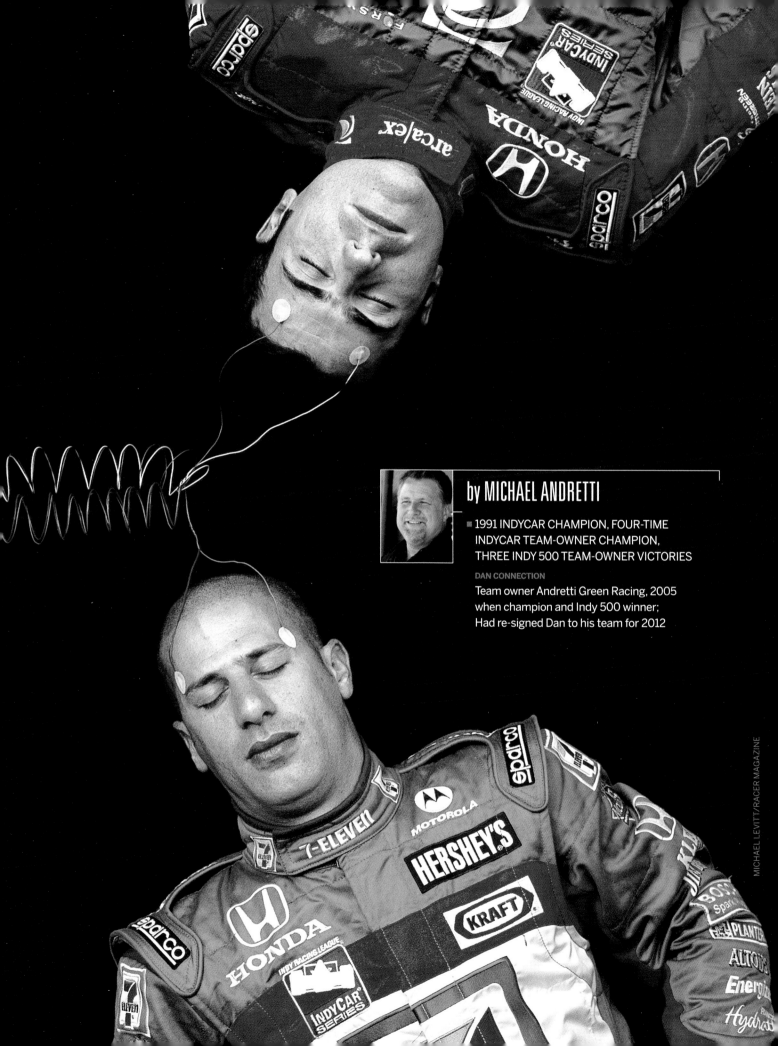

by **MICHAEL ANDRETTI**

■ 1991 INDYCAR CHAMPION, FOUR-TIME
INDYCAR TEAM-OWNER CHAMPION,
THREE INDY 500 TEAM-OWNER VICTORIES

DAN CONNECTION
Team owner Andretti Green Racing, 2005
when champion and Indy 500 winner;
Had re-signed Dan to his team for 2012

The first time I met Dan, he had just tested for Panther Racing and had done very well. At that point, his deal was only ovals and we looked at him as a really talented oval racer. We thought he had a lot of potential and we wanted to get a young kid on our team to replace me once I retired. We thought he would be the perfect choice to go after, so that's what we did.

Before he even raced for our team, he did miles and miles of testing for us. We were just starting in the IRL, so he tested for us constantly. He did an excellent job, giving us great feedback and good knowledge as to what the cars did and how they reacted to different situations. The cars and the series were new to us, so we needed as much knowledge as we could get. Dan was crucial to our early success in the Indy Racing League.

The plan was to move him up to a full-time ride once I retired, but when Dario Franchitti hurt his back in a motorcycle crash in 2003, we put Dan in Dario's car at Motegi. He did a solid job, finishing seventh. From then on, he took over for me and just kept getting better and better.

My early recollection of him was that he was a great kid who was a bit cocky, but that's what you want in a young driver. We felt like he was going to fit right in, and he did. Dan got better and better the longer he was with us. He was working with three veterans – Dario, Tony Kanaan and Bryan Herta – so he was able to absorb their knowledge. Every race he was able to improve and you could actually see it.

"The plan was to move him up to a full-time ride when I retired. He took over for me and kept getting better"

Wheldon's precison and ability to "lean" on his car was a natural gift; AGR team burnouts at Watkins Glen to celebrate his 2005 title; flying the flag after winning the Indy 500

"**He was always happy and always positive. He was a good guy to have around. He lifted our team and brought everyone closer**"

The big test was road courses. We tested at the Daytona road course as the IRL prepared for its first road/street race in 2005. By the end of the session, he was quickest. That was a shock to all of us. We hadn't seen road racing to be his strength, but he performed very well at that test. Then he went out and won the first IRL street-course race at St. Pete. The team finished 1-2-3-4 in that race, and Dan was in front. The fact that we were that fast can be traced back to Dan's testing with us. He gave us a great understanding of the car and how it would react to road and street racing.

But Indianapolis Motor Speedway is where he really stood out. Dan and Marco are the two best drivers I've experienced at Indy. They both took to it like fish to water. They both ran the car so neutral there. I've never seen any other drivers do that. If you watch the in-car cameras from Dan's win at Indy for us in 2005, you can see how loose that car was. He carried it all the way for 500 miles. He just had a real knack for Indy.

The other thing about Dan was his charisma. He was a magnetic guy. The room always lit up whenever Dan came in. He had a strong personality that drew people to him. He was always happy and always positive. He was a good guy to have around. He lifted our team and brought everyone closer together.

He always was very anal and obsessive about order and the way things had to be around him, and that led the other guys on the team to play practical jokes on him. When they did it, he would freak out,

which only enticed them to do it more. He had a big target on his back, but it was always done in a playful way; it wasn't mean-spirited.

There were times when Tony would get into his locker at Indy and turn everything upside down. Dan wouldn't just laugh it off; he would get seriously angry about it, which only made the other guys laugh harder, so they'd play jokes on him more often. Eventually Dan learned how to get back at them, but it was his over-the-top reaction that led them to continue doing it.

We were all set to have Dan return to the team in 2012. I was truly looking forward to the second time around with him. I felt like he was reaching his prime and had championship potential and more Indy wins ahead of him. He was so much more mature at that point. He had gone through a tough time and didn't have a full-time ride, but he had proven that he was still extremely capable with his win at Indy in 2011. He was coming back with a sense of appreciation for what he had and what he had accomplished.

When he first started out, he was young and everything just happened so quickly. He earned it, no doubt, but I'm not sure that he appreciated his initial success. He was coming back humble but confident. He was going to be a very positive addition to our team, and we couldn't wait.

Through it all, Dan remained positive. He was so looking forward to coming back to us, and we were so excited to have him return. It would've been fun to see it happen. ▮

Putting a whole new spin on "milking the moment" in Victory Lane after his first Indy 500 win in 2005

By MARINO FRANCHITTI

- WEC SPORTSCAR RACER,
  FORD CHIP GANASSI RACING TEAM

DAN CONNECTION
Cadet kart, Daytona 24 Hours teammate, 2005

Dan was only two weeks older than me. I remember our first race was at Shenington in karts. It was the first cadet race in the UK. Three of us were battling when he broke down in the race, I've got a picture somewhere of me, and you can see Clive pulling on the starter of his kart in the background!

I didn't do karting to the level he did but we always kept in touch and, as we got older, we started to go out and socialize as young men. We started to cause some proper chaos, as I'm sure Kristian

beautifully laid out. So, just as a matter of course, we would go in and mess it up. You know, just as you walk past, pop your hand in and move stuff about. He'd come in and he'd fix it perfectly, then you'd walk back past and move it all around again. It had to be done. He took that pretty well, considering...

Also, in endurance races, there are all these stories about drivers peeing in the race seat during their stint, so you can imagine.... Dario and I were winding Dan up the whole time, telling him that's what happens and it was just inevitable. We would tell him we'd done it and obviously we hadn't. Just the look on his face when we were discussing it and the discussions we had after were so funny. The clean freak couldn't even cope with thoughts of that.

I was with the boys in Japan when we did his room over, and that was funny (I maxed the heating out), but I also remember the bus trips back to Tokyo from Motegi after the races. Those were always

WORK HARD. PLAY HARD.

They had their first kart race together and over two decades on, shared a ride in the Daytona 24 Hours

Kolby has said. You grow up together but might not see each other for six months at a time, maybe longer, yet you get to experience so much of your formative years together. So many things like getting drunk the first time, going out to clubs, we did all that.

So, to have done all of that growing up and then eventually getting to drive together in 2005, was an absolute treat – and in the Daytona 24 Hours. Me, Dario, Dan and Milka [Duno]. The car wasn't the fastest, but we got everything out of the thing and we were right up at the front most of the race.

One of the best things about that whole deal was working with the Crawford team. They were great people, a lot of fun. In the other cars, you had Tony Stewart and Jimmie Johnson, who are great guys, in fact we all went to watch a dog race the night before the 24. The camaraderie between all the drivers was incredible.

Once you get into the race you barely ever see each other because you're rotating through stints. But the three of us were sharing a motor home as well, and it was just hilarious. I remember cracking up from start to finish, even at things that you maybe shouldn't be laughing about...The motor home was almost like a frat house, all our friends and everyone else just dropping in. We were taking it very seriously, and we were really focused, but on our down time, we just had so much fun.

Of course, Dan would have his helmet bag and it would all be

hilarious. We would load the bus up with drivers to wind down with a cold beer or two, playing cards and games. By the second year, we discovered how to get the karaoke machine working....

That was the thing though, we had a lot of good times but we worked as hard as we played. Not so much these days, but in our younger days that's what we did. We were all very serious about what we did, but we had a lot of fun once the job was done.

I also think Dan redefined what guys were doing on ovals. He was one of those guys, like a Marc Marquez in MotoGP, who comes along and finds a new edge to live against. That's certainly how it looked to me. The rest saw that and knew they had to catch up.

I think now, though, the things I remember more are from when we'd grown out of the special nights when we were younger. Dan was a father before I was but it was like someone flipped a switch when he found what he was looking for in life, with Susie and the boys. I remember talking to him before Sebastian was born and asking, "How are you going to cope with this; with the OCD and with a baby?" But he really did, you know? It was the one thing in the world that stopped him from twitching.

That was Dan. Thinking back to when we were young and as much fun as we had, that was the Dan I was most fond of and most proud of. Dan as he was in his later years, with his family – the person he'd become. That was a pretty special person. ■

Above: Two Franchittis and a Wheldon teamed up for Daytona's 24hrs. The legendary Motegi-Tokyo bus, with Bryan Herta, DW, Darren Manning, Marino, Buddy Rice and Vitor Meira

BROTHERLY LOVE

As teammates they were close, yet TK's and DW's
relationship was sometimes more like sibling rivalry

The different sides of Dan Wheldon most people didn't know about were discovered by the three of us – Dario Franchitti, Bryan Herta and I – when Dan joined us at Andretti Green Racing in 2003. There was a fun side of Dan, a crazy side, and a complicated side.

When I first met Dan, he was exactly like my young son Leo. I took Leo to the park today, and he kept saying, "Dad, are we there yet? Dad, are we there yet?" When we got there, he said, "Dad, when are we leaving? Dad, when are we leaving?" When I first met Dan, he was just like that. He asked me 4,000 questions a day about racing. "What do you do in this situation? How do you save fuel? What do you eat? What time do you go to bed?"

He was always eager to learn, and I think he thought if he did exactly what the rest of us did, he would become a champion. At

the time, he simply wanted to get better. Personality-wise, Dan and I were similar, or at least our personalities were closer together than his was to Dario's or Bryan's, so we bonded right away.

But as I got closer to Dan, I discovered odd little quirks about him. He was anal to a bizarre degree. Every shoe he owned had to be in a box and sorted, probably in alphabetical order or by color. He knew where everything he owned was at all times. If it got scratched or messed up somehow, he threw it away. He was insanely organized about things that really didn't matter, and I simply could not understand that.

How could I like this guy? In many respects, despite the similarities in our personalities, I had absolutely nothing in common with him. I have no hair; Dan was obsessed with his hair. He had 15 hair products with him at all times. It took him longer to get ready

to go out than most women. He had face creams and anti-wrinkle serums. I was like, "Who cares?" But that was Dan. It was part of what we all started to enjoy about him, if for no other reason than to give him a hard time.

He spent a lot of time at my home in Miami in those early days, and he started taking an interest in some of the things I was into. I'll never forget the time we were looking at cars at a local Ferrari dealership before the 2006 Indianapolis 500. He really wanted an Aston Martin they had in the showroom. I went to help him with the negotiation, and when they settled on a price, the salesman said, "Do you have a car to trade?"

Dan said, "I have four."

The salesman thought he said, "I have a Ford." No, sir, he had *four cars* to trade for the Aston Martin. What's really funny about

by TONY KANAAN

■ INDYCAR SERIES CHAMPION, 2004;
   INDY 500 WINNER, 2014

DAN CONNECTION

Andretti Green Racing teammate, 2003-2006

the story is that he got money back from the deal. Afterward, he thought he was the king of all car dealers.

Dan was Dan. If he was happy, he was happy. If he was mad, he was mad. He didn't speak to me for more than a year and a half at one point. He thought I was trying to take his seat with Chip Ganassi's team, which wasn't true. Chip had talked to me about the possibility of joining the team, but it had nothing to do with Dan. I told Dan at the time, "I don't have the power to do that, bro. Chip was the one who approached me." Dan was like, "Well, he should have told me."

I also never heard Dan apologize. After a year and a half passed, he just started talking to me again. There was no production, no apology, and no explanation. It was as if it never happened.

He had a very strong personality. If you were his friend, you were his friend for life. If you were not Dan's friend, he could be a complete jerk. That's just the way it was. He was great with race fans and with most of the people around him, and he had a clear vision of what he wanted to be and what he wanted to accomplish, but there were

times – especially early in his career – when he could come across in a bad way.

We all can be jerks at times, but early on when he was with Andretti Green, Dan was pretty full of himself, so much so that Dario and Bryan and I had to set him straight. Three times in the first three months we were teammates, we had to sit down with him and tell him what was what. The last time, Bryan made him cry. We basically had to impress on him that his nonsense wasn't going fly with us. He listened to us, and he grew up quite a bit after that.

If Dan was going to be something, he was going to be the best he could possibly be at it, and in those early days, there were times when he was the best jackass around. He could also be the best person around. I've never seen anyone as attentive or responsive to fans. He truly got that part of it – that the fans were responsible for what he did for a living and the life it gave him.

One of my favorite stories about Dan involved a trip to New York City. Back in the day, all the drivers in the Indy 500 would do

In 2004 Tony Kanaan was IndyCar Series champion. In 2005 it was DW's turn. Animated discussions (below left) after the 2011 Indy 500

"I'll always be grateful that Dan decided to start talking to me again. We were right back to where we were before"

a media tour in New York the day after qualifying. Well, one year we all qualified on Saturday, so we decided to go to New York early because Dan wanted to party. So Dario, Bryan, Dan and I rented a plane and flew there.

Dan was not a very good drinker, and since I'm not much of one, I was often in charge of babysitting him when we were out. This was one of those nights. We went out and had dinner and drinks, but we couldn't get a taxi to stop for us. Dan started getting mad. At one point, Bryan was trying to hail a cab, and Dan jumped on his back.

Well, that didn't sit well with Bryan, who shoved him aside. Dan, being half lit, decided he was going to fight Bryan in the middle of a Manhattan intersection. I had to referee. Needless to say, the night was wrecked, but somehow we managed to find three different cabs to take us back to our hotel.

On the track, I always felt like Dan raced me harder than he raced the other two guys. I never asked him about it, and I never really spoke about it with the other guys. He'd known Dario since he was a kid, and he respected Bryan because he was the oldest, but I always felt like he saw me as the competition. That said, he always knew what he was doing on the track, and he was always fair.

When he won the Indy 500 the second time in 2011, he passed

ROOM SERVICE?

When teammamtes pranked Dan at their Japanese hotel they did it big. The reaction was seismic

I'M SURE MANY people have heard the Motegi story – the massive prank we pulled on Dan during our race at Twin Ring Motegi in Japan, in 2004 – but here is my version. Well, my PG-rated version, anyway.

For drivers, our goal on the annual trip to Japan was to travel with carry-on luggage only. It was a week-long trip, we didn't really have to pack many clothing changes, so it wasn't a big deal to avoid the lines and the hassle of checking baggage and just carry everything on the plane.

Dario, Bryan and I got to the airport with our carry-on luggage and here comes Dan with two giant bags – one for his clothes and another for his shoes. I said, "You should have been born a girl."

(What's truly funny about that is, when we all actually did dress up as girls for Halloween one year, Dan was a really ugly girl. I told him, "I may be an ugly man, but you are an uglier woman.")

We started planning our prank on the flight to Tokyo. At Motegi, all the drivers stay at the hotel on site, so we asked Al Larsen, our public relations guy, to figure out a way for Dan to disappear for a while. Twin Ring Motegi is a fantastic facility – hotel at one end, oval and road course in the middle, and the famed Honda museum on the other side. We asked Al to take Dan away to the museum for an hour or two, and he did.

As soon as they left, I went down to the lobby and told a clerk, "Hi, my name is Dan Wheldon, and I lost my room key." She gave me his key, no ID, nothing. That policy changed by the time we returned in 2005...

Dan's room was right next to mine. The original idea was to get to Dan's shoes and steal the right one of each pair and ship them back to Indianapolis. He packed, and I kid you not, five pairs of shoes. Once we got into his room and saw that, we decided we needed to make a bigger statement.

So, we pulled the mattress out of his room and put it in mine. We went through his bag and found all of his face creams and hair products and messed them up. You would not believe how organized Dan kept his beauty products. The labels were all facing forward in the bathroom, everything was measured just right, all perfectly neat and clean. We wrecked it. Let's just say he didn't look quite right the rest of the weekend.

The next installment of the prank I really can't describe accurately in a family book, but let's just say we all left him a present.

> ## "We pulled the mattress out of his room. We turned the heat up as high as it would go and shut off the water"

Then, we turned the heat up as high as it would go, shut off the water, and removed every light bulb. We all went back to my room. I called Al and told him to stall as long as he could so the room would get as hot as possible, and then we waited.

We heard him coming and heard the door click as he opened it. About 15 seconds later, we heard this shrill scream and words I can't repeat. He had only seen the missing mattress and shoes. He came out into the hallway screaming and swearing. He went back into the room and saw the rest of it, and came out of the room screaming for Kim Green, our team's co-owner. He sounded like a little kid. Meanwhile, we sat in my room and tried not to let him hear us laughing.

By this time, every door on that floor of the hotel was open. People came out of their rooms to see what was going on. I heard him scream, "KANAAN!" I was like, "Hey, why me and nobody else?"

Dan went down to the lobby and told the clerk he was Tony Kanaan and had lost his key. Of course, he got a key to my room, not knowing that we were in it waiting for him. He opened the door and we were all sitting there laughing. He was really angry. In fact, Kim got mad at us because Dan refused to stay in that room and the hotel was full. The hotel had to send up a cleaning crew, and Dan made Kim switch rooms.

But do you want to know the best part? Five shoes – all for the right foot – arrived via FedEx the following week at the Andretti Green shop in Indianapolis. ■

Whether teammates or rivals, hugs, showers and cake would frequently be on public display in victory celebrations; TK was the self-voted "best looking woman" of the gang

me with about 15 laps left in the race. I didn't know it at the time, but he thought I chopped him a couple of times during the race. I hadn't, but he perceived it that way. While he passed me, I saw what appeared to be a wave. I thought, "What the hell? Why is he waving?"

He ended up winning and I finished fourth, so I walked to Victory Lane to congratulate him. I went to hug him, but he swore at me. He started yelling at me that I had cut him off. I said, "Dan, you just won the Indy 500. Let it go." He wouldn't, so I had to apologize. "I wouldn't do that to you," I said. "You know me."

Then I said, "Didn't you wave when you passed me? I thought you were happy."

He said, "No, I was flipping you off."

At the awards banquet the next night, I congratulated him on the win and had some fun with our little moment. I said, "I noticed you waving when you passed me. Sometimes when you stick your hand up at 200mph, you can't control all of your fingers. It looked like you lost a few of them."

I'll always be grateful that Dan decided to start talking to me again in 2011. It happened out of the blue. No explanation, no apology, just a simple greeting that washed away 18 months of silence. We were right back to where we were before. Best of buddies, brothers who occasionally tangled but always got over it, two guys who were alike and unalike.

Most of all, we were friends for eternity. ■

by RUBENS BARRICHELLO

- FORMULA 1 GRAND PRIX DRIVER,
  11 WINS (NINE WITH FERRARI)

DAN CONNECTION
Granja Viana 500-mile kart enduro-winning
teammate, 2004 & and 2005

Dan joined us twice for the big end-of-season kart race in Brazil, the Granja Viana 500-mile enduro just outside Sao Paulo. The event is great fun, and drivers from different categories all over the world come. I was in Formula 1 with Ferrari at the time. In 2004 Dan came, and our team was me, Tony Kanaan, Felipe Giaffone and Dan. Helio Castroneves and Gil de Ferran were in that race too. We had no pressure to perform, and Dan jelled with us so well. He drove the karts very well indeed.

Dan was great fun himself but, of course, we took it seriously! When I say that we had no pressure, that was because we could

Four Indy 500 winners and a Formula 1 star had "competitive fun" and a laugh at the end of season 500-mile kart race in Brazil

MAURICIO LIMA/GETTY IMAGES

Receiving the 2003 Autosport Rookie of the Year Award from Mark Webber

PETER SPINNEY/LAT

by MARK WEBBER

- FORMULA 1 GRAND PRIX DRIVER, NINE WINS (RED BULL RACING)

DAN CONNECTION
Fellow Brands Hatch Racing school instructor, 1996

I worked with Dan as an instructor, mainly at Brands Hatch back during 1996. Our lunch breaks were the highlight of the day in many ways, as we'd get a break from the customers! We were part of a group and used to bring in our packed lunches and sit down and tell each other how awesome we were! Dan always impressed the women and loved the bling. I liked him because there was always a bit of banter involved.

Our group usually included Jamie Spence, Matthew Davies, Mark Marchant, Johnny Mowlem, Karl Jones and myself – so, between us, there was more than enough mischief available to cause plenty of mayhem on a racetrack. In actual fact, the best part of our job was when we were given marshaling duties, which we all had to do, as we only had to sit and wave flags at various flag points around the track. It was easy

work. We'd know who was instructing in which car so we'd generally take liberties and wave all the different flags.

I look back now and think those poor people actually paid for the privilege of riding alongside us. They were literally passengers in our hands – I remember one time Jamie doing a "moonie" out of the window with a pupil alongside and then getting his ass stuck... Thank God there was no social media, or mobile phone cameras in those days – our careers would have been finished before they started!

Before instructing at Brands Hatch, Dan was part of the Early Drive scheme

set a good time in practice and then relax and have a churrasco ready to eat. While doing that, we had great meetings to set up the kart better!

I knew of Dan's name early in his career in England as he raced against younger Brazilian friends of mine, but it was only when TK showed me how special a friend he was that I took notice. They were best friends and so he became special to me too.

We had plenty of funny moments especially after we had a caipirinha together. Big laughs... I miss seeing him with TK, Dario and Herta when I would visit the races. They were so special together and I feel blessed to have been a part of it. ■

How Dan Wheldon won the 2005 Indy 500

This story ran in the IndyCar Series magazine that the RACER group produced for IndyCar in 2005. These interviews were conducted a few days after Dan Wheldon's first Indy 500 win, once the dust had settled, Dan and the guys had time for the news to sink in, the TV and press had left them alone, and they had time to absorb the experience. It is a wonderful blow-by-blow record of their whole event, with fresh memories of victory at the 89th Indianapolis 500. Starring: Dan Wheldon (DW), Eddie Jones (EJ), John Anderson (JA), Kim Green (KG) and Michael Andretti (MA).

Dan Wheldon takes the checkered flag to win the 89th running of the Indianapolis 500, flanked by Vitor Meira (second) and teammate Bryan Herta in third place

MICHAEL KIM/LAT

Dan Wheldon was patient all day long, pushing when he needed to, adjusting the car as he went. Opposite page: Celebrating the win with Honda personnel

PHIL ABBOTT/LAT

THE EUPHORIA HAS subsided and the milk's been drunk. Now Dan Wheldon and the key men behind his 2005 Indy 500 triumph tell the story of his incredible climb through the field to victory. Words by Andy Hallbery, IndyCar Series magazine, August 2005.

As Dan Wheldon poured the milk over himself in Indy's Victory Lane, the impact of what he'd achieved by winning the 89th Indianapolis 500 had already started to sink in. Only minutes after the checkered flag, he had climbed from the cockpit of his Andretti Green Racing Dallara-Honda surrounded by camera crews and photographers, already reduced to tears. He said it was the first time he's ever cried in a racecar.

Then, in a symbolic gesture, he handed the milk to his team co-owner Michael Andretti, who, as a driver, came close but never did win in 14 attempts. Andretti wasn't sure what to do. Did etiquette allow a team boss to drink the milk? What the heck, he decided, and took a big celebratory gulp. "It's the sweetest milk I've ever tasted," beamed Michael.

To get to Victory Lane, Wheldon and crew worked hard all month. Here is the rollercoaster story in the words of the men at the center of it all, as they look back on winning the biggest race in the world.

QUALIFYING MAY 15 2005

Wheldon's qualifying run to 16th was disappointing, compounded by the fact that two of his AGR teammates were quick: Tony Kanaan on pole and Dario Franchitti in sixth. Bryan Herta was 18th.

EDDIE JONES: (Wheldon's race engineer): We got it wrong on our first qualifying attempt. We improved the car and got the speed in the afternoon, but there wasn't enough time to get our run in. That was disappointing.

DAN WHELDON: I let the team know how I felt afterward! I was frustrated. Michael asked: "Does the car feel good?" I said, "Yes, but it's slow." He said, "Then don't worry. You don't need to have the fastest car to win this race." I hate to admit it, but he was right.

RACE MORNING MAY 29

A bright, sunny day greeted the 33 drivers. Wheldon had been third on Carb Day, and again felt he had a good racecar.

DW: In a strange way, qualifying 16th was a blessing in disguise, because it made me work on the car. After I calmed down, we just got on with it, and I got the most comfortable car I'd ever had in traffic; and I was very, very calm.

JOHN ANDERSON (AGR team manager and Wheldon's racecar chief): Dan's blood pressure was coming up, but he also knew we'd be OK if he stayed out of trouble. Starting 16th was just something he had to deal with.

THE START

Green flag: Wheldon loses two places on the first lap and is 18th, as Kanaan, Sam Hornish Jr. and Franchitti set a frenetic pace out at the front. Wheldon progresses, slowly but surely...rising to 14th by lap 18.

EJ: I felt good just a few laps into the race. Dan is a guy who wants to make up six or eight places on the opening lap, and that didn't happen. But he settled into the race and began picking them off one by one. My feeling early on was that if we could have a mistake-free race, we would be near the front by the end.

LAP 21

The whole field makes its first pit stops under yellow. The #26 crew makes minor changes to the tire pressures, and Wheldon beats three other cars out to emerge 11th. Seven laps later, he passes Tomas Enge and hits the top 10 for the first time. His inexorable rise is happening, but the midfield is still treacherous.

DW: There were some close shaves. One time I was behind another car – I can't remember who it was – and it got understeer between Turns Three and Four, and so did I. I thought it was gone, to the point I pulled my legs back, because I thought I was going to hit the wall. Somehow I managed to save it.

LAP 38

Wheldon exchanges places with Bruno Junqueira and Vitor Meira for 20 laps, but even when he loses out and drops back to 10th he is still the model of patience. The leaders, Kanaan, Hornish and Franchitti are continuing to lap quickly, but in Wheldon's pit, the key men are calm.

JA: I was a little concerned about the pace at the front, while Dan was still back in traffic. But that's when patience comes in, and I was very impressed with Dan.

LAP 48

From lap 48, Wheldon begins making inroads toward the top five. That lap he passes Helio Castroneves. Two laps later he is by Meira and then picks off Scott Sharp on the next to take seventh place.

EJ: Whatever is required at any time, be it pace, composure, or speed, Dan's able to give it to us. That part of the event was the time for pace. Dan's skill in doing that was a big component to winning the race.

LAP 57

Wheldon pits under green for his second stop along with the rest of the front-runners. Rapid pit work, including another tire pressure change, gets him out ahead of Junqueira and Buddy Lazier. He emerges fifth, and his stealthy but safe rise from the midfield is complete. Patience is paying off.

EJ: There's no doubt Tony, Dario and Sam were extremely competitive at the front, but our progress was steady, relentless, and inevitable. I knew when we got Dan into the top five we had a real shot at the win.

LAP 79

Wheldon runs fifth until the next round of pit stops during another yellow on lap 79. This time Wheldon's crew adds more front wing. As it turned out, the wing change wasn't the right one, but Wheldon hovers in sixth and fifth, trading places for the next 27 laps with Meira.

JA: It's not a gamble changing a car in a race as long as this one is. It's more of a good opportunity. The track conditions were changing and we could chase that with our changes at the stops.

LAP 114

Another yellow, and it's a perfect time for the whole field to pit. Wheldon's crew takes out the wing change, and he returns to the track in sixth behind Meira and Sharp. Still, the leading trio is now within striking distance.

JA: Our big concern was Hornish, who was swapping the lead with Tony and Dario. But we felt Sam needed to keep himself out of traffic as much as possible. If he had a car as comfortable as ours, he'd have been in the draft.

LAP 127

The changes transform Wheldon's car. On lap 127, he's past Sharp, a lap later he is by Meira, and five laps on he's past Hornish to move into the top three for the first time. He's behind Kanaan and Franchitti, making it an Andretti Green 1-2-3.

"I will remember that day for the rest of my life" Dan Wheldon (2005)

KIM GREEN (AGR team co-owner): Dan did a great job using the tools in the racecar – his roll bars, his weight-jacker – to help set up his car each time to pass the cars he was racing against.

LAP 149

A key turning point: As suspected by Anderson, Hornish struggles in traffic and on lap 146 he crashes out. The leaders pit and Wheldon's crew excels. He emerges first ahead of Meira and Franchitti. Fifty laps to go, and he's made it to the front.

KG: A good thing for Dan was that he had a very clear pit entry. Dario and Tony struggled – especially in the last few pit stops – getting around another car to get in or out of the box. Dan hit his marks every time and got great track position.

LAP 165

When they're back to green, Meira passes Wheldon, but three laps later Wheldon is back in front. They now appear to be the most threatening for the win, while Kanaan is struggling down in seventh with a vibration. In the lead, Wheldon looks strong on his own.

DW: The car was handling well in traffic, but it was also quick on its own. So I was able to take advantage of the opportunity.

LAP 171

Another yellow alters the order. All of the leaders pit for their final fuel stop, except Danica Patrick and Wheldon's third teammate Bryan Herta. Crucially, Wheldon's crew decides to change all four tires – the only team to do so.

EJ: We calculated that, with 28 laps to go, the amount of fuel we needed would give us enough time to get four tires. Danica and Bryan stayed out, so there was nothing we could do about them. We came out sixth behind Meira, Bourdais and Franchitti. But we had fresh rubber, and that was all that mattered.

MICHAEL ANDRETTI (AGR co-owner): It was a good strategy. They gave up track position, but I knew it would pay off. It made the difference.

KG: Bryan and Danica stayed out gambling on a fuel mileage based on two more yellows, and they got them! Certainly for Bryan, fuel wasn't actually an issue at the end.

LAP 174

On the restart, crucially, Bourdais and Franchitti delay each other and Wheldon is straight up to fourth behind Meira – and he is the one with a tire advantage.

JA: Danica and Bryan just went with fuel, no tires. I was very comfortable with the fact that, during the sprint to the finish, we were going to be there with a good set of rubber on the car. We had put ourselves in a very good position.

LAP 179

With four fresh tires, Wheldon is on the move. He is fourth and then passes Meira. Six tours later, he's made it past Herta…with only crowd favorite Danica Patrick to go.

KG: It was obvious to me that Dan was faster than Bryan, who had a touch more downforce on his car. Bryan realized Dan was faster, and certainly didn't get in his way.

LAP 186

Wheldon gets a run on Patrick and gets underneath her exiting Turn Four to edge into the lead. At that moment, the yellow flag waves after Kosuke Matsuura hits the wall. Wheldon is leading by inches as they cross the line. Wheldon is now first for the restart.

MA: I would rather have had Dan second on the restart. We pretty much knew he was going to get passed. But we knew he would be stronger because Danica had older tires.

LAP 190

With 10 to go, Patrick drafts Wheldon over the line at the restart and moves back into the lead. Despite his tire advantage, Wheldon still has to muster everything he has.

DW: I knew I could pass her, it was just a case of timing. But having just done it, she was aware of where I was good, so she made it a bit more difficult for me.

LAP 194

After a few aborted attempts into Turn Three, Wheldon makes the final pass for the lead into Turn One. He then makes a small break as she fends off her teammate Meira.

MA: Meira had a strong car as well. I was worried about it. When he had a problem getting past Danica, giving Dan a gap, I felt a little bit easier. And Bryan was all over Meira, too, and that helped slow Meira down a little too.

MICHAEL KIM/LAT. INSET: F PEIRCE WILLIAMS/LAT. OPPOSITE: MICHAEL LEVITT/LAT

Kissing bricks never tasted so good. Wheldon made headlines by becoming the first British winner at Indianapolis since Jim Clark, 40 years before

LAP 198

Meira passes Patrick for second, but half a lap later, before he can challenge Wheldon, Bourdais hits the wall, and the yellow flies. Wheldon simply has to cruise the final two laps to complete a remarkable Indy 500 triumph. He takes the yellow and checker with Meira to his left and teammate and 'wingman' Herta to his right. In the cockpit emotions were catching up with the winner, knowing his face would now grace the Borg Warner trophy.

DW: It was such a proud moment for me, the proudest of my life. Michael and my teammates were a big part of the win, and there are lots of people who helped me get there. But Kim Green's a special one – he took a flyer on me.

I'll remember that day for the rest of my life. ∎

MOODY BLUE

One photographer's endeavor to get all creative with our hero

by ROBERT LABERGE

■ PHOTOGRAPHER, GETTY IMAGES

DAN CONNECTION Official team photographer, Andretti Green/Chip Ganassi Racing, 2003-'08

Spring Training Media Day. It happened every year. The teams would get two days of testing at Homestead, Miami. The third day was media day, when all the TV, radio and print media could get their preseason material. The photographers could get the portraits, too; drivers in suits, with caps, without caps, facing left, facing right, facing straight, smiling, serious... over and over again. You get the drift.

I was doing a long exposure, so everything had to be dark and blackened out. It was basically a 20x20ft box with a hole and black cloth, so anybody around couldn't actually see what was going on inside. The camera was outside, and I shot through the hole looking in. So, being digital, people could actually see on the back of the camera what was being shot.

The drivers had a schedule, where they had to be from a certain time to the next certain time. It was a long day of interviews and photo shoots. Dan showed up earlier than he should have, and basically didn't seem too excited about it; he just wanted to get it done quickly. Some guys were waiting in line and coming back and forth. Scott Dixon was already there, Dario, Tony – the usual guys – but they were on schedule! They were there first but Dan just wanted to get it done and out of the way.

The photo was one six-second exposure. I dressed in black jeans a black, long sleeve shirt and gloves with one pop of the flash on the driver's face. Everything else was me walking around them with strips of colored lights from Home Depot. The kind you find strung up outside a restaurant at Christmas. I would move for those six seconds around them, and that would create that light effect. It's funny because the drivers didn't really understand what I was doing until I'd done four or five of them and they could see the result. It's one of those shots you only do once; you don't repeat it.

As I shot, The driver would only see what I was doing after we'd finished, as the camera body was fixed outside the box. Then they started to get interested, Scott in particular got pretty excited about it, and I kept busy, shooting and doing everything.

The only thing I remember from Dan is that he was kind of upsetting me a little bit. He had an attitude that day that he just didn't care about it, but wanted to get it done and move on. I hadn't realized while I'd been shooting he'd been watching the other drivers and had developed an interest in what I was doing with them. So, he walked into the box, and I shot one frame, maybe two, and said, "OK, we're done." He looked at me and said, "What do you mean 'we're done?'"

I told him I thought he wanted it to be quick and I was granting him his wish. The PR and competitive side of Dan kicked in, and he suddenly wanted to do it for much longer. He was comparing himself to them, asking why they had all these nice pictures, and realizing he had to do the same thing.

Actually, I think that one frame worked out pretty well. I think after a year or two he was definitely seeing all of the usage we were getting out of these "strange" pictures, and that it was worth spending time with it. Some guys are OK with it, some are not bothered by it, and others hate it. With Dan, it always worked out. ■

> ## "He had an attitude that day that he just didn't care about it, but wanted to get it done and move on"

A racing driver's job is not only about going quickly. It is also about rising to the media's artistic requirements

by MIKE LEVITT

■ PHOTOGRAPHER, LAT USA

DAN CONNECTION

IndyCar photographer 2002-2011

On your first visit to IMS, it's loud, bright, and full of people and action. There are a multitude of things to look at, and your attention is drawn by the cars, the people, the movement. Race day is overwhelming with the huge crowd and pre-race/post-race madness.

Walking around looking for photos, you are constantly lost. "Is this the gate I used to get to the photo hole last year?" The gates look the same. The corners look the same. You wander and try gate after gate, and eventually find what you were looking for. In the process of being lost, you also find things you were not looking for. Open gates, interesting angles, shortcuts and passageways.

This photo is one of the things I found.

For more than 20 years, I've been at the track almost every day in May that it's open for action. Rookie tests, practice, qualifying, race. The day starts late and the pace is slow. You arrive an hour or two before the track opens and look at the sky. If it's raining, you edit, hang out and talk to your friends. If it's sunny, you head out to one of the corners with a big lens and shoot some cars. Usually, it's overcast. Some years the sun never comes out.

Quite often you are just standing around, as there are only a few cars out at one time, and they spend a lot of time in the pits between runs. You have time to watch, and think. A few weeks of this and you somehow end up with a shot of every car.

When you have a sunny day, you try to take full advantage of it, starting the day in Turn 1 by the fence, moving to Turn 3 inside and outside, and then back to the Turn 1 grandstand. You chase the light, and hope the clouds stay away and the cars run.

As the day progresses, you watch the sun move. By about 3 p.m., Turn 1 is completely in shadow and all of the other photographers leave. But for some reason, you wait – for the box of light.

I can't remember when I first saw it, but I remember the feeling I got. Something important was happening. I saw it just creep onto the outside of the track, far from the racing line. In the course of 20 minutes, it marches across the track as the sun sets, spending five minutes illuminating the racing line. If you are lucky, those are your five great minutes.

Occasionally, there are many cars running, and you get dozens of shots. Sometimes there's a caution and you spend the entire time watching safety trucks as the box travels across the line and onto the grass. Some years it's never sunny. Or the sun comes out a few minutes before you need to be outside, and you don't have time to make the 20-minute walk out to the corner.

There are many things that can go wrong, but everything must go right to make the shot work; the time, the cars, the light, the line, and you.

In the film days, you had to make a calculated guess at the exposure, since the track was black and there was nothing to meter. Guess wrong, no photo. You have to focus on an empty section of dark track. You have to be in the right place, at the right time, with the right car on the right day with the right weather. And, guess right.

You only win when you get everything you control right, and are lucky enough that the things you can't control are also right.

I wonder if Dan had similar feelings about winning the 500? ■

"I can't remember when I first saw it, but I remember the feeling I got. Something important was happening"

STEVE SWOPE

SMILING FOR THE CAMERA

One racing lensman remembers Dan Wheldon as a fashionable and charming gent with a permanent smile

The Dan Wheldon moment I remember most was actually the first time I met him. It was at Richmond, and he was in Indy Lights. There are a couple of photo stands inside the racetrack there. One was on the inside of Turn 3 where I decided to photograph an IndyCar practice session.

I looked up at the stand and saw a bunch of people who didn't belong there. I went up and politely asked them to leave because I needed the space to work. Dan was in the group. He asked me if I needed him to go, too. I said, "No, no, no. I know who you are. It's fine." He said, "OK, mate. Thanks!"

He stayed up there on the photo stand with me and watched the session. He was polite and respectful, and from that moment on, we were friends. That sums up Dan, just the fact that he was a gentleman and respectful.

We always had a good laugh. I had a deal at the time with Hugo Boss, so Dan would tease me about my Hugo Boss clothing. He'd always say, "Hey, Steve, why don't you get a job with Hugo Boss?"

Dan was very much into fashion. I always hear the expression with regard to golfing that half the battle is to look good on the golf course. Well, Dan always looked good in pit lane. It didn't matter if it was white sunglasses or silver shoes, he did the complete opposite of what all the other drivers did, and he made it work.

by STEVE SWOPE

- CART AND INDYCAR PHOTOGRAPHER
  DAN CONNECTION
  Indycar photographer from 2002

The morning after his first Indy 500 win, in 2005, I arrived early at Indianapolis Motor Speedway to shoot the victory photographs. It was 7am, and Dan was walking out of the media center all by himself with a big smile on his face. He'd just finished doing ABC's *Good Morning America*. He looked at me and said, "Holy shit." I said, "Yeah, you just won the Indianapolis 500." It was like he still couldn't believe it had happened.

Dan was one of the easiest drivers to photograph. It was always fun to take pictures with him. He was a good subject, very comfortable around a camera. He never over-posed, but even when I was shooting him candidly, he knew I was there. He knew the game.

He was really fun to photograph when he was with Andretti Green Racing. One of my favorite moments was photographing Dan, Tony Kanaan and Dario Franchitti on the podium together in St. Petersburg in 2005. I decided to go off to one side of the podium in a severe angle in pretty strange light, but the photos turned out very well. It wasn't your traditional podium shot, but Dan's reactions made the photos work.

I never saw Dan mad. I caught him with some serious looks, but never angry. I'm sure he got mad, but I never photographed him while angry. It seems like every photo I took of Dan involved him smiling. That's the way I will always remember him. ∎

STEVE SWOPE

DAY & NIGHT WATCHMEN

A win in the prestigious Rolex 24 Hours of Daytona was another milestone in DW's career

by CASEY MEARS

■ NASCAR RACER

DAN CONNECTION
Chip Ganassi Racing teammate with Scott Dixon, Rolex 24 Hours of Daytona winners, 2006

He was a great teammate and we had a blast. All three of us had a really good time throughout that whole event. What we did was very, very serious, but he was always making it light, making it fun. I just remember him having quick one-liners to help everyone relax a little. Things tend to get so serious; it was cool to have a guy like Dan around. He was serious about what he did and was very focused but, at the same time, he could help make it fun. I just remember laughing a lot. ■

HITTING THE TARGET

When Chip Ganassi signed his man, he couldn't believe the instant, race-winning, effect the whirlwind had on his team

by Chip Ganassi

- OWNER CHIP GANASSI RACING

DAN CONNECTION
Race-winning team owner in IndyCar, 2006-8 and Daytona 24 Hours, 2006

When I think of Dan, the first thing that comes to mind is the time we started talking to him about joining our team. He had an infectious, dynamic personality, and at first I thought, "Am I the only one who's seeing this?" Turns out I wasn't. *Everybody* saw it.

I was excited about having Dan join our team. You never want to hire someone based only on your personal feelings about them, but Dan was different. As he met more people within our organization, I started getting the same response from other people about Dan's electric personality, his smile and his enthusiasm.

So, once we all saw it, agreed that it was a positive thing, we started to turn our focus to his driving. What would he be like in the car? Honestly, it was the same exact thing as his personality – bold, compelling and effective. His first race for us was the Rolex 24 at Daytona in 2006 and, of course, he went out and won it. His next race was the IndyCar season opener at Homestead-Miami Speedway, and he won that, too. He beat Helio Castroneves by something like two feet. They were side by side for the last 12 or so laps.

Here it was the end of March, Dan had been part of the team for just a few weeks, and already had won two races. That, coupled with the fact that everyone on the team was impressed by him as a person and caught up in his personality and energy. Those two things together – the on-track skill and the off-track personality – set the tone for his following years with us.

What he did for our team you could never buy for any amount of money. That was the great thing about Dan Wheldon. He basically plugged our team into 440 volts. He took the whole team and stuck the plug in the wall. It just electrified everybody in the organization.

> "He went wheel to wheel with one of the sport's best oval racers and didn't back down"

It was a full step change in the team in terms of our competitiveness and approach.

Quite frankly, he also helped Scott Dixon become the racer he is now. I think Scott would be the first to tell you that Dan helped him as a driver. Guys like that don't come along every day in this business. It's hard for racers to share their knowledge with others, including teammates. But Dan wasn't like that. He wanted the team – not just himself – to succeed.

When you have an opportunity to look back years later, you realize that you may have missed, at the time, just how special something or someone was. You don't fully grasp the impact a driver is having on your organization at the time it's happening.

Dan was invaluable to our team during the three years he raced for us. Whether we understood it or even noticed it at the time, he was taking us through a huge change for the better. Obviously it was good for our entire team, but it was also good for Dan. He grew as both a driver and a person while he was with us, and we grew, too.

While he was with us, it seemed like every oval race became a battle between Dan and Scott. They'd check out from the field and be gone. It happened everywhere – Texas, Kansas, Chicagoland. It seemed like every time at Indianapolis, we'd be far in front by lap 175. I can't tell you how many times we won the Indy 450 but weren't there for the full 500 miles.

In all, Dan won six IndyCar races in those three years with our team. He tied for first with Sam Hornish Jr. in points in 2006, but lost on the tiebreaker, then finished fourth in 2007 and 2008. When Dan was behind the wheel, he rarely got beat. We might have lost races because of our mistakes, but he rarely got outraced.

That first IndyCar race at Homestead in 2006 still stands out to me. He went wheel to wheel with one of the sport's best oval racers and didn't back down. Lap after lap, they were inches apart. I was thinking, "Who is this guy? That's my car out there, but who is this guy driving it?" There were many other moments throughout his time with us and throughout his career that were memorable, but that was the moment I realized just how good he was.

That ability, and the infectious personality that brought it out, are still with us. ∎

Chip Ganassi (right) and his team knew they had a winner in Dan straight out of the box with victory in his first race at Homestead in 2006. Photos: Dan Streck/LAT

TAKING THE HOT SEAT

Stepping into the shoes of his hero was everything he expected... and more!

by MARCO ANDRETTI

- INDYCAR SERIES & INDY 500 ROOKIE
  OF THE YEAR, 2006

DAN CONNECTION
Successor at Andretti Green Racing
in 2006, and friend

From the moment I first met him, Dan was one of my mentors. I was in Indy Lights at the time, and he was driving for Dad's IndyCar team. He was always interested in what we were doing in our Lights program. He really cared about it and was very supportive of it, so I started shadowing him.

I'll always remember him with the white shades, the white shoes and the cool hair. He was somebody I wanted to be like. He was charming and hilarious. There was always a laugh to be had with Dan; something was always going on. His energy was positive and light, but when the visor went down, he was a fierce competitor. That's all you can ask for as a driver.

He also was a great spokesman and ambassador, not only for the sport as a whole but for any company that became his sponsor. He knew the entire picture of racing, that it was about more than just driving a racecar. He knew how to put all of the pieces together

to make a team jell. He was uncanny when it came to that, and everyone involved with the team looked up to him for that reason. All of those qualities are admirable, but the bottom line for me was that Dan was a fun guy to be around.

The first time we came together on the racetrack – literally – happened at St. Pete in 2006. He had moved to Ganassi that year, and I had moved into the No. 26 car, which had been his car from the year before. I threw it in on him in Turn 2. We collided, but he saved it off the barrier. I passed him and we continued on.

Later that night when we got back to Indianapolis, we went out to get a couple of beers, but he wasn't happy. In fact, he was furious with me. I'll never forget that. He was mad, but he still went out. He got over it eventually, but I think in that moment we gained respect for each other. We didn't crash. We bumped wheels. I think he respected the aggression in what I did, even if he wasn't happy with it. And I respected his ability to save it – as well as his ability to want to work through it.

Dan would race you right up until the last inch, but he was extremely fair. He was one of those guys you were comfortable to be around on the track. He raced you as hard as humanly possible, but he was always clean about it. Those are wonderful, rare traits.

Some of my best moments with Dan involved pranks. I learned from him what not to do in that situation. When I was coming

Marco makes an impact in his first IndyCar race – with Dan

up, the IndyCar side of the team was Dan, Tony Kanaan, Dario Franchitti and Bryan Herta, and it was a non-stop prank machine. They were constantly scheming and coming up with new ways to get each other.

Dan was the target of most of it because of his reactions. He would get so annoyed and upset, which only made them do it more. I figured out right away to act like nothing bothered me. So, when I moved from Lights to IndyCar, I was cool to every prank. It wasn't fun for them anymore, so they eventually stopped. With Dan, if you moved one shoe just a millimeter, he'd notice it and make a scene.

"I was in the changing room getting undressed. Dan opened the door with a crowd of Japanese fans behind him and said, 'Who wants to meet Marco Andretti?'"

But he was a prankster himself, another reason their running battle went on as long as it did. Once, in Motegi, I was in the changing room getting undressed. Dan opened the door with a crowd of Japanese fans behind him and said, "Who wants to meet Marco Andretti?" Then he brought all of them into the room as I changed.

There were times when we'd be out in Indianapolis and he'd walk up to complete strangers and say, "Hey, do you know who Marco Andretti is? This is him, right here." Whatever he could do to put me on the spot, he'd do it. It was hilarious.

One night I was sitting at a table in the window of a restaurant on Illinois Street in downtown Indianapolis. Dan walked by on the sidewalk. I didn't see him at first, but he saw me. A few minutes later, I hear a knock on the window. I look up and it's Dan with a bunch of girls. "Who wants to have dinner with Marco Andretti?" he said, and then he brought all of them into the restaurant.

He was always up to something. In 2008, two weeks after my 21st birthday, we both finished on the podium in the season opener at Homestead-Miami Speedway. I was doing a post-race press conference when he joined us. The first question for him was something about the race. He said, "I don't want to talk about that. I want to talk about what happened on Marco's 21st birthday." He totally disregarded the question in order to put me on the spot.

One of my favorite things about Dan was that he was always moving and evolving. Every time I saw him, he had a different look – long hair, short hair, new sunglasses or shoes. He loved fashion, and he was able to pull off all of his different looks. Being in the background and watching him constantly grow and mature was a life lesson for me.

He made 180-degree change in the time I knew him. He became a devoted husband and father, a very committed person. I was able to see all of those changes in him first-hand. He was an admirable guy, one of my best friends, and my hero. ■

SIDE BY SIDE

Dan Wheldon and Sam Hornish Jr. tied on points for the championship in 2006

by SAM HORNISH Jr

- THREE-TIME INDYCAR SERIES CHAMPION, 2001, 2002, 2006* INDY 500 WINNER, 2006

DAN CONNECTION
IndyCar teammate (2002); rival, 2002-2007

Tied on points with Dan Wheldon, champion with more races won

People were captivated by Dan, and I was among those captivated. He showed a lot of emotion and flair, and he was always positive about it. I'm a little less flashy than Dan was, but he was always genuine about his personality. I found myself intrigued by him. If I couldn't win a race, it didn't make me mad to see Dan win. I can't ever say I'm glad to see someone else win a race, but I was always happy for Dan when he won – especially at Indy.

Neck and neck was how
the IndyCar world saw
championship rivals Sam
Hornish Jr. and Dan Wheldon

We were teammates briefly, in 2002, at Panther Racing. He competed in the last two races of the season – Chicago and Texas – before he moved on to Andretti Green Racing in 2003. You know the rest of his career – Indianapolis 500 wins in both 2005 and 2011, the IndyCar championship in 2005, and 16 wins in 10 years. And we tied in 2006.

But those are just the statistics. There was much more to Dan Wheldon than numbers on a sheet of paper. He was smart, clever,

funny, a devoted family man, and, yes, a fantastic racer. And, because of that 2002 season at Panther, he was also my friend.

When Dan won the Indy 500 the second time in 2011, he understood it all. He truly got it. He knew what it meant to be there, and it showed. He probably appreciated it more than he did in 2005. For me, that was so gratifying. I joked afterward that now I wasn't the only guy to win the race with a pass on the final lap, but at least the car I passed had all four wheels on it.

Sam says knowing Dan changed his outlook on life, and being friends helped him become more social

NICK LAHAM / GETTY IMAGES

Some people talk about how brash Dan was when he was younger and first arrived in IndyCar racing, but I never had that experience. I was one of the first drivers to deal with him when he got to Indianapolis, and he never acted out of line. Maybe he hid it from me or didn't feel like he needed to be that way around me, but back in 2002 he was just a driver who was in the same place I had been a few years before. He was getting where he wanted to be and learning everything he could in order to get there.

I'd met Dan a few times as we were coming up through the various open-wheel ranks before we both ended up at Panther and, to me, he was just another driver on a journey. Sure, he had the flashy shoes and the big personality, but that's part of what I liked about him, largely because it was so different from me.

Whenever he showed up with those silver racing boots, I'd give him grief. I'd say, "Dude, when are you going to show up in a suit made out of that stuff?" Maybe it was my personality, but I never interpreted what he did at that time as cockiness. Perhaps I found him entertaining because I had enough confidence in myself. I never took his shoes and his flamboyant behavior as arrogance. I thought he was confident.

Most of all, though, Dan made me laugh. He brought me out of my shell at times. I've been described as aloof, which I'm not, but I am quiet and generally keep to myself, and sometimes that gets misinterpreted. I don't know why, but Dan was one of those people who could bring me out of that. He's one of the few competitors I would consider a true friend.

It always seemed like Dan was sincerely interested in getting to know me. I don't hang around much with other drivers, but Dan and I hung out together. We did things outside the racetrack and beyond the commitments we had to the team and sponsors. We didn't *have* to hang out together back then. We just did.

Through hanging out with Dan and talking to him, I opened up to other drivers. I got to know Dario Franchitti and some of the other racers a little better, and that was Dan's doing. He was very social and, by being his friend, I became more social.

That's why what happened at Las Vegas in 2011 was so hard for all of us. He had become the social instigator, the guy who

brought all of us together and made us smile. He was a huge figure in racing in general, but in IndyCar he was the one person we all had in common. He was the one who was friends with everyone.

I'll never forget that day. I was racing in the Nationwide Series at the time, so I had Sundays off. I was at home building a tree house and a gazebo swing set for the kids. We had gone to the Renaissance Faire earlier in the day. Eliza was just under a year old, and Addie was getting ready to turn 4 years old. They were playing in the driveway, and my in-laws and my brother were there, helping me build the swing set.

My wife, Crystal, called out to me and said, "Hey, the race is getting ready to start," so I went inside and got a glass of water and watched the beginning of it. As soon as I saw the accident, I knew it was bad. I was reasonably sure what the outcome was going to be, but I didn't know who it was. I went back outside to work on the swing set. People asked me if I wanted to watch more. I was like, "I don't need to watch it. I already know."

Somebody came out and said they were going to make an announcement, so I went back inside. Crystal was sitting there with both girls on her knees. When I heard, I was devastated. All I could think about was Dan's wife, Susie, and Crystal. Our kids were about the same age. I couldn't imagine Susie being in that situation. I couldn't imagine Crystal being in that situation.

I still get emotional when I think about that day, and I probably always will. Our careers were so similar. Dan had lost his ride but had come back and won Indy; I had lost my Sprint Cup ride and was racing in the Nationwide Series, trying to get back to where I was. We were both getting into broadcasting. It wasn't just about being his teammate for a short period of time in 2002. There was always a deeper connection to Dan in terms of our lives and the direction and similarities of our careers.

It's still unbelievable to me. But out of the sadness of that day, I began to think about how Dan made me laugh. I try to keep that in mind whenever I think of him. That's one thing that has helped me make sense of all of this. He changed my life – and the lives of thousands of others. I truly believe that was his purpose here. He accomplished it in more ways than we'll ever know. ■

> **"Whenever he showed up with those silver racing boots, I'd say, 'Dude, when are you going to show up in a suit made out of that stuff?'"**

INTRODUCING...

Dan Wheldon had his own ways of keeping the media on guard

by JEFF OLSON

■ USA TODAY

DAN CONNECTION
Writer, Lionheart – Remembering Dan Wheldon,
RACER magazine, USA Today 2002-2011

I met Dan Wheldon shortly after he skidded on his roll hoop through the north chute at Indianapolis Motor Speedway in 2003. Most young racers would have been rattled by the sparks and noise and fear of their first big shunt at Indy, but not Dan.

Dan was angry – truly angry. Annoyed at himself for making a mistake, at people like me for asking about it, and at the world at

that moment. He looked at me as if he'd just encountered a colossal hillbilly, and told me so.

Our relationship didn't immediately improve. Every time I approached Dan, he pretended he didn't know me. I'd counter by opening with "Jeff Olson, *RACER* magazine." The next time I'd see him, usually a few weeks later, he'd look at me as if he didn't know me, so I'd open again with name and publication.

While doing interviews for this book, I relayed Dan's faux confusion to Tony Kanaan, who laughed heartily: "That was Dan," Tony said. "He did that to *everyone*. It was his way of feeling people out and putting them off guard."

So for years, Dan Wheldon was trolling me for a reaction, and the reaction often went from irritating to comical, sometimes in a single meeting. During one interview at Richmond after Dan won the Indy 500 for the first time in 2005, he threw a fit about a moment of miscommunication between us. He stormed out of the transporter, then returned, then stormed out again, and then returned.

Once I was able to explain the misunderstanding, he agreed to the interview. He laid down on a couch and put an arm over his eyes. I turned on my recorder, I asked one question and didn't speak again. He did 15 brilliant minutes that made for an unforgettable story.

But my favorite mixed-up moment with Dan involved his silver

Head above the crowd: DW keeps
an eye on another Indy 500
tradition: the Pit Stop Challenge

boots. He showed up at Texas Motor Speedway one year wearing glorious, wonderfully awful silver racing boots. Everyone was taunting him about them – especially his teammates – but I thought the boots were cool. It took courage to wear something that far out, so I tried to break the ice after qualifying by telling him as much.

One problem. I hadn't been paying attention to his qualifying run, and didn't realize he'd just put himself deep in the field with an uncharacteristically slow effort. So, as he approached the media bullpen, he wasn't in the mood for me.

"Jeff Olson, RACER magazine," I said, expecting a smile and not receiving one. "I like your boots, dude." He looked straight through a colossal hillbilly again, not saying a word. Just glaring.

"Seriously," I followed. "I like them. I'm being sincere. They're cool." Glare. For what seemed like five minutes. Then, without saying a word, he walked away.

The wonderful silver boots were certainly a talking point. Or not, depending on timing

STEVE SWOPE

"I turned on my recorder, I asked one question and didn't speak again. He did 15 brilliant minutes that made for an unforgettable story"

BENITO SANTOS

In the years that passed, things between us improved dramatically. I came to consider Dan a friend – as much as a subject/reporter relationship can be considered a friendship, anyway. He was sincere, genuine and enthusiastic in interviews. He was clever and funny, intelligent and warm. He turned into one of my best, most quotable subjects.

In October 2011, USA TODAY asked me to ghostwrite a series of columns surrounding his attempt to win the $5 million challenge at Las Vegas Motor Speedway. The premise was straightforward – I transcribed phone conversations with Dan, turned them into columns and sent them to him for corrections and final approval.

Everything leading up to that weekend was upbeat and positive. Dan saw it as an immense challenge – starting from the back and winning to claim the bonus – but he thought it was an attainable goal. When I e-mailed him the final column before the race, he sent a text saying he loved it. I answered by saying thanks, and he shot back: "Don't get too drunk tonight, mate!"

To which I replied, "Too late. Already there." Dan answered with a smile emoticon.

Until the most recent phone upgrade, when I forgot to ask to have my old texts saved, that exchange had stayed with me for nearly four years. When I told Scott Dixon that story, he said he still has voicemails from Dan on his phone. He doesn't listen to them, but he can't bring himself to delete them.

We aren't the only ones who carry memories. They are good ones, all of them. ■

SOLE LOVE

DAN WHELDON'S FASCINATION for footwear was legendary. Tales of immaculate scuff-free training shoes abound as he used his feet to make a statement, and not just on the track. His silver race boots caused a stir, his pink ones were for a good cause in cancer awareness, and his yellow ones were...well, a violent, luminous yellow. In 2005, DW became the first British driver to win the Indy 500 since the legendary Jim Clark 40 years before, and he was always proud of his home country. At Indy in 2008, there was no doubting his patriotism with his Union Jack colored "Boots of my Roots."

DIFFERENT STROKES

They may not have been regular adversaries on the racetrack but the Dan Wheldon charm still left its mark on the NASCAR champion

by Jimmie Johnson

■ SIX-TIME NASCAR CHAMPION

DAN CONNECTION
Daytona Rolex 24 Hours rival, 2005-2008

My experience with Dan is limited compared with everyone else in this book, but Dan was such a unique individual that the moments we had together will stay with me for a lifetime. We shared a bond and a friendship, especially while racing in the Rolex 24. There were a lot of great laughs in a short period of time.

Dan competed in the race from 2005 through 2008, winning it in 2006 with Chip Ganassi Racing and teammates Scott Dixon and Casey Mears. I remember one year, the night before the race, we found ourselves at Daytona Beach Kennel Club, the dog track that used to be located behind the main grandstand at Daytona International Speedway.

It was Dan, Tony Stewart, Dario Franchitti, Tony Kanaan and myself just sitting there betting on the dogs and laughing. It was great hang time and stress relief the night before a big race, and Dan was the center of it. We all had stories, as racers always do. We might race in different vehicles and different series and come from different backgrounds, but we all share the bond of racing.

My other interactions with Dan were at other racetracks and appearances away from the Rolex 24. I remember seeing him a couple of times in Las Vegas and at a few other tracks. He'd pop in, and make a quick appearance and say hello, but I was always drawn to Dan. He always had a smile and a way about him that brought everyone to him. His love of life was contagious. You wanted to be around him.

Dan was already well known and had a name before I met him for the first time in 2005. I was really stoked to meet him, too. He had finished third in the 2004 Indy 500 and finished second in the IndyCar championship that year, so all of us from other types of racing were aware of how good he was. He was hauling ass at that point, so I was anxious to put a face and a handshake to the name. I couldn't wait to meet him.

ERIC GILBERT/MOTORSPORT.COM

"**He always had a smile and a way about him that brought everyone to him. His love of life was contagious**"

The Target car of Wheldon's team shared the Daytona track with Johnson's Lowe's machine

Dan and Jimmie both shared their successes at the Indianapolis Motor Speedway with their children on the famous bricks

GREG ALECK/LAT

FAR LEFT: PHIL ABBOTT/LAT. LEFT: NIGEL KINRADE

Without a doubt, Dan's personality transferred to the racetrack. His appearance, his energy and his motivation could all be seen in the way he drove. He was definitely flamboyant – and a character that was full of life.

I can't recall dealing with him on track in those four Rolex 24s we raced in, but that's not unusual. It's a long race with teammates, so it wouldn't surprise me if we were never on track at the same time. Or, if we were, we never raced door to door.

But every time I saw him, he was wearing the wild-colored racing boots. Then one year he showed up with his new teeth, these big, bright pearly whites that you couldn't ignore. When he walked

they finally started talking again, it was like nothing had happened. I imagine it would've been hard to stay mad at Dan.

On that October Sunday in 2011, we had raced the night before, so we had a rare Sunday off and were having a cookout while watching the IndyCar race on TV and just hanging out in the backyard. As with any wreck, there's a level of concern, but this one was bad. When you know somebody and you know they're in trouble, it goes to a different level altogether. We just stopped and watched.

I remember being in total shock and just holding out hope. It went on for so long, so we were just hoping and praying that he survived the

> ## "Big smile, a goofy pair of sunglasses and a Hollywood hairstyle. He *lived* life. We should all aspire to do the same"

Radical styling was never far away

CHRIS JONES/IMS

around with those new teeth for the first time, everyone was like, "Whoa! What happened?" He just rocked it.

A lot of times you'll meet a driver you've never met, and shake their hand and they'll be very quiet. It's a moment in time, and you're left wondering what to say or how to say it. With Dan, it was always rolling. It was always quick and clever. He always had a joke or a story. You were never bored when you saw Dan. He never stopped being Dan.

The thing that always struck me most about Dan is that we could go a year without seeing each other, yet it would be as if no time had passed. Whenever I bumped into him again, it was like we had just seen each other the day before. He was one of those guys who picked up right where you left off.

I've heard stories about teammates or competitors who got into it with Dan and wouldn't talk to him for a period of time. It happens to all of us at some point. But in Dan's case, when the feud ended and

crash. When we found out he didn't, we were devastated. Everyone throughout the racing world – IndyCar, NASCAR, Formula 1, NHRA, sports cars – was devastated. As racers, we're all connected.

That's what made it so real on so many levels. We're all racers, and we're all brave, but what happened to Dan shook us all. I'd just started my family around the same time. It made things so brutally real. It's still something that shakes me to think about. I still feel for his family, and I think about them often.

But I'd like to think that if Dan was here or talking to us from above, he'd say, "Pull it together. Go have some fun. Live life." That's what we're all trying to do and trying to remember about Dan. I can't ever imagine Dan not smiling and not going about his day with everything he had.

That's how I'll remember him: Big smile, a goofy pair of sunglasses and a Hollywood hairstyle. He *lived* life. We should all aspire to do the same. ■

The tribute Dan Wheldon-liveried helmet that Johnson used at Talladega was later sold at auction

GAME FOR A LAUGH

Good for a giggle is how rival Danica Patrick remembers Dan Wheldon

by DANICA PATRICK

■ INDYCAR WINNER, NASCAR RACER

DAN CONNECTION
IndyCar rival 2005-2011

The thing I remember most about Dan is how nice he was to me. That's not always common among racers, so it stood out. He always respected me and treated me well, and I've always been grateful for it.

It started when I lived in England early in my career. It was hard being away from home. I was a young woman starting out as a professional, and I didn't always feel as if people fully supported me.

At first, I didn't know if I could trust Dan. He would try to give me advice and tell me things and talk to me, but I didn't know how much of it was to be believed. After enough time, I started to realize that he was sincere. Some of my initial mistrust may have come from being so jaded by what happened when I was there. It wasn't Dan, it was me. My experiences while I was there weren't always positive, so some of that seeped into my initial perception of him.

But once we were racing together again in the U.S., I came to understand that he was being honest with me and he was actually a very nice person. He was always kind and funny. He also was very easy to make fun of, which I did often. There

Dan and Danica were always good for marketing and a photo opportunity

"He left the door open for us to joke with him, but he always took it well"

Danica stole the headlines by leading the 2005 Indy 500

F PEIRCE WILLIAMS/L4T

were quirky little things about his personality – his orderliness, his obsession with his appearance, the girlish things he did – that made him an easy target for some playful kidding.

Dan was a bit of a metro sexual, so I had fun with that. I joked with him about his hair products and his white sunglasses and other aspects regarding his appearance. At one point, Dan and I both had a deal with the same sunglasses company and we started off with the same style and color. That's when he switched to the white frames. And, of course, he went on to make those his signature.

He left the door open for us to joke with him, but he always took it well. In fact, he was really good at taking the jokes. If somebody doesn't take jokes well, you can't keep doing it. But Dan was always a good sport about it, and he was always able to give it back in the same spirit it was intended. I wasn't the only one who made fun of Dan in a friendly way. I'm sure Dario and Tony have hundreds of stories about playing pranks on him.

I can remember him being at my birthday party when I turned 25. I called it my golden birthday because I turned 25 on the 25th of March in 2007. We were racing at Homestead, so everyone went to a club on South Beach. Dan and I sat on a couch and just talked for hours as the party went on around us. He was authentic, real and genuinely nice, and that's the way I'll always remember him. ■

STEVE SWOPE

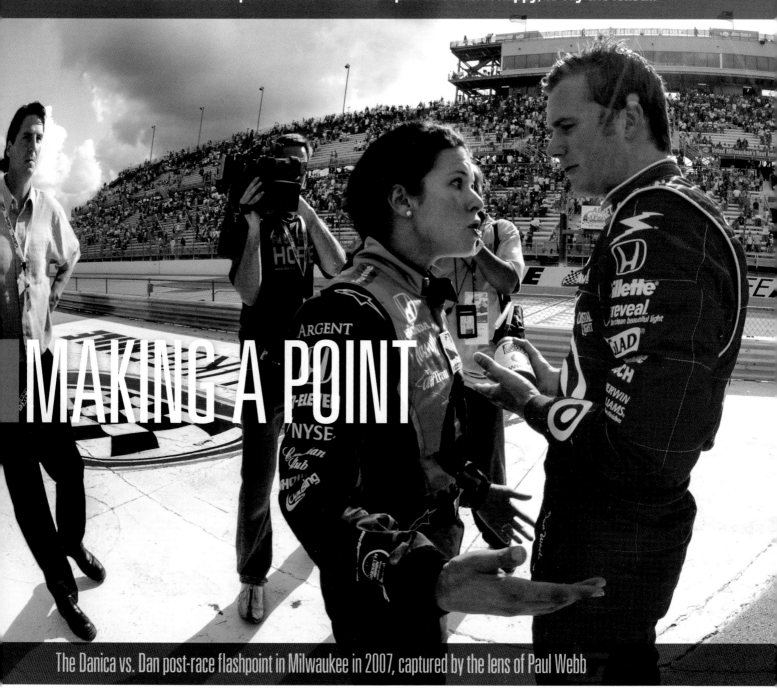

PHOTOGRAPHER PAUL WEBB was in the right place at the right time at the IndyCar Series race at the Milwaukee Mile in 2007. In pit lane, post-race, Danica Patrick made her feelings known about an incident during the race when she believed Dan pinched her into a half-spin. She wasn't happy, to say the least…

MAKING A POINT

The Danica vs. Dan post-race flashpoint in Milwaukee in 2007, captured by the lens of Paul Webb

One of the problems after races is that you don't always see people. At Milwaukee, in 2007, I was angry. Dan had chopped down on me at a key point in the race, and – even though I didn't crash – it ruined what could have been a good finish.

After the race, I was in the pits talking to my team. I saw Dan across the way. I was like, "There he is. This is my chance."

I finished talking to my team, and – with a completely level head – I went over and talked to Dan. I even asked my guys if it was OK. Nobody said no, so I went. Obviously, I was frustrated and mad about him nearly wrecking me, but I was also calm and collected.

I was extremely fast in that race, which only added to my frustration. Qualifying was terrible, but I'd worked my way up to fifth. After he chopped me, I went into the grass, and that sent me to the back of the pack, but I worked my way back to eighth by the end.

I can't remember exactly what I said to him, but I'm sure I expressed my displeasure with something like, "Didn't you see me?" He started walking away, and that's when I put my arm around him in the "most unfriendly" friendly way possible. I imagine he felt it in his right trapezius muscle for a while after that. I grabbed him hard as I was walking, and I continued to lecture him.

The Verdict

SCOTT DIXON AND Dario Franchitti both have opinions on the dust-up. Scott was a witness, and Dario was Danica's teammate. Time has moved on, but the pictures still raise a smile for the pair.

SD: I'll never forget that dust-up between Dan and Danica. I saw both parts of it – the on-track incident and the off-track incident – up close. Shortly after a restart, Danica tried to go to the inside, but Dan closed the door pretty heavily. I knew she was going to be angry, and I figured she was going to confront him. So, I positioned myself where I knew I'd be able to see it.

DF: (Laughs) Oh my God!! Look at him just...I mean that was wrong.... Look at Scott!

SD: She marched up. This was going to be comedy gold, and I had to see it. She got to him and started poking her finger in his chest. Being on the wrong side of Danica is a place no driver ever wants to be, and Dan obviously did not want to be there.

DF: Yeah. It was just a bad situation. Danica and I were team mates at the time and I said to her after, if I'd have

gone up there and started pushing and shoving Dan he'd have punched me in the mouth. He couldn't do that to her, she put him a very awkward position. He just had to stand there and take it.

SD: You could see by the look on his face that there were 100 different places he would rather be than right there at that moment. For a bystander who had seen what had happened on the track, I couldn't help but enjoy myself.

DF: It's one thing verbally giving somebody a hard time, but pushing them, too? He can't in any way respond. She played the sexism card; flipped it over, played it backward. That is two fiery characters there. Those two actually were good pals though.

SD: The look on Dan's face was priceless. He had no idea how to respond. I had a bit of a laugh and a bit of a smirk over that one. What was he going to do? There's nothing you can possibly do in that situation. If he could have crawled under a rock at that point, I'm sure he would have. However, Dan being uncomfortable was always hilarious.

Scott Dixon (right) makes the most of his prime vantage point for the "discussion"

Talking isn't always the best way to get your point across or to effect any change in on-track behavior. Sometimes you have to make your point on the track. But, in this case, I think he got my point. After that incident, Dan always raced me fairly, and I always felt comfortable around him.

From Milwaukee we went to Texas, and Eddie Gossage, the promoter at Texas Motor Speedway, made a big production of what happened between us in Milwaukee. He called it "The Rumble at the Speedway" and made banners and scheduled press conferences to drum up interest for his race.

In all, it was entertaining and fun afterward. Yes, I was angry at the time, but once it was over, we were cool. I've been told Dan was uncomfortable being confronted by a woman, and I've also been told guys get confused and nervous in that situation and don't know what to do. Clearly most guys have been taught well by their mothers and know they can't hit a woman, but they don't really know how to respond.

I could tell he was uncomfortable at the time – I seem to have that effect on people, don't I? But he listened to me. Dan always respected me. In turn, I respected him. ■

THAT SMILE?

They fought hard on the track and laughed about it after, memories that made a mark on Helio

by HELIO CASTRONEVES

THREE-TIME INDY 500 WINNER,
2001, 2002, 2009

IndyCar Series rival from 2002

The first year Dan was with Andretti Green Racing in 2003, he came over to visit me at my place in Miami during the Homestead race weekend. At that time, I was living in an apartment. I opened the door and he said, "Man, I thought you were going to live in a huge palace!"

I had never really given it much thought. My mind was always focused on racing. My apartment was just where I slept when I wasn't racing. I said, "I never thought about it that way. You're

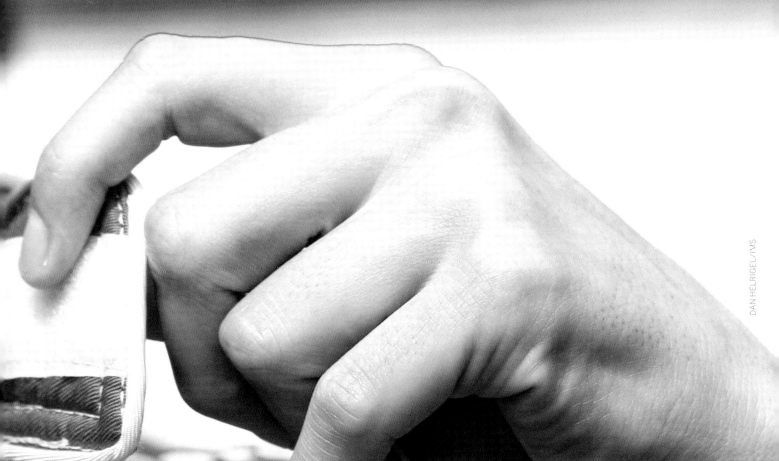

Two of IndyCar's most popular stars were never far away from a laugh or a joke. Dan and Helio share more stories

The 2006 opening race at Homestead saw this kind of trust and racing from the pair lap after lap for the win

JIM HAINES/IMS

F. PEIRCE WILLIAMS

"He had left his home for a place he'd never been, uprooting his life and pursuing his dreams, and all the while doing it with a smile and a unique brand of fun"

MICHAEL VOORHEES

right, I should step up my game." Not long after that, I bought a home. That showed me that Dan was already thinking big. From other people, that might have come across the wrong way, but I got what he was saying, and he said it in a fun, lighthearted way.

If you want to be a winner and a champion, you have to think big. Your attitude has to be different. You have to dream, and you have to work to achieve those goals that get you to your dream. That's exactly what happened with Dan. He had big dreams, and he worked hard to make them come true.

Dan's strengths shined through on ovals. For someone from England, where the classic training is geared toward road racing, that was a remarkable feat. There, ovals are a specialty, and when he got to IndyCar racing, he didn't have much experience with that type of racing. But, right from the beginning, he was fearless and fast on ovals. He was at his best.

He reminded me of myself when I was younger. He had left his home for a place he'd never been, uprooting his life and pursuing his dreams, and all the while doing it with a smile and a unique brand of fun. There was something about Dan that drew people to him, myself included.

My best memory with Dan was at a race weekend shortly after my daughter Mikaella was born in 2009. We were both staying on the same floor of a hotel and had our families with us. Dan's oldest boy, Sebastian, was playing with my daughter. It was the first time she had interacted with another child. It was the sweetest thing to see.

One of my other favorite memories was when the mayor of St. Petersburg, IndyCar officials, Susie and the boys gathered with other people to honor Dan by naming a portion of the track Dan Wheldon Way before the 2012 season opener.

It was a very emotional ceremony. I was there with other drivers, all of us dressed in our fire suits, and Sebastian saw me and came running up to give me a big hug. I couldn't contain myself. I tried my best to hold it together, but there were so many emotions that swept through me at that point. It's a good memory, though, an incredibly beautiful moment.

I'm glad I have those remembrances. They help me stay positive about Dan and what he contributed to the world around him. What he meant to me is extremely personal. He was someone I looked forward to seeing at the racetrack. As a competitor, he made me better. As a friend, he made me feel welcome.

But most of all, when I think of Dan, I think of that smile. It was and remains the smile of all of us in racing. I will keep that smile in my heart forever. ■

UNFORGETTABLE

After their first meeting Mike Hull knew that Dan Wheldon was a unique and very special individual

by Mike Hull

■ MANAGING DIRECTOR,
CHIP GANASSI RACING

DAN CONNECTION
Team boss, Target Chip Ganassi Racing
2006-2008

When Chip and I were interested in hiring Dan late in the 2005 season, we asked him to drop by a hotel room in Sonoma, California, after he got done with a sponsor function for Michael Andretti's team. It kept getting later and later, and still no Dan. Chip and I were thinking, "Man, is this guy ever going to show up?"

At one point I said to Chip, "I don't know if he's going to want to meet with us. He's got to race tomorrow. It's getting late." But we kept waiting and talking about racing and the team. Around 11 o'clock, there was a knock at the door. It was Dan. He'd spent every minute he could at the sponsor function; something we'd later learn was common with Dan. He gave everything he had to all aspects of what he was doing.

I'd spoken with Dan before, but never in depth until that night. He came into the room and fully engaged us by talking about nothing but racing. He *loved* motor racing. He loved all facets of motor racing. And, since that's who we are, we hit it off immediately. We're

a bunch of kids who never grew up, in a way. I know we have to be responsible individuals, but the reality is that we love motor racing on the same level Dan did. We knew then and there that we were going to make him an offer.

One of the things we've been able to do over the years at Chip Ganassi Racing is match the resources we have with the sponsors, the people, the crew, the drivers and the owner. We're able to put all of that together and have it flow onto the grid and work to win motor races. That was the high point of Dan. He was a master at helping us meld those elements together.

The only downside of Dan's contribution to our team is that when he didn't perform to his expectations – and he had enormously high expectations of himself – he went into a massive state of depression. It would take us several days of working with him to get him back to center. But once he was there, man, he was on top of it. He was a perfectionist, and when he didn't feel like he was living up to his own standards, he'd go into a funk.

From the moment he joined us in 2006 until he decided to join Panther Racing in 2009, Dan was all in. He always tried to make himself better. He never pointed fingers at the team. For him, it was always about making himself better and making the team better and learning from his teammates. He was very unselfish with his teammates – primarily when it came to Scott Dixon. He worked really hard with Scott to help both of them understand what we refer to as a frictionless driving style.

Dan was a master of oval racing. He was incredibly talented at not turning the wheel on an oval. If you looked at the data after his oval races, you would swear he wasn't turning the wheel at all. He would do fast laps below the line in qualifying and then, during the race, he'd find ways to get around people who were very special. He was a uniquely gifted oval racer.

The excitement he provided transcended through the team. Every crew member on his team gave everything they had for Dan. It's because he gave back an equal amount. It's not uncommon that crew members on race teams have little or no contact with their driver. He's considered the "talent" who just comes in on the weekends and drives the car. That was never the case with Dan. He made a sincere connection with the guys on his crew. They worked hard for him because of that, but also because they knew he was giving his all for them.

Dan also was known as a prankster, and everyone knew. The result of that was, we liked to have fun with him, too. At his first Rolex 24 at Daytona with us in 2006, I sent him out for coffee and food at 4 a.m. It was a bit of a hazing, and something he could have said no to, but he did it with enthusiasm. He didn't just go out and find coffee and food, he made sure it was the *best* coffee and food he could find.

lit up the room or engaged everyone in the room, but he had enough heart for everyone in the room. That was Dan. That, to me, was truly special.

The attention to detail he had in his personal life, fell into the attention to detail he had in his professional life. That was a distinct trait of Dan's. He was extremely organized, and it made him a better racer. It created avenues for betterment professionally. The positive fallout from that went all the way through the team. He didn't go out of his way to upset anyone on the team with hyper-organization, but he went about his business in his own way, very precisely and detailed, and the positive element of that raised our game as a team.

A good example of that (and it has nothing to do with motor racing) is that he helped me – in a roundabout way – find someone to build a home. I'm in the process of building a new home in St. Pete, and we were trying to decide whom to hire to build it. Dan and Susie had a house built, and they hired a builder, so I went over and looked at his work and was blown away by his attention to detail. That worked for Dan, they thought and worked the same. He had passed the Dan test. It's important to find someone who thinks the same.

If you can do that, you're special. Dan would wear you out with detail. If you understood that going in, you knew how much better it would be when you were done with the Dan test. It was terrific to have that perfectionism going for us.

People often would come to me and ask quietly about Dan. He was this larger-than-life figure, so people were sometimes cautious

"He was a perfectionist, and when he didn't feel like he was living up to his own standards, he'd go into a funk"

Dan was just a terrific person. In my position, I have to keep our drivers at arm's length. They become friends but, at the same time, they work for us. It's a boss-employee relationship. You want it to be cordial and friendly, but you don't want to get too close. You don't dig into the relationship side of it like you would if it were an interpersonal relationship.

However, Dan was such an engaging individual, it was hard not to become his friend. I really thought I had done a good job of that – keeping things professional and maintaining some distance – but the truth is I really became his friend.

After Dan left our team, I bought some property in St. Petersburg, Fla., where Dan had settled with Susie. My wife, Melinda, and I ended up spending an enormous amount of time with them when we were there. We became really good friends. I saw him in a completely different light than when he drove for us. I became aware of all the things he went out of his way to do for other people. He had such a big heart.

That's probably what I miss most. Dan may not have always

to approach him. They thought he must have an enormous ego, but he was exactly the opposite. He had a lot of self-confidence, but the self-confidence didn't create ego. That's a rare quality.

Dan remembered where he came from. He owed a lot of that to his mom and dad, but he remembered how hard it was and how much he struggled in his early years. He remembered what it meant to earn a dollar in the United States for the first time. He understood what it meant when he accomplished something. He always thanked everyone. He was responsible to and respectful of everyone.

He never stopped being that kind of person his entire life. That is such a rare quality in a person. We all know people in this business who go off the deep end once they find success. Some of them come to their senses, and some of them never do. Dan was the same person from the first day I met him until the last morning I talked to him in Las Vegas – absolutely the same person.

I truly believe that is his legacy. He was himself, and that person was unforgettable. ∎

WORKING THE SPOTLIGHT

When it came to photo shoots Dan Wheldon was as much art director as he was model

by Andy Hallbery

■ EDITOR, LIONHEART –
REMEMBERING DAN WHELDON

DAN CONNECTION
Writer and art director

One of the joys of editing magazines is creating ideas for photo shoots. One of the downsides of that is persuading the star of the shoot, Driver X, to agree it's a good idea and act out the role we have invented for the story.

With Dan, that was never an issue. In fact, quite often he took over, suggesting ideas, looking at test shots, Polaroids, and generally getting right in the swing.

One such shoot was for *IndyCar Series* magazine, which RACER Communications published on behalf of the League. My role there was to help out with production, especially on the ground with the ever-more-complex shoots dreamed up by Editor-in-Chief Laurence Foster and Editor Tim Scott. For the IndyCar Spring Training test at Homestead, Miami, I had 15 minutes booked into Dan's schedule for a story to be headlined "The Running Man," based on his new focus for the season, diet, fitness, and such. It was Olympic year, so the athletic angle and theme were apt. Foster suggested that we have a lot of motion in the shot, and that was my brief for Dan.

Working with Dan was always fun, whether I was interviewing him or organizing specific photos. Right from the early days he always got involved, unlike many drivers who would just as soon be somewhere else, rather than make time for a photo. He often thanked us for "making me look good" in shoots we did when magazines were published and, through them, he and I became friends. In 2006, when his U.S. visa needed to be renewed, I had no hesitation in writing a letter of support for him, citing his "unique athletic skills". He did the same for me – also being an ex-pat Brit – when time came for my renewal, his confirming that I was "… an alien of extraordinary ability."

At Homestead, photographer Laurence Baker and I arrived at the track, scouted for locations and found a great spot in the tunnel under Turn One. The lights were set up, and I, being the dummy, pretended to be Dan and stood in to make sure we were getting the images we wanted.

Our allotted time came and went. Motorsport is 90% waiting, and the IndyCar media day had drivers going here and there with interviews and other shoots to be done in plans ordered by the 15-minute slots. Our 2pm "slot" was long passed when Dan, our subject, emerged from an interview to meet me. He apologized profusely, ("Man, that went on a bit, so sorry….") as we walked to our location. We knew his schedule was tight, and he was obviously already late for his next appointment.

He looked at our test shots, wasting no time pointing out that I was no athlete. Instead, according to Dan, I portrayed a "jogging man," and he would do so much better at running than I had.

Not surprisingly, he did. Time after time he ran through the tunnel, stopping to see how it had come out, then trying again, but faster, or harder, with more energy. He then asked what it would be like jumping instead of running. I'd tried that earlier, too, and my test results had him laughing even more.

With time edging way past our 15 minutes, he was still thinking. "What about this, or that?" Finally he knew he had to go, but he wanted to try one last image. He wanted to stand stock-still. It was totally against the theme of the story we were doing, but Baker, behind the lens encouraged it. He stood still and, pictures taken, thanked us for our time (yes, really!) and then set off for the next part of his media day.

The running image and its motion worked very well, and "The Running Man" was published in the 2008 preview issue of *IndyCar Series* magazine as planned.

In November 2011, after Dan's passing, I was asked by *Autosport* to contribute to the magazine's tribute feature. Instantly I thought of that unpublished – mostly unseen – image we took right at the end the day in 2008. Dan's own thought and effort in front of the camera, his contribution to our work.

Silent, still and content as he was then, the picture of peace took on an entirely new and poignant meaning. ■

> "He wanted to stand stock-still. It was totally against the theme of the story we were doing, but Baker, behind the lens encouraged it"

THE RUNNING MAN

On your mark, get set, go go go! And don't let up until the final lap or the final race. That's Dan Wheldon's simple philosophy after a disappointing (by his standards) 2007

The final shot of the day, Dan's choice ;
the planned image (inset) as published in
IndyCar Series magazine in 2008

SHARP SHOOTER

Team photographer recalls the time that the planets aligned in his camera's viewfinder

by DARRELL INGHAM

■ PHOTOGRAPHER, GETTY IMAGES

DAN CONNECTION
Official team photographer, Andretti Green/
Chip Ganassi Racing, 2003-2008

I've worked in racing from the mid-1980s and taken thousands of images in that time. One particular photo I took of Dan stands in my all-time top 10. It was taken on Carburetion Day at Indianapolis in 2006.

Everything came together for this. Practice and qualifying were done, I'd already been there all month, and I certainly didn't need another picture of a car on the track. That day, I was looking for something else that would tell a little story for Target Chip Ganassi – a preview. I was just hanging around on the overhang in Gasoline Alley, waiting for something to come through. There was a huge throng of people down there. And, suddenly, Dan comes through. Perfect!

Everything fell into place for me: I've got a news picture, I've got our team guy, I've got Wheldon – the reigning IndyCar champion and the reigning Indy 500 champion – the "10" on his back, his arm is up waving, the throng is separating like a sea. Perfect. I prefer the black and white version – any distractions are taken away.

Try imagining that picture as if it were taken today as opposed to more than 10 years ago. Everyone there would have their arms up as well with their cell phone cameras pointing at him!

"Everything fell into place for me: I've got a news picture, I've got our team guy, I've got Wheldon"

That picture says a lot about Dan. He's there, reaching out to the fans. He was always doing that, signing autographs and stuff. He was the same with us photographers, too. When I was working for CART and he was a kid in Formula Atlantic, he always made a point of saying hello, being nice. "Hey guys! How's it going? How are you doing?" He knew who we were, what we did and what we represented.

He was always very good to work with because of that attitude. I took a lot of pictures where I've dropped the camera into the cockpit, in his face, so you get that tighter helmet picture as opposed to the front of the car. He was always great with that, didn't make a fuss. I was always very aware it could disturb things – I'd never do it in qualifying, obviously.

With Dan, if you wanted him to flip the visor down, he'd flip the visor down for you. He was well aware that pictures were there to be made, and something was going to come from those pictures. I think there was something about the attention he liked as well. ◼

TRICKY STARTERS

They became great teammates and friends but that wasn't how it always was

by SCOTT DIXON

■ THREE-TIME INDYCAR CHAMPION

DAN CONNECTION
Target Chip Ganassi teammate 2006-2008 and friend

A t the very start, Dan and I didn't see eye-to-eye. I first met him in 2000. He was in USF2000 at the time, and he came to PitFit in Indianapolis to train. He was this skinny little dude, and my first impression was that he talked a lot and liked himself too much. I thought, "Oh, God. Here's another one. Here we go."

I didn't see him for a long time after that. The next time I ran into him, it was 2003 at Indianapolis Motor Speedway when he was filling in for Dario Franchitti with Andretti Green Racing. He had a massive crash at the 500 and flipped over. From that point, he was a regular in IndyCar, but we didn't really have too many altercations on the track. We always raced together fairly well. He won the championship in 2005 in dominating style.

Toward the end of that season, we caught wind that Chip was talking to Dan about joining the team, which is what happened for the 2006 season. It had been a rough couple of years for our program. We were down on power with Toyota, and we were constantly getting beat by Honda.

At our first team test at Phoenix, before the 2006 season, Honda was starting its first season as IndyCar's sole engine supplier, and the chassis were the same for everyone. It was my first experience with the Honda engine, so I was getting a new engine, but Dan had been with Honda from the start. At that first test, Dan and I were 1-2 on the speed chart. Dan was quickest in the first session, but he got out of the car and said, "Man, the power sucks on these things." My comment was, "Are you kidding me? This engine has great power compared to what we had the last two years."

We had a few moments adjusting to each other that season. We didn't really click or agree on many things at first. At Indy, we had a major dustup during one of the practices. We were working together, but we were really annoying each other. When we would go through Turn 4 and he was leading, he would lift in the middle of the corner. We were doing race simulations, but it would totally mess me up and ruin the run.

Since he was doing it to me when he was leading, I would do it to him when I was in front. After it got really bad one day, the team leaders sat us down in the truck and said, "Hey, this has to stop. You guys are hurting the program."

There was some time off between practices at one point, so Dan and I went out drinking. We had a pretty big night, actually. From that moment on, we became a lot closer. We started hanging out together more often, and we both made more effort to work together and stop antagonizing each other.

The morning after our night out, we had a commercial shoot at the shop. We were both about three hours late, but that was the moment it all changed. We started enjoying each other's company more and communicating better. That season was fought closely to the bitter end. Dan and I each won two races, and Dan tied Sam Hornish Jr. for the championship. However, Sam won the tiebreaker because he'd won four races that year. I finished fourth, but it all came down to that last race at Chicago.

The next year, IndyCar added road courses, so Dan and I started working even closer together through testing and trying to develop a solid road-course program. We both came close to winning that championship – I finished second behind Dario, while Dan was fourth – but we really bonded that year, as well as in 2008.

In 2007, I knew that Dan and Susie, who had been working with him on public relations, had been seeing each other off and on. It became more serious throughout the year and I was seeing Emma

Fun and a laugh were never far away once the ice was broken; nobody was immune to a cake in the face; even when not teammates, time for smiles

"Dan was a lot of fun, and I think that's what people should remember about him"

at the same time. We got married in February 2008, and Dan and Susie got married in March. That was the time we started hanging out together as a group, just the four of us, taking trips and such.

The thing about Dan that inspired me was his attention to detail. There are tons of funny stories about his clothing and how he organized things. You could move something very slightly or put something in his locker that wasn't supposed to be there, and it would send him sideways. That was a continuous prank with us, but his detail and organization is what set him apart on the racetrack.

Yes, he was a funny guy and a joker and prankster himself, but I've never seen anyone who was more organized and thorough. Dario is probably the only one who comes close as far as debriefs. After each session – practice, qualifying and races – we would meet with our engineers to debrief. We discussed the car and its performance, how it responded, what it felt like, how it changed through the course of the session. Usually we just talked about it, but Dan would talk about it *and* write it down.

He would have pages of detail for the engineers. Nine times out of 10 he'd be the last guy to leave the track. He provided an enormous amount of insight and detail about the cars. It's true that he was very good in some areas and struggled in others, but he made sure he put in the time to try to help that situation and try to make himself a better driver. It wasn't just about sorting out the car for Dan. It was about improving his part of the car-driver equation.

Once we bonded together and started working together completely, it was magical. I have to credit him a great deal for my championship in '08. He helped a great deal in that.

We both grew up during the time we knew each other. We were

in funny transitions when we met. I was very quiet and shy when I was younger, while Dan was talkative and brash. Dan's personality was very welcoming, while people often misinterpreted my shyness as aloofness. I changed a lot through Dan, and I think we found common ground. We also found confidence in ourselves through each other.

We were almost on the same path, really, but just going about it in different ways. I started quiet and gained more confidence and became more open and talkative, while Dan started loud and cocky and became more humble as he got older. We changed from young guys who didn't know much, to grownups getting married and starting families. As people we grew at the same time, and that's what brought our relationship closer.

The other thing I admired about Dan was his ability to represent his sponsors. You couldn't get a better representative for the company putting its logo on your car. He was very much in the mix of what was going on with the companies, and he always insisted

"We were headed in the same direction, at the same point in our lives, at the same time. He became a wonderful friend"

Great friends and teammates who shared success together in IndyCar (left), at Daytona, and downtime with their families away from the track

point in our lives, at the same time. He became a wonderful friend.

There are so many funny stories about Dan. In 2007, at a test at Texas, he showed up with his new teeth. Man, we would not let that go. You could see the transition from when he first got them – they were huge – and then he had them ground down so they weren't as large. After the initial surgery, his lips wouldn't go back to normal, so he was constantly smiling.

When I got to Texas for the test, I hadn't seen him yet, but the other guys on the team had. They all wore fake teeth the first time they saw him. It was hilarious. Honestly, Dan was living the dream at the time. He didn't give a shit what people thought of him. He had that way with clothing or anything else about his appearance. If he liked it, he wore it, and he wore it proudly.

Dan was a lot of fun, and I think that's what people should remember about him. Yes, there were down times at certain points, but overall he was a very positive person and always funny. I keep thinking back to the final weekend in Las Vegas and how upbeat and happy he was that entire time.

The night before the race, Dan and Susie went to get tattoos. I had picked up Emma from the airport, and we were thinking about going out to dinner, but we just ended up getting room service and staying in. I remember waking up and looking at my phone and seeing about six texts and 10 missed calls, all from Dan. My first thought was, "God, what's happened?"

So I called him at about 7 in the morning, and he was like, "Man, you've got to come over and check out my tattoo! We got matching tattoos!" I said, "Dude, I thought you were in jail or something."

I remember sitting in the drivers' meeting that morning and chatting with him. He was typical Dan – upbeat and happy. It wasn't really any different from any other race weekend. Racers usually have some lulls, or they have bad weekends or show up on race day pissed off. Dan had his ups and downs, but you never really saw the lulls. He was rarely down, but that weekend he was especially happy and enthusiastic.

That's the way I remember him, because that was the Dan I knew. He was a great racer and teammate, a great father and husband, but most of all a great friend. Not just to me, but to everyone. ∎

on going above and beyond what they needed. The best example of that are the years he spent with the National Guard sponsorship at Panther Racing. He put everything he had into representing soldiers, and he truly loved it.

He also made a connection with fans. When you met Dan as a fan, you felt like you were really his friend. That was something that came naturally to him, and it was because he genuinely liked people and understood that, without fans, he wouldn't be racing. That's why he was so loved. I saw it again and again. Wherever we went people really reacted to Dan. It was his personality. For the sport, that connection was massive.

Once we had kids and started taking family trips together, we really got closer. Whenever the St. Petersburg race came up, we'd go down there the week before and hang out with Dan and Susie. Sometimes we'd stay with them. We'd go to the pool and the zoo with the kids and just enjoy life. For me, those are wonderful memories. We were headed in the same direction, at the same

LIFTING THE LID

When you consider how OCD Dan was, leaving something as personal as his helmet design to someone else seems unthinkable. But his trust in Jason Fowler was both complete and well placed

by JASON FOWLER

■ HELMET PAINTER AND AIRBRUSH ARTIST

DAN CONNECTION
Helmet Designer 2003-'11

first started painting helmets for Dan back in 2003. He hadn't been in the U.S. very long and wanted to update his now iconic Lionheart theme. We painted a few helmets for him and started chatting about designs. Dan liked the idea of changing the look a little each time, giving each helmet an individual style and feel. Half-jokingly, I asked if we could surprise him with each one, having free rein to come up with fresh ideas for each new design. To my amazement, Dan agreed! This was so unusual in a sport that gets more restricted every year, and we couldn't wait to get started.

The outline brief for his helmets was very loose. All we had to do

was keep the relevant sponsor logos in the correct position, have a union jack somewhere and, of course, feature the Lionheart Knight on the back. Beyond that, we were allowed to do whatever came into our heads. The only time we had any prior notification was when Mattel made miniature models of Dan in his racecar, so we had to keep the overall design the same for several races. Even then, each one had variations to make them slightly different from each other. We'd sometimes think of new techniques or ideas and try them out first on Dan's helmets, meaning he often got styles and effects that hadn't been used before.

Dan started featuring the Lionheart Knight as a small emblem on the back of his helmet during his karting days. Apparently his mechanic, Mark Rose, thought Dan drove with such courage and bravery he was like Richard the Lionheart going into battle, so Mark suggested he feature the logo on his helmet. Over the years, we made the Knight more detailed and eventually gave him a life of his

There was no brief for the helmet designs; some were fun, some embraced his UK home, and others reflected the heritage and history of his prized Indianapolis 500

own when we began doing special designs that related to particular races. He was finally able to get off the horse and do other things!

I think those race-specific specials suited Dan's personality most and they are some of my favorite designs, too. They were fun, spontaneous and not made to fit any usual ideas or parameters. Helmet designs can often be like a boring corporate meeting to sell a sponsor's product, but Dan's helmets were more like a party! The various Indy 500 specials we produced, and many others such as the Miami-Homestead helmet with the Knight driving a custom car from the beach to the track, were so much fun to design. A real change from the majority of work we're asked to do.

One of my favorites to paint – as it was so different – was a helmet created for the 2011 Surfers Paradise V8 race, which, unfortunately, Dan never got to wear. The design featured a surfing Knight with aboriginal patterns and was very intricate. The only theme we ever

> ## "Helmet designs can be like a boring corporate meeting to sell a sponsor's product. Dan's were like a party!"

had a problem with was one painted for a race in Canada where we had the Knight as an ice-hockey goalie, wearing the colors of the local team. Unfortunately, someone in the hockey team's legal department must have been having a bad day and banned the use of the helmet due to it being an infringement of their trademark.

I have so many great memories of Dan. I was lucky enough to

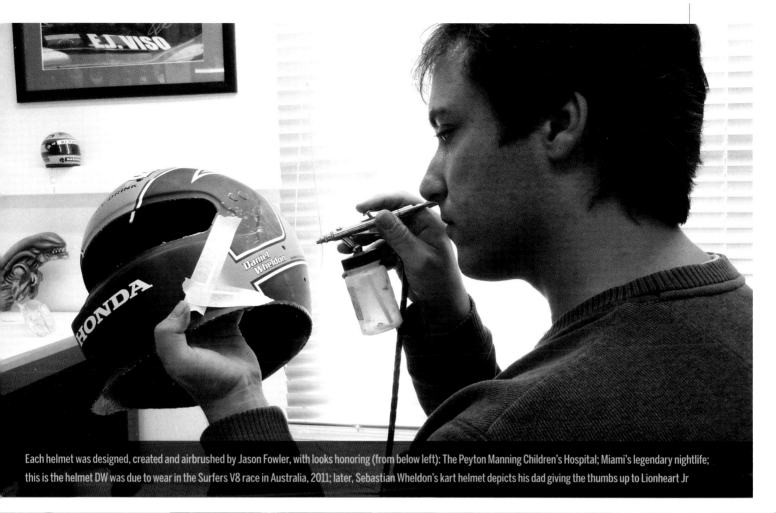

Each helmet was designed, created and airbrushed by Jason Fowler, with looks honoring (from below left): The Peyton Manning Children's Hospital; Miami's legendary nightlife; this is the helmet DW was due to wear in the Surfers V8 race in Australia, 2011; later, Sebastian Wheldon's kart helmet depicts his dad giving the thumbs up to Lionheart Jr

finally meet him at the 2010 Indy 500 race after working with him for so many years. Lots of races stand out, especially his first Indy win. I'd always been a fan of the race and watched it every year on TV all the way over here in the UK, and as Dan did the victory lap it suddenly made me realize how lucky I was to be a small part of something so big. His second Indy win was special, too, after he'd had such a difficult year. For some reason, I couldn't watch it here so I was following live timing on the Internet; just watching the laps count down. He was in second starting the final lap, and then, as the last lap finished, he jumped to first on the timing screens! I couldn't see what had happened in that incredible finish but I was cheering while sitting in front of the laptop in my kitchen.

I always look back at my time working with Dan as the most fun part of my career. I deal with a lot of drivers and teams and, at the top of the ladder, it can occasionally be very restrictive, intense, and in some cases unnecessarily difficult. It was always the opposite with Dan; he was easy-going, appreciative and gave us freedom to have fun with the designs, which is rare at such a high level. He always made sure we had the helmets in plenty of time, as he knew the number of hours involved in creating them and wanted to make sure we had the time to do as good a job as possible.

In 2014, we came up with the design for Sebastian's karting helmet, as Susie wanted to feature the Lionheart on it in some way. We thought it would be a nice tribute to Dan to have them both on the helmet, him passing the baton to his young son. We used colors and elements from Dan's past helmets in the overall scheme as well, almost like a crossover between the two. We had a lot of comments about the cartoon and it seemed to go down well. It was hard painting a "Dan" style helmet again but, at the same time, it brought back some good memories. ∎

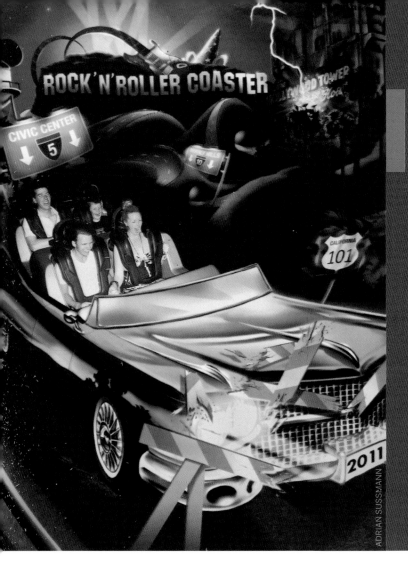

ADRIAN SUSSMANN

BEST MAN FOR THE JOB

A driver's career can be dictated by crucial decisions. Having faith and trust in the guy making the deals is a huge part of that

by ADRIAN SUSSMANN

■ MANAGING DIRECTOR,
GP SPORTS MANAGEMENT

DAN CONNECTION
Manager, 2000-2011; best man at Dan and Susie's wedding

et me just say, before I start the stories, the thing about Dan was that he loved everything about motor racing, every aspect of it. He loved the cars, the racing, and the driving. He also loved the fans, the interaction with the media and the business around racing. A lot of the drivers put up with this other stuff, but for Dan it was a massive part of racing. He loved it all.

Not only that, he knew how to work every aspect of it as well. People thought he was cocky or arrogant but it wasn't that. He was just so confident. You learn from someone like that, when you watched him walk through the paddock with this big smile, with something funny to say to everyone. He got the same reaction back because the world is a reflection. Like all careers he had his ups and downs. When you go through the downs you appreciate the ups even more. That's what made his last win at Indy so poignant and so spectacular.

We started working together the summer of 2000. Dan was racing for Cal Wells in Toyota Atlantics. I got him the ride with PacWest (in Lights). That was a great deal – he was the only kid in Indy Lights to actually get *paid* to race.

Dan thought that was just fantastic. At the start of the season, I told him that to progress to IndyCar he had to win two races...one race could be considered a fluke, but two races would prove he

was for real. Of course, that was a stupid thing to say to Dan! He won his first oval at Milwaukee halfway through the season and I was starting to sweat. At the next race at Road Atlanta, on the last corner of the last lap, he made a banzai, around-the-outside move on Townsend Bell for the win. He called me straight afterward and said, "Right, I just won my second race, where's my IndyCar ride?"

There was nothing. It was 2001, and racing in America was falling apart. That was when Penske moved over to IndyCar from CART and the teams were disintegrating. Unless you had four or five million bucks, you weren't doing anything. That wasn't a good enough answer for Dan, of course, and he would phone me four or five times a day asking, "What are you doing now? Where's my ride? I won my two races, what's going on?"

That would happen *every single* day.

We went to all the races at the beginning of 2002 doing the tours of all the transporters. At Indy, with some financial help from his dad, Clive, we agreed to a deal for Dan to test and do the last two races of the season with Panther. The great thing for me was it meant that Dan would now spend his days at the Panther race shop, so instead of bugging me five times a day he would now be bugging the Panther guys!

Doing those two races was the right thing to do. A lot of the CART

While on the pace with Dan's career, Adrian was one of the last to know Susie and his charge were dating

MICHAEL VOORHEES

teams and Honda were all wandering around the IndyCar paddock, plotting their moves. Our attitude was, spend a bit of money and get a couple of late races in so it's fresh in people's memories.

Dan finished fifth at Chicago, and was high up at Texas even though he had radio issues. The Andretti guys, Kim Green and Kevin Savoree were at Chicago, Robert Clarke from Honda, too. They spotted Dan. We had already been working closely with those guys for Dario, and we were telling them to watch Dan.

Andretti landed the Jim Beam sponsorship and wanted a new kid with a bit of personality. They felt that Dan fit the bill and, sure enough, he did. Doing those two races did work; those performances led to his drive at what became Andretti Green Racing.

We did a three-year deal for 2003, one year with a two-year option. They were taking a bit of a risk on an unknown kid with a big new sponsor they wanted to make sure was happy. But you couldn't have put two better groups together. I think they all had a pretty

"Unless you had four or five million bucks, you weren't doing anything..."

good time. Keystone Sports Marketing had the Jim Beam account, and they signed Susie to it. She was handling all of Dan's PR and scheduling and such.

It all went great but – like everything – nothing's ever quite as easy as you think it's going to be. There were definitely some moments where it could have all gone horribly wrong. He was so meticulous and particular about everything. He wouldn't leave the house – would even miss flights – if his desk wasn't properly tidied first!

I didn't tell Dan off very often because he knew naturally what to do, but he got into an argument with Kevin Savoree, one of the founders of Andretti Green Racing, about some expenses that hadn't been reimbursed – it was probably a couple hundred bucks. It was the stupidest thing and the timing nearly cost him his ride. I had to pull Dan aside and go a little ballistic with him. I said, "What are you doing? You've got to let me handle that stuff. Your job is to drive the bloody racecar!" I think he got the message after that and realized

131

DAN HELRIGEL/IMS

GLEN DUNBAR/LAT

This page: Dan was courted by BMW's Mario Theissen (below) for a future in Formula 1 in 2006; on stage at the CMT Music Awards with John Rich and Gary Busey; stars are out! Bryan Herta and daughter Cali, Dan, Big Machine's Scott Borchetta and Adrian meet Taylor Swift

that's how the game works. When drivers try to negotiate their own contracts or handle the admin, it can quickly have a really negative effect on their relationship with the team.

He was IndyCar Series Rookie of the Year in 2003 but he didn't win any races. Then the second year, obviously it was important for him to win. AGR took up the option on him and he won Motegi, Japan. His first win and Honda's first there, too, so that cemented the relationship. That was the first of three wins and he ended up second to AGR teammate Tony Kanaan in the championship.

The team wanted to extend his contract, because he was about to start the last year of the three-year deal. We were at the Rolex 24 at the beginning of 2005 and Kim Green showed up with his offer of what the next contract would look like. Let's put it this way, it wasn't quite good enough! But we were very polite to Kim and said we'd think about it and thank you very much. This was where Dan's timing was immaculate; because he went and won the season-opener at Homestead. So, we get an offer that's a little bit higher. Second race at St. Pete, Dan wins that too and then we get another offer that's a little bit higher. And so on…it just carried on like that as Dan won four out of the first five, including the most important one at Indy. His stock was getting higher by the race.

At that point, Formula 1 came on the horizon as well and my partner in Europe, Julian Jakobi [Ayrton Senna's and Alain Prost's manager] was talking to BMW and Mario Theissen. That was actually quite comical thinking back as we tried to schedule a meeting. There was one point where Dan and I were going to have to fly to Japan for 24 hours to meet with Mario then fly back to fit in with Dan's race schedule. Luckily, Dr. Theissen was on his way from Brazil to

Japan via LAX. So Dan and I, at a moment's notice, flew to LAX and met him in the food court at terminal five to discuss a possible F1 contract! It was hilarious – not very "Formula 1" at all! We're there an hour talking. They put a contract on the table but they wouldn't make a firm race commitment. It was a test drive which would turn in to the race drive if Jacques Villeneuve didn't carry on, which no one would say for sure if he was or wasn't. Dan wanted to race. That F1 offer ended up being the deal that Robert Kubica took and sure enough, Villeneuve was replaced!

In the meantime, Chip Ganassi's team had not been doing very well and was about to switch to Honda, and he, too, was suddenly really interested in Dan. At end of the day, the relationship is between the driver and the team owner, so you have to put them together. That was another one of those "interesting" meetings. The only time we could find was around 10 o'clock at night in Chip's hotel room in Sonoma on race weekend. There's Dan and I tip-toeing along the corridors, hoping nobody sees us, ducking into a room and Chip's there in his bathrobe. It was just one of those classic scenes in racing! Mike Hull was also there, not in a bathrobe I must add…

It's nearing the end of 2005 and we had three options on the table, stay at Andretti, go to Chip, or BMW Formula 1. Our job as managers is to negotiate the best contracts we can and get as many good options as possible for the driver to choose from. But it's always the driver's decision what they want to do. If they don't like the deal that's on the table, they're not going to do it. It's not about the money as much as it is about the feeling in the team.

I also think Dan wanted to prove that he could win in two different teams. That is a statement, similar to the winning two races thing

KEVIN MAZUR/GETTY IMAGES

RICK DIAMOND/GETTY IMAGES

It was a great wedding at The Vinoy Renaissance Hotel in St. Pete. After I'd toasted the bride and groom, I had three items for the happy couple in my speech. The first was freeze-dried astronaut food because in all that time in his house he'd never used his kitchen. The fridge literally just had Fiji water and some San Pellegrino lemonade, and nothing else! The second were covers to go over shoes, not for walking in the house – because you're obviously already not allowed shoes in the house. The covers were to walk in the garage, where Dan had just had the concrete floor polished. Finally, no couple should be without a "his and hers" toothbrush set...Dan had recently had his English teeth replaced with a large, gleaming white Hollywood grill...so, I had a normal toothbrush for Susie and then a giant gag one for Dan!

For whatever reason, and I don't understand it, Dan did struggle on the road courses. Scott would regularly be in the top six and Dan would struggle to even get past first qualifying. That's the thing with racing, you go from hero to zero so fast, and it's all confidence.

Chip kept saying through 2008, "Yeah, yeah, don't worry we're going to renew the contract." I remember we got to Richmond and Dan had heard rumors that Tony Kanaan was talking to Chip. I was telling Dan "No, I just saw Chip and he said there's no problem, relax..." We got to Kentucky where Robin Miller broke the story. Tony had obviously been re-upping with Andretti and the contract was done but it hadn't been signed. I think Andretti saw the rumors, literally marched into TK's motor home and held a pen in his hand to make him sign the contract.

So, that was Tony off the market. I was with Dan and Susie in his motor home, and Dan's phone rings. He shows it to me and it's Chip. He answers and says, "You got the wrong number, this is Dan. It's not Tony, it's Dan!" He wasn't happy about the situation and told me to see what else was out there. You don't want to drive for someone, if they don't want you to drive for them.

I was chatting with John Barnes during that race and he came back to me, all of a sudden, sounding quite interested for Panther and National Guard. OK, Dan wasn't American but he was pretty close, and he was the type of

earlier in his career – just one could be a fluke. He loved the idea of the challenge of coming to Chip's team and obviously Chip really wanted him, so that's what happened.

Dan made his decision just before the last race of the season at Fontana, and we had to tell Michael, Kim and Kevin what he was doing, and they weren't very happy. Obviously, Andretti Green wanted to keep him and it was really difficult for Dan as he was so grateful to them for giving him his big break. (Dan remained great friends with Michael and Marco and was due to return to the team in 2012, with the contract finalized just hours before the tragic Las Vegas race).

The first race at Homestead in 2006 was the incredible battle between Helio and Dan; when they were literally wheel to wheel for 30 laps. Dan won it by five centimeters, or whatever it was. Chip was screaming, "That's why I signed that guy!" And that's what his team was missing. I won't forget the look on the

> "Dan and I flew to LAX and met him at a food court to discuss a possible Formula 1 contract"

Target guys' – all of that team's faces – they were blown away. Dan lifted the whole team and that's what a good driver can do.

During Dan's second year at Ganassi, he and Susie – who had left Jim Beam and was now his personal assistant – called me up to say they were getting married and wanted me to be best man, which was a real honor. It was also a surprise! Call me perceptive (err...not!), but I had no idea they were even dating....

personality that National Guard would be looking for, and a proven winner at Indy. Things moved quite quickly. Dan and I went to Indy and met with John and he showed us his new race shop that they were going to move into. They put a big offer on the table and we started negotiating. In the meantime, Chip had come back – finally – with a contract extension and we had a choice to make. It was a really difficult one.

It's up to the driver to decide. No one else can make that decision. Was Panther the right decision or the wrong decision? That's a hard one...Dan did say afterward that he felt he made his decision with his head rather than his heart. I think he regretted not staying, because the equipment was just so much better at Chip's.

I think he really enjoyed his time at Panther, off the track, anyway. It raised his stock again because he was doing things with that car that shouldn't have been done. To finish second at Indy twice – that was pretty amazing. The second time was to Dario, in the ride that Dan had stepped out of at Ganassi, and I was managing Dario, too.

I remember going to greet Dan after he got out of the car at Indy, and he basically just looked at me and said, "Well you had a better day than I did." Typical Dan.

At the end of the day, it was Dan's decision what he wanted to do. He could have stayed where he was but he decided he wanted to move on. I don't think drivers think about that. When you leave somewhere, you're leaving a vacancy for someone else. Perhaps he hadn't really thought about that, how he would feel if he was following his old car across the line at Indy. Which is sadly what ultimately happened in 2010.

That's the other thing about Indy; it's always got a twist to it. For Dan to win it the year after, in 2011 – having gone through all of the heartache of not having a ride – it was special.

He really loved and enjoyed the television work he did while sitting out. It brought out the best of him. All of a sudden he was the contemporary of all the drivers. They would give him material that other people would never get and he did it in such a cheeky way. He was just a natural presenter, very eloquent and had such energy and passion behind a microphone. It was great to watch.

We were about to sign with KVSH Racing for the 2011 Indy 500. I had the contracts all done on the table, ready to go. Then, literally, the next day, before we had signed them, Bryan Herta called saying that he'd managed to put a deal together.

They'd been teammates at Andretti Green Racing and Dan had a really good feeling about what Bryan was capable of doing, so we went with Bryan instead.

Dan again, did what he always did in every team he was with. He got the best out of them, believed in them, and gave 100 percent for them. Dan told me that the last stint he drove was the best he'd ever been around Indy, and his engineer confirmed that. It was literally just perfect every lap, getting the best out of the car and being in position to win on the last corner of the last lap...it was incredible.

Dan was also clever at maximizing every opportunity. Think about this... He'd won the 2011 Indy 500 in the most extraordinary circumstances and he's completely overcome by emotion. When he gets out of the car, all the microphones are thrown in his face and he does his interview with ABC TV in tears, thanking all the sponsors and telling them all how happy he is. Then, at the end of the interview, he looks at the camera, and says, "I'm going to take my kids to Disney World."

It's basically tradition in the U.S. that the winner of the Super Bowl goes to Disneyland and Dan knew that. Sure enough, the next day I got a phone call from this guy, something like the Executive Vice President in charge of parks at Disney. "Hi!! I'm from Disney. We saw Dan Wheldon's interview on ABC television yesterday when he won the Indy 500 and we'd like to invite him to Disney!" So I said, "Fantastic, he would love to come, and can his manager come, too?" and he said, "Sure!"

So we all went to Disney World in June for Dan's birthday. Coincidentally, it was my son's birthday the next day. They put Dan, Susie and the boys up in their nicest hotel at Disney World. Then they gave us a guide so we didn't even go through the entrance to the park. We didn't have to wait in any queues because they didn't take you to the front of the line; they put you on the ride where everyone's getting off. It was unbelievable. We had two days of, "Can we do that one again?" "Yeah, sure," and we'd just get straight back on it again. They had him as the Grand Marshall in the parade, with Susie and the boys at the front; they did a bunch of interviews. The whole thing was fantastic.

No other driver I know would think to say "I'm going to take my kids to Disney" at the end of their race, it's the last thing they'd think about. But Dan had it all figured out.

That race was also the start of the relationship with Scott Borchetta of Big Machine Records. I introduced myself to Scott on the grid before the race. He'd been going to the 500 since he was a kid, but this was his first time sponsoring a car. He was on board because Bryan had sponsorship from Cary Agajanian and Mike Curb (Curb Records). Bryan was still looking for extra funding to complete his deal and, as they were both in Nashville, Mike knew Scott and the fact that they shared a passion for racing.

When Scott found out that Dan would be the driver, he was in! The funny thing was that Curb Records had been sponsoring an Indy 500 car for 20-odd years and never won it, and Scott comes in for the first time and wins it.

After the win at the 500, Scott invited Dan and me to Nashville.

> "His phone rings, and it's Chip. 'You've got the wrong number. This is Dan, not Tony'"

Two Indy 500 wins, and both celebrated with the guys from GP Sports Management; Disney days

Not knowing much about country music, we didn't really know who Scott was, but we had nothing else to do so we went. We were there for 48 hours and it felt like the longest two weeks of our lives!

We realized very quickly that Scott was Mr. Nashville and he literally had it so there wasn't a second that Dan wasn't doing something. It was amazing.

It was the Country Music Awards and they had Dan as a presenter with musician John Rich and actor Gary Busey, it was hilarious. He was giving an award; they had him walk the red carpet. Every single country music station around the country could interview the stars. Dan did that, too. We went to the awards after party and then the "after after" party at Big 'n' Rich's house where they treated Dan like a superstar…. Awesome!

The second day was more of the same. At the end of that, Scott says to Dan, "There's just one last thing I've got for you. You've got to do an intro, because there is going to be a highlights show for the country music festival on ABC and you just need to do the intro for one of the bands." Dan was, "Yeah, cool, no problem."

We show up at the Tennessee Titans football stadium and Dan's like, "What the f*** are we doing here?" There were 70,000 people in the stadium! He had to walk out on stage, in front of 70,000 people without a cue. They casually said, "Here are some lines you've got to say and you've got to memorize them… All right, go! It's the only time I ever saw Dan scared – and he was terrified. He was pacing around at the back of the stage, saying, "I can't do this, I can't do this! What are the lines again?"

The call comes, "Right, Dan you're up. Here's the microphone." They announced him to the crowd, too, "Ladies and gentlemen, the 2011 Indianapolis 500 champion, put your hands together for Dan Wheldon…" Everyone's cheering as Dan walks out to the crowd, and there's cameras on booms and such. A short pause for effect, and soak it in, "…Good evening, Nashville!"

They did three takes in the end and the third one he nailed it. He came out and he was so pumped up, just from the energy from the crowd and the adrenaline, he was like, "Woohoo!" It was just great. When Dan was pacing around before, Scott said, "This isn't as bad as Turn One at Indy with Matsura on your outside." and Dan said, "No, it's worse than that!"

I had no doubt that Scott was going to be a big part of Dan's future, because he saw the whole kind of "rock star" quality that Dan had and wanted to build it up. Scott's idea was apply to a race driver what you do in the music industry. You make stars, and no one's doing that in motor racing. Scott saw in Dan the perfect person to do that with. In fact, he was going to be one of the sponsors on Dan's return to Andretti Autosport that had been agreed for 2012.

Scott invited Dan, Bryan and me to go to the Brickyard 400 as he was title sponsor, presented by Big Machine, and was providing the music. So we went. We didn't have anything else to do because Dan wasn't racing. Taylor Swift – who Scott had discovered and signed – was playing in Indianapolis that night, by pure coincidence, and we met her. So, thanks to Dan, I got some credibility at home with my daughter! She once got a fortune cookie and I always remember it. "The best things happen to the people who make the best of the things that happen to them." And that could sum up Dan. There was never a dull moment around Dan, and that's the thing – he made the absolute most out of every opportunity.

He was a great champion, a great person and a great friend. It was a privilege to have been along for the ride. ■

ADRIAN SUSSMANN

WHAT A RIDE!

Success breeds celebrity invites and amazing experiences

By MICKEY RYAN

- VICE PRESIDENT, NORTH AMERICA, GP SPORTS MANAGEMENT

DAN CONNECTION
Manager, 2003-2011

When I started, I was like an apprentice learning the trade. I wasn't doing the big deals and the contract negotiations in those early years. A lot of what I was doing was on the day-to-day driver management; helping with websites, travel, making sure that if we had a sponsorship deal, all the helmets and fire suits had the right logos, that sort of thing.

I'd joined in December 2002, and Dan had just signed for Andretti Green Racing as a test driver, but was scheduled to replace Michael Andretti after the Indianapolis 500 that year. Then Dario [Franchitti], who we also looked after, had his motorcycle accident. Initially, he'd planned to race at Motegi with a broken back and all, so I was heading to Japan in case he needed help. While I was mid-flight, Dario's doctor said he couldn't race, warning him that another crash could be really serious for him.

So, while I'm midair, Dario is yanked, Dan was thrust into the role, and I had no idea. I took a train to Tokyo, and walked into the hotel lobby where the team was staying, and Dan was there with them. He was sitting there having breakfast with Kim Green, I said, "Dan, hey! I'm Mickey." We'd spoken on the phone, but the first time we met was halfway around the planet, and that was it. Suddenly we were thrust into working with each other for his first race with Andretti Green, and that's where our friendship began.

> **"He did little things for the staff working their butts off behind the scenes, and they loved him for it"**

At the end of that year, Dan was 2003 IndyCar Rookie of the Year, and was voted for an award back in England by the readers of Autosport magazine. I went over to London and was kind of Dan's "date" at the banquet. There were a lot of big names from world motorsport there that night, and he was holding his award at the table, so excited, and very pleased to have won. There was an after party, and we got back to the hotel as the sun was coming up, and ordered room service. Dan fell asleep before it arrived, shirt half undone, but still clutching that award!

Motegi, the following year, was the backdrop for more great memories. It was his first win, and the first win for Honda, and it was in Japan! How sweet was that? We went out so big that night in Roppongi. At that race, the drivers get together and charter a bus back from the Twin Ring circuit. Everybody was on it, drinking beers, and there was a microphone and karaoke. It was pandemonium.

We ended up in this place called Geronimo's Shot Bar, and it was a really popular place with ex-pats. It's this tiny little darkened bar you'd never even know was there. There were a lot of soccer players and Kiwi rugby players, and there's a wall of fame. Dan was hell bent on being on that wall. So, he just bought shots all night! There were a lot of other drivers in there, crewmembers and so on. Geronimo's sure knew who won that day's race...even if by the end of the night, Dan didn't! He was absolutely gone to the world. It was so cool to be there for his first win, and to see how big he celebrated it, and just how happy he was.

As he got a little older, he became that little brother you loved... but you wanted to beat up, you know? He would have his little jokes, steal your phone; but really he was this kid nobody knew and he just blew up on the IndyCar scene and endeared himself not only to the fans, but also to teams and the media.

Jet set travel, TV, cell phone photos on red carpets, '80s popstars... What was there not to like about working with Dan?

We got to do some really fun things, like the ESPY awards, and we were invited to the Playboy mansion.... It was great that we got to share those experiences together.

Even after '05, he was always in contention and he was still invited to the ESPYs. He was so charming and so nice to people who organized the event; whether he had a good year or a mediocre one, he would always be invited back. He'd say hi to everyone, bring hats and shirts with him. He did little things for the staff who were working their butts off behind the scenes, and they loved him because of it.

I got to do some crazy stuff because I was with Dan at some of these things! We did a New York media tour after his 500 win in 2011, and we were doing a whole bunch of stuff for Sirius Satellite radio and various programs. There, we ran into Debbie Gibson in the lobby as we were leaving. Both Steve Shunck, the fix-it guy who was there for IndyCar, and I spotted her right off the bat. I have a younger sister, and Debbie was one of her idols and role models growing up – so I knew exactly who she was.

I whispered something to Steve, like "Holy cow...that's Debbie

Gibson, I used to listen to her because of my sister." Before you know it, Steve's shouting, "Hey! Debbie! Do you mind getting a picture with Dan and Mickey here!" Dan, meanwhile just turned and said, "Who's Debbie Gibson?" I had to explain, "Dan...she was huge in the '80s man. My little sister loved her." Definitely an '80s moment for me, and s enough for him to make fun of me for the rest of the day.

I have to say 2003 and 2004 were great; and 2005 was just the icing on the cake. I look back on those years with such fond memories. I count myself fortunate to have been around at that time – it allowed me to spend important time with Dan in his young career, and do the really fun things that I know I will always remember, and that Dan would, too. He was winning everything and he was just such a charming guy, and everywhere we went, people loved him.

That we were still having fun and enjoying success in 2011 was fantastic, and as much as I cherish the early years, standing on the bricks with Dan, the Borg Warner Trophy and Adrian again for the second time in 2011 was so sweet. ■

Honda engines powered every single one of Dan Wheldon's 16 IndyCar victories, and made special memories, too

BEAUTIFUL DAYS

by T.E. McHALE

■ MANAGER OF MOTORSPORTS
COMMUNICATIONS, AMERICAN HONDA

DAN CONNECTION
Winner, Indianapolis 500,
2005, 2011

Among my fondest memories of Daniel involve the moments before and after he won the Indianapolis 500 in 2011.

From the circumstances of how Dan took the lead – in the final 1,200 feet of the race – and the fact that he did it with a one-car team on a very small budget, it may have been the most unlikely Indy 500 victory ever. But he was fast throughout the month and started on the second row, so when we were both on the grid before the race, I looked at him and said, "Why not you?"

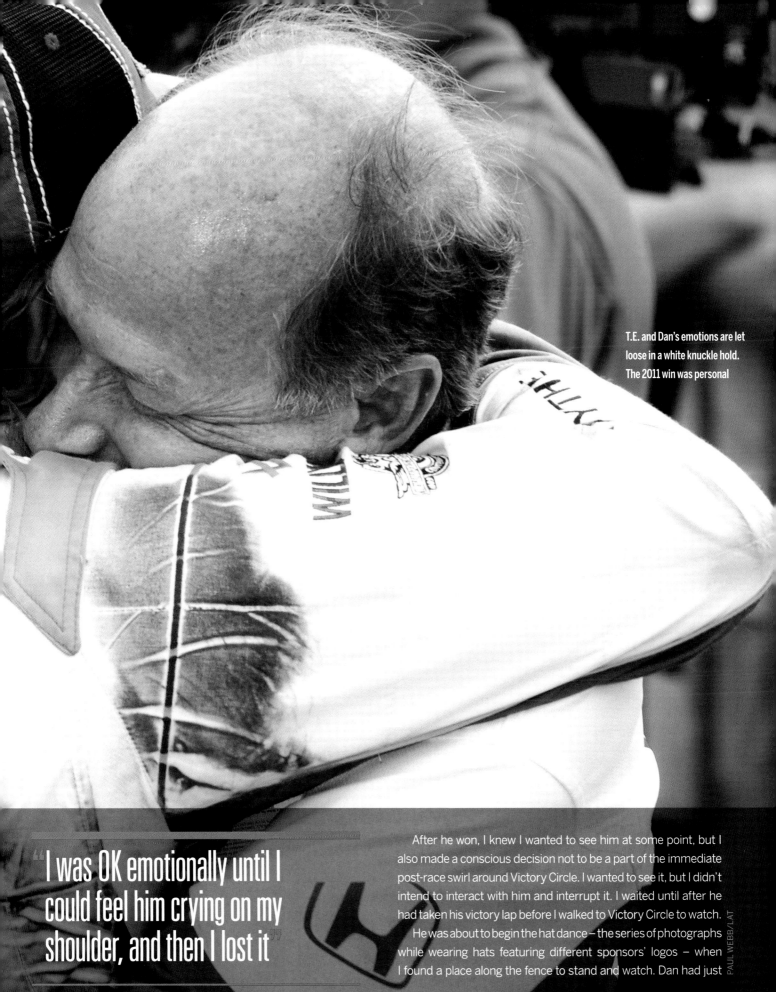

T.E. and Dan's emotions are let loose in a white knuckle hold. The 2011 win was personal

I was OK emotionally until I could feel him crying on my shoulder, and then I lost it

After he won, I knew I wanted to see him at some point, but I also made a conscious decision not to be a part of the immediate post-race swirl around Victory Circle. I wanted to see it, but I didn't intend to interact with him and interrupt it. I waited until after he had taken his victory lap before I walked to Victory Circle to watch.

He was about to begin the hat dance – the series of photographs while wearing hats featuring different sponsors' logos – when I found a place along the fence to stand and watch. Dan had just

stepped into the cockpit of the car – ready for the first of many photographs – when he saw me.

He stepped out of the cockpit, put the hat he was next to wear down on the nose of car and walked over to me. I looked at him and said again, "Why not you?" He gave me the biggest bear hug. I was OK emotionally until I could feel him crying into my shoulder, and then I lost it. We were both a bit of a mess for about 15 seconds.

He thanked me for everything Honda had done for him and everything I had done for him personally. One of the things that stands out to me about that moment was a group of people – about 15 or 20 – were standing in the bleachers overlooking Victory Circle when this moment played out, and they cheered and applauded when Dan came over and hugged me.

As he walked back to resume the hat dance, I looked up at the group of people expecting to see familiar faces, but I didn't recognize a soul. They were people we didn't know who applauded an emotional moment between two good friends celebrating an unlikely victory, and it resonated with them in some way.

Dan had that effect on people, and we certainly felt it at Honda.

After that victory, he worked as a color commentator for NBC Sports – a role he was born to fill, by the way. One of his assignments was the race at Iowa Speedway. At my request, he got up early the next morning and flew to Monterey, Calif., to do an appearance in front of 10 people who had won an Acura contest. He did it, without complaint (and without being paid beyond travel expenses), and he made 10 people extremely happy.

He easily could've turned it down, but he didn't. It was a month after his Indy victory, and he was arguably the hottest driver on the planet. The Iowa race was a night race, so he probably didn't get away from the track until 11 or 12 a.m., and then got up early the next morning so he could catch a flight from Des Moines through Denver to Monterey to greet 10 people who had won a contest.

In the days leading up to the race at Las Vegas later that year, I had been working very hard to put together a personal services agreement that would help pay for Dan's 2012 ride. It wasn't going to be money going directly to a team that would help buy the ride for him, but instead an additional source of income to help defray his salary and keep him in the Honda family.

The deal had gone through several levels of management before it fell through. I called Dan around 11 a.m. PT on the Tuesday before the race to tell him that. Between then and the end of the day, Dan called me back three different times to make sure *I* was OK. He knew how much effort I had put into trying to make it happen.

Instead of protesting or asking if I could try something different or questioning the decision, Dan was checking on me and making sure I knew how much he appreciated the effort and how sorry he was

From left: Recognizing Honda's first IndyCar win, Japan 2004; he won again at Motegi, the company's home soil in 2005; dinner for a winner – T.E. serves up the pasta, Indy 2011; DW in action at the early IndyCar tests, December 2002

for me that it didn't come together. Not how sorry he was for himself, but how sorry he was for me.

The following year, Dario Franchitti won the Indy 500, so it was an emotional time for everyone. I hadn't attended the 2011 Indy 500 championship banquet – and Dan had mentioned our moment in Victory Circle during his acceptance speech – so I decided to attend the 2012 banquet.

In the two weeks leading up to the Vegas race in 2011, I had U2's greatest hits collection in my car's CD player. Every day on the way to and from work, I listened to "Beautiful Day." After Dan died, that song became the focal point of my grief. At a certain point, I decided I was never going to listen to it again. It was just too painful.

> "Dan was checking on me and making sure I knew how much he appreciated the effort"

I went to Indianapolis in 2012 with an idea that I'd find closure. The way the race played out, with Dario winning, was perfect in my mind. The following night, I attended the banquet.

It's televised live locally, so the entire program is tightly structured. It includes a live band that plays into and out of commercial breaks. The band that night was Al Chez and The Brothers of Funk, who played exactly the kind of music you would

expect from a band called The Brothers of Funk – old Motown, Earth, Wind and Fire, R&B, soul standards, and jazz.

The program was about to go to a break when Jeff Belskus, then the president and CEO of Hulman & Co., made a presentation about Indy 500 winners who had died in the previous year. One was Jim Rathman, and the other was, of course, Daniel. It included a three-minute video tribute to Dan.

As the video finished and the show moved to a commercial break, The Brothers of Funk – without expectation or explanation – played U2's "Beautiful Day." My jaw hit the floor. There was no reason that song should've been part of the band's repertoire. My brain tells me it was coincidence, but my heart says it was Dan telling me it was time to move on.

To those close to him, Dan was our beautiful day. He had an immeasurable effect on us. He endeared himself to people inside the sport as well as the fans who made it all happen.

But to some, he was more than a sports star and champion. To some – more than people may know – Dan was a dear friend and a genuine, kind soul. ∎

COOL RUNNINGS

Natural skill, great racing and a curious bobsled incident

I met Dan in August of 1999. He'd come to the U.S. to run in the F2000 Championship with Jon Baytos, whom I'd known for a long time, and his Primus Racing operation. At Mid-Ohio, the F2000 cars were a supporting race for the CART Indycar weekend, and Jon had introduced me to the "skinny, young, can't believe he's shaving yet" Dan earlier in the weekend.

During the F2000 race, I watched Dan and an Irish driver, Jeff Wright, battling wheel to wheel. It was pretty entertaining, the pair going side by side down the back stretch, lap after lap. Good fun.

Although Wheldon finished second, he went on to win six races and the title that year. I filed him away as one to watch in the future.

As champion, Dan got a good deal to move up to Formula Atlantic, another CART support series, and he signed with a top team: PPI Motorsports. He won the opener at Homestead and again at Laguna Seca to finish second in the championship to Buddy Rice.

by DAN LAYTON

■ HONDA PR REPRESENTATIVE

DAN CONNECTION
Worked together throughout IndyCar career

I'm sure others will have stories about the successes that followed for Dan with Honda: the thrilling Indy 500 victories; our first (and second) wins at Motegi; his IndyCar championship.

But here are the things that spring into my mind when I think about DW: The funny thing about outwardly self-confident athletes – at least the ones I've known – is that beneath the bluster, there's also a layer of self-doubt and a need for positive reinforcement. Dan was no exception. For all the outward cockiness, he would still

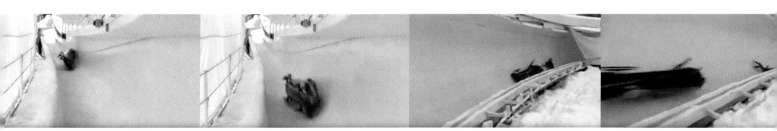

Vicki O'Connor, the series organizer, was another friend who was quick to sing Dan's praises, and made sure Dan and I met a couple of times during the season.

He was obviously talented, and a bit cocky, too (not that there's anything wrong with that!). Even then, Dan was always "on," entertaining anyone within earshot – and would crank it up another notch or two if there were any pretty girls in the immediate vicinity. He never lacked for confidence...

After 2000, I lost track of him for a while, as he ran a season of Indy Lights and then signed a test/limited IRL race deal with Panther Racing. At some point, he picked up Adrian Sussmann as a manager and, by late 2002, was back in our (Honda's) orbit.

We'd already announced Honda's intention to leave CART for the IRL in 2003. Meanwhile, Michael Andretti was in the process of taking over Andretti Green Racing and planning to retire after the 2003 Indy 500. Wheldon, with race-winning potential, test mileage and race experience in an IRL car courtesy of Panther, was a good fit for Honda and Andretti Green – and Adrian knew it. He was soon signed, sealed and delivered to Andretti Green, and I gradually got to know the real Dan Wheldon.

privately question himself. He always wanted to improve, both on track and off.

There was that tough, tough day at Homestead in 2006. Paul Dana had been fatally injured in a warm-up crash, although his death had not yet been officially announced. In his first race with Ganassi, Dan had qualified eighth, but Homestead was always a good circuit for him and I think he had a feeling it might be a good day.

When we chatted that morning, his first thoughts were of Paul. He asked me if I had any word on his condition, and the only thing I could think to tell him was "It didn't look good, but you need to focus on what you need to do today." We looked each other in the eye for a moment, and he understood without another word being spoken.

That afternoon, Dan drove a stellar race, beating Helio Castroneves with a high-side pass coming off the last corner. His first race as defending series champion, first IndyCar win with a new team, yet he was composed and compassionate in victory circle.

"Well, I think what's very important about today is that our thoughts and prayers are with the Dana family and everybody at Rahal Letterman. It's a very, very sad day." Then he paused, before following with the usual, "Great race, Helio was tough, but fair with

Clockwise from main; Mid-Ohio 1999, and DW shines in a frantic USF2000 race; Layton's FF career aided by a gifted HANS; High speed bobseld wipe out caught in style

"He sent me a link to a video of the crash, a crack about 'gangster bruises' and some more quotes that can't be repeated..."

me, and I hope I was fair with him." It set the proper tone, and I've remembered it to this day.

Fortunately, there were many far happier times to remember. A post-race celebration in Tokyo that ran into the next morning. I had no problem sleeping on the long flight home after!

Once, at Watkins Glen, he decided to go visit the F2000 race paddock, taking time out of an always-busy IndyCar race weekend to say hello to old friends, and encourage the future hopefuls who now looked up to him as someone who had achieved their dreams.

When Dan heard that I was going to get back into an F1600 car myself for "one last crack at the whip" in 2010-'12, he gave me a HANS device to use. A small thing on his part, I'm sure, but it saved me over $1,000, and was a priceless gesture to me.

Then there was the voicemail that popped into my phone that year, with Dan laughing about a bobsled crash he'd had while attending a fundraiser for the USA Bobsled Team. He followed that with a link to a video of the crash, a crack about "gangster bruises" and some more photos and quotes that can't be repeated. I laughed my ass off, called him back and we cracked jokes and laughed for a long, long time. Gawd, how I wish I had saved that message.

One last snapshot, the one that's been in my head all day while writing. It's the night before the Las Vegas race, and I cross paths with Dan and Susie in the lobby of our hotel. I'm headed out one way to have dinner with a friend, and they're going out the other way. I think that may have been on the way to get their matching tattoos. We stopped for a second, embraced, exchanged a few words, and they were on their way, smiling and holding hands.

It's my favorite image of Dan and Susie, and one I will always carry in my head with a smile. ∎

ORIGINAL PRANKSTER

One man's love-hate relationship with the practical joking side of great friend DW

by BRENT BRUSH

■ MOTORSPORTS SALES &
MARKETING EXECUTIVE

DAN CONNECTION
Great friend of Dan and the Wheldon family,
and practical joke target

There are a million and one stories to tell about the friendship that Dan Wheldon and I had. Not all of these stories are rated PG, in fact, many of them aren't. But they all carried a common theme. Just like Dan's racing, he did everything with all of his heart.

I met Dan in early 2006. I was blessed to have sat next to Dan's (and Dario's) manager, Adrian Sussmann, on a flight to Denver. Adrian invited me to a race after I shared with him that I worked in the Consumer Products industry. Dan was racing for Target Chip Ganassi Racing, and Target was one of my major accounts.

From the moment I met Dan, there was an immediate special bond. I remember within the first couple of hours of meeting him Dan asked me, "Where are we going for dinner tonight?" I remember thinking to myself, "Why is this guy, who had recently won the Indianapolis 500, interested in going to dinner with me?" But that was Dan. He was kind to everyone, and treated you as if he had known you for years.

That didn't mean he was always kind. There was the time in 2008 when, after the final race of the season in Miami-Homestead,

Dan decided on a celebratory night out in the VIP-hosted area of some trendy Miami Night Club. Close family – Susie, Holly, Elliott – and several others were there. About every 10 minutes (or, so it seemed), a cocktail waitress, dressed in a washcloth, would emerge from behind a door, holding over her head a bottle of champagne garnished with a fiery sparkler. These weren't just bottles of champagne, these were magnums of champagne... Cristal champagne.

After what seemed more like a four-hour parade of sparklers that would make any city in America proud to be celebrating the Fourth of July, I came back from the restroom to find that everyone had left and the only person still there was the cocktail waitress. Looking petrified, I asked, "Where has everybody gone?" She looked up at me and said, with something close to joy: "The gentleman ordering said that you had the tab covered." She then handed me a $17,000 bar tab.

The next morning, waking up to what can only be described as Black Monday, I went down stairs to the Miami Ritz-Carlton. I heard this roar of laughter from across the pool from one over-zealous little Englishman. As he lay on his lounger overlooking the pool like some sort of king, he laughed. "Those were some expensive sparklers, huh?"

As I said, there are a million stories to tell about Dan. Many of my stories of Dan end with me being the brunt with of one of his warped jokes, or me being stuck with some meal tab, or simply a new nickname that Dan convinced the entire IndyCar paddock to start calling me. Most would've turned and run for the hills, but Dan

"'The gentleman ordering said that you had the tab covered.' She then handed me a $17,000 bar tab"

had this way of drawing you in close to him, he tested his friends and, more so, he tested their loyalty to him. In return, you learned that Dan's friendship with you was fiercely loyal. The testing, I firmly believe, kept him humored as he watched you squirm, but more than that, it was his way of showing you that you mattered and that you were, in fact, his friend.

Dan loved people...He loved his family, he loved his friends, he loved his fans, he loved being a celebrity, and he embraced it like nobody else.

As Dan's and my friendship grew and we spent a fair amount of time together, I used to watch people react around him. When Dan would walk into a public place I would watch how people, who

didn't even know what he did for a living, would gravitate toward him. Those who knew what he did wanted to meet him and speak with him, and they quickly learned that it was his personality and the interest that he took in them, that made them instant fans of DW.

I can't tell you how many times I would be sitting with Dan eating in a restaurant, and see a kid and his or her Dad staring at Dan from across the room. More times than not, Dan would call the kid over to our table, push his warm meal aside, and sit and talk to them for an hour. That was Dan. He was kind to the core, without an audience, without reward... and many times, without dinner.

There's no question that Dan was one hell of a racecar driver; competitive is an understatement; his ability to win is indisputable. But it was Dan's love of people, his kindness, and his friendship that I miss the most.

While I don't want to forgive Dan for sticking me with $17,000 bar tabs, or nicknaming me in front of the IndyCar world, the truth is, I know that it was the love in his heart that pushed him to do all the things he did. He was a great friend, and he taught me more about being a person than anyone else in my life. Dan filled every person's life that he came across with love; he filled mine with unforgettable memories and love in a way only he could. ■

FANS FOR LIFE

Everyone mattered to DW and he would go all-out to make sure they knew it, whoever they were, whatever they did. That's why he meant so much to them

by MIKE KITCHEL

■ COMMUNICATIONS DIRECTOR, INDYCAR

DAN CONNECTION
COMMUNICATIONS DIRECTOR,
PANTHER RACING, 2009-2010

My youngest son is unbelievably particular. Everything must be organized perfectly or he gets irritable and restless. He's very selective about what he wears and refuses to put on any piece of clothing he doesn't pick out himself. His shoes, specifically, must always be immaculate. Any time he's in a room, he's the center of attention with no exceptions. He's disarmingly charming and a damn good-looking kid – which is complicated by the fact he knows it.

Max Daniel is 3 years old.

My son's similarities with the behavioral nuances of Dan Wheldon, while eerie, are merely a coincidence. His name is not. It serves as a constant reminder for our family to embody the distinctive qualities that made DW's impact on us so profound. The race wins, championships and Indianapolis 500 victories made him a legend, but there is no statistic for what made him truly great. It wasn't just the charisma, the compassion, the engaging sense of humor and the legendary practical joking. Or the relentless drive for excellence, meticulous attention to detail or brutal unwillingness to accept anything less than perfection.

What always amazed me most about DW was the amount of time he invested in his innate ability to make people feel special. It wasn't just for his friends, teammates, sponsors or the hordes of race fans he saw at the track. It was volunteers, cashiers, hotel clerks, waitresses, janitors and the countless other people who crossed his path each day – many of whom had no idea that he

BENITO SANTOS

JOE JACOBSON

From top: Helmet design by children's hospital patient Jama; Sourdough IndyCars by Chef Dan; clicking with a dedicated young race fan at Motegi, Japan; author Kitch gets a special pat on the back from the boss

MICHAEL LEVITT/LAT, BENITO SANTOS

drove racecars for a living. Yet, somehow, he managed to find some laughter in all of them.

Once, with a night race on the slate at Kentucky Speedway, we had an afternoon to kill and the two of us plus Panther Racing colleague Benito Santos and Dan's assistant Misty Gibbs stopped for lunch near the track. Our usual recipe of laughter, insults and storytelling were in full swing when, out of the corner of my eye, I noticed DW had been spotted by a family of race fans who had just entered the restaurant.

They eventually approached the table, somewhat sheepishly, but it was clear their enthusiasm was difficult to contain. They'd come from Chicago, they said, and never missed a race at Kentucky Speedway. Their excitement was tempered by the obvious sense that they were uncomfortable interrupting our lunch. They wrapped up the conversation quickly, wished Dan luck, and found their seats on the other side of the restaurant.

Dan's wheels were turning. We knew what was coming.

"How far is Chicago from here?" Wheldon asked, clearly awed at the length they'd driven to see an IndyCar race. "That's like a six- or seven-hour drive with traffic, right?"

We all pulled out our phones to find an answer, but by this point it didn't matter. Dan reorganized his lunch onto its tray and excused himself from the table. He knew an easy way to ensure the drive was worth their time. Before our phones were back in our pockets Wheldon had found another seat and was having lunch with his new friends from Chicago. Suddenly the laughter that had been present at our table was coming from the other side of the restaurant.

One of the first appearances we did together was the SKUSA SuperNats go-kart race in Las Vegas. Dan loved karting, and the SuperNats is the sport's Indianapolis 500. The National Guard was a sponsor of the event which included a ride for DW to compete in the race. What I figured was a chance for him to get a free weekend in Vegas to spend some face time with his primary sponsor was much more.

The first practice session of the weekend was quickly approaching, and Dan was holding court outside his team's garage with a group of kids all wearing firesuits and holding their helmets. He was two feet taller, and nearly 20 years older, than everybody in the crowd, and the only one who didn't seem to notice. From the outside he was a superstar racecar driver doing his part to give back, but in that moment Dan Wheldon was just another kid at a go-kart track talking shop with his competitors.

He knew most of their names and what divisions they were running in during the weekend. He pointed out specific on-track passes, forgettable mistakes or otherwise memorable moments he'd seen while watching them compete. He joked that they should take it easy on the old man on the kart track but he wasn't going to return the favor if any of them made it to the IndyCar Series. The crowd of young go-kart drivers all tried desperately to play it cool, but their eyes were wide.

As Dan finally broke away from the crowd to rush to pit lane for practice, a young boy and his father had been waiting patiently around the corner to ask for an autograph. The signature was quick, but the recipient had a few questions about karting, and the green flag on Dan's practice session was imminent.

He apologized profusely as he quickly wrote down his e-mail address next to his autograph with explicit instructions to send him all of his karting questions and a promise that he'd get a prompt reply to all of them. The boy's father clearly appreciated the gesture, but couldn't withhold his skepticism.

"Those e-mails," the father asked, leaning in to speak to me. "Do they go to a personal assistant or something?"

I could only smirk.

"We sent his IndyCar contract to the same e-mail address," I replied. "Make sure your son uses it."

Every year in Indianapolis, Dan would make a personal appearance at Peyton Manning's Children's Hospital at St. Vincent to visit with sick children. At each of these visits, DW would meet with the kids, get to know each of them, and leave behind a

worksheet with a blank template of a race helmet for them to draw any design they wanted. Once the appearance was completed, he would select the kid that inspired him the most and have his helmet painted with their design for a race later in the year.

When the hour scheduled for our appearance concluded, and we were finished visiting all the rooms that were planned, Dan asked if he could see more kids. Once we'd cleared another hospital floor, he directed our group back to the elevators so we could visit another. When the nurses finally convinced him there were no more kids he'd be allowed to see, he wanted to make a return to one young cancer patient he couldn't get out of his head.

Jama was sassy – a self-assured adult spitfire trapped in an 8-year-old's body. Her medical prognosis was bad, but she showed little interest in dwelling on it. We spent the rest of the time hanging out with Jama – she gave us a tour of her hospital floor

> "An elderly woman working the desk wasn't impressed. That only provided additional encouragement. The more awkward it got, the more fun it was for Jama and Dan"

DW scored two determined second places for Panther at the Indy 500

A family man and a fan favorite, DW shone wherever he went

and introduced us to almost every nurse and doctor in the building. We wore out our welcome at approximately the same time DW took her to the front desk of the hospital and instructed her to answer the receptionist's phone each time it rang. An elderly woman working the desk wasn't impressed, but that only provided additional encouragement. The more awkward it got for everybody else the more fun it was for Jama and Dan.

When Dan finally left – which only happened because he was late to pick up his wife Susie from the airport – he'd been at the hospital for more than five hours.

One of my few PR mentors, the late John Cardinale from Sonoma Raceway, had arranged for a media tour that included an event at the iconic Boudin Bakery in San Francisco. Dan was going to make "an IndyCar out of sourdough bread" which, normally, would draw a laugh and rejection – but with John you always said yes because he could seemingly make anything a national news event. In addition to the bakery, we were scheduled to make other stops at TV and radio stations in the area. John, knowing it was important for DW to arrive in style, arranged for a limousine to take us around for the day.

Our limo driver was a gentleman named Dave who was extremely shy, to the point it bordered on being socially awkward. But Dave was a genuinely nice person, clearly going out of his way to keep us on schedule during a hectic day. Dan engaged Dave in every conversation, including a few inappropriate ones, for the entire day. When we stopped for lunch, Dave joined us, and was not permitted to stay in the limo as his boss typically requires. It's entirely possible that, throughout the course of our tour, DW asked Dave more questions than he'd received from media the entire day.

As the media tour concluded, Dan assured our new friend that he'd have a pair of VIP passes waiting for the race in Sonoma later that year. We didn't get a chance to see Dave until the cars were on the grid. But DW ran up and gave him a hug, met his wife, and relived a few quips from our ride together. As Dave walked around the car to take a few pictures I went to introduce myself to his wife. When I got closer I realized she had tears in her eyes.

"Nobody acknowledges Dave when he's driving, but all he talks about is how cool it would be to become friends with the celebrities who ride in his limo," she said. "This time he really did." ∎

AN INAUSPICIOUS START

Their working relationship started off on the wrong foot, but they became firm friends

My story with Dan was rather unusual. It started when I came to the United States from Brazil to work for Vitor Meira. Vitor and Dan didn't see eye to eye because of an incident in Formula Ford when Dan took Vitor out as he was leading the series' biggest race one year. Vitor never let that one go.

When they got to IndyCar, Dan beat Vitor fairly regularly, but it was always close. They became pretty intense rivals. Remember that Vitor was runner-up to Dan in the 2005 Indy 500. It was heated, to say the least.

I have to admit that I wasn't a fan of Dan's in the beginning either. One time, during my first year with Vitor, I was taking photographs of his and other cars during a practice session. Dan saw me, pointed at me and sent one of his crew guys from Ganassi over to tell me in no uncertain terms I wasn't allowed to take pictures of Dan's car.

Fast forward to 2008. I knew Vitor's contract was up at Panther Racing and wouldn't be renewed, but I had no idea who would be replacing him. Dan had never smiled or said hello to me or Mike Kitchel, Panther's public relations boss at the time. But, in Detroit, he walked by us and said, "Hey, guys. How are you doing?"

I was like, "What the...?" I looked at Kitch, and I believe he knew at the time that Dan was about to be Vitor's replacement. Sure enough, a week or so later, Dan signed with Panther and I was offered the same PR position with the team I had with Vitor.

Kitch was like, "You need to make a decision about this. If you can't get along with him, it's not going to work." I told him, "Of course I want to stay here. I don't know the guy, and I'm not sure I

by BENITO SANTOS

■ MARKETING DIRECTOR, KANAAN RACING

DAN CONNECTION
PR/Marketing Manager, Panther Racing 2009-2010

like him, but don't worry about it. I'll be a professional."

During the first teleconference we had with everyone – Panther owner John Barnes, Dan, Kitch, Marketing Director Chris Bowers and myself – we were introduced. When he got to me, Dan said, "Benito? Who's Benito? Is he that guy who worked for Vitor?" Immediately I thought, "This is not going to work."

The first time Dan came to Panther, he came into my office and said, "So, you were the guy who took care of Vitor's helmet, right? You'll be taking care of my helmet now." I was like, "Dude, no. I work in PR. You can handle your own helmet."

He knew exactly which buttons to push and, in the beginning, he pushed them all. But it didn't take long before I realized he was doing it mostly for effect and to get a reaction from me. The more we hung out together, the more our friendship developed. It wasn't long before we were genuine friends.

When Dan wanted to be difficult, he could be extremely difficult. Not only could he be difficult with other drivers, but he also could be difficult with the people he worked with. At the same time, he could be wonderful to people. I realized that this guy had nothing to do with the guy I thought he was until I actually got to know him.

I started to respect him a lot, but he could still be a tool. By the end of 2009, there were rumors that he might leave Panther, and he had an option in his contract that would allow him to. I asked Bowers if they had a plan in place if Dan actually did leave. He said, "Dan's not leaving." I said, "But is there a plan in place if he does?"

As soon as I walked out the door, Bowers called Dan and said,

From left: Affection for the Panther PR guy; entertaining the troops who were guests of the team; a warm British gesture from the cokpit; transparent frames, purple lenses...

500 with a team that nobody imagined could even finish in the top 10, let alone win the race. I saw him every day in May, so I knew what he was going through. It didn't look possible, but Dan was so meticulous with everything he did. He got that car where he wanted it through his attention to detail, and he won the race.

It was the sweetest victory. I was still loyal to Panther, so I felt their pain when JR Hildebrand crashed in the final turn. However, when I saw Dan cross the finish line, the sadness went away quickly. I was so happy for him.

One of my favorite memories about him involved his obsession with shoes. One day before the 2009 season, I got a call from his management team saying they were about to ship his racing boots. A few days later, a box as big as a table arrived. There were 22 pairs of shoes for a 17-race season. Not just ordinary shoes, but the wildest styles and colors imaginable. He had ordered one pair in camouflage, another pair in purple camo. I was like, "Dude, if you're ever in a purple jungle, your feet will be invisible."

Dan owned his style, and his style was intended to shock. If you ever paid him a compliment on his wild clothing or shoes or hair or sunglasses, he would change it. One time he showed up wearing these wild designer sunglasses. The frames were transparent, but the lenses were purple. They were hideous. I said, "You're not going to wear those, are you?" He said, "Dude, these are mega." He wore them, and he rocked them. I constantly taunted him about them, which only inspired him to continue wearing them.

"Benito says you're leaving us." Dan didn't speak to me for five months after that. He only started talking to me after his wife, Susie, explained to him that I didn't say he was leaving, I just asked if there was a plan in place in case he actually did leave.

He broke the silence by calling me one day and saying, "Yo, Santos, bro, we need to talk." I was like, "You haven't talked to me the entire off-season. Why was that?" He said, "I don't know. I miss you." No apology, no explanation. It was over, and we were pals again.

By the end of Dan's second season with Panther, I was talking to Tony Kanaan about becoming his manager. I knew that Dan and Tony were tight, so I asked Dan if I should pursue it. Dan was fully on board. He said Tony was awesome, and that I should do it.

But when I first started working for Tony, it was nothing like I expected. I had doubts about whether I'd made a mistake. I'd moved from Indianapolis to Miami, my wife was seven months pregnant, and I seriously wanted to quit, but I couldn't. Dan knew what was going on, and he called me every day to make sure we were OK.

At the time, he didn't have a ride. Here was a driver of his caliber without a job, but his concern was with me. Part of it was that he had encouraged me to do something that I wasn't enjoying. He'd call just to chitchat. It made me feel good, and eventually things got better.

After that, we had the fairytale story of him coming to the Indy

> "At the time, he didn't have a ride. Here was a driver of his caliber without a job, but his concern was with me"

One day in 2010, he showed up while I was packing his gear for the race in Brazil. He saw what I was doing and asked if he could do it, so I said: "Sure, it's your stuff. Have a go at it." It took him two hours – keep in mind this was just his race-related gear, not his personal things. He went through everything; helmets, suits, boots, HANS, gloves. With each one, he'd explain why he was choosing it over the dozens of others. I never saw a man so happy. I told him he was a piece of work. He laughed and kept packing.

Another time, I had to pick him up for a PR function. Dan was usually punctual, but for some reason he was running late. I walked into his bus. He saw that I had my shoes on and he flipped out. I had to take my shoes off, even though we were late. That was Dan. He had his ways, and his ways were often hysterically entertaining.

The happiness that Dan brought with him was unmatched. Whether he was being facetious or playful, unintentionally funny or intentionally funny, he made you feel good about life.

For me, he still does. ∎

NATIONAL TREASURES

Fighting for the spotlight was not on the agenda when two
of America's favorite racers got together

by Dale Earnhardt Jr.

■ NASCAR HERO, DAYTONA 500 WINNER,
2004, 2014

DAN CONNECTION
National Guard sponsor colleague

I met Dan when we shared the National Guard sponsorship in 2009 and 2010. I'd seen him a couple of times at Guard functions and appearances. We got to know each other through that relationship, and later we got together at Indianapolis Motor Speedway. I remember how nice he was to me that day. Indy was his home turf. NASCAR guys are often the considered visitors at Indy, but he was really nice and welcoming.

Every year we did a dinner together in Washington, D.C., for the National Guard Youth Foundation. We all had to get up on stage and speak, so I was able to see more of the person Dan was through that interaction and by listening to him talk. It was through those speeches and meetings that I realized what a likeable guy he was.

I had just a handful of opportunities to be around him. You

assume that other drivers – whether they are in NASCAR, IndyCar or Formula 1 – are very confident. A lot of times when your confidence and their confidence are in the same range, it might create a little bit too much ego for one place. But with Dan, it was never like that.

What I appreciated most about him was that he was really approachable. Having a conversation with him was really easy. At the appearance at Indy, they had an Indy car there. I could've felt like a second fiddle, but Dan made me feel completely comfortable. The promotion was centered a little more around his team's relationship with the National Guard than mine, but Dan made a point of making me feel like I was a part of the process.

He was the focal point that day, but he made me feel at home because of his interaction with me in front of everyone. He included me in the conversation throughout the day and kept me updated about what we were doing. He didn't have to do that. Honestly, I look back at that day and don't know if I would've been able to do what Dan did.

He made sure that everyone in the room was having a good time. He had a great disposition, very upbeat and positive, and it rubbed off on everyone around him. I really appreciated how

"What I appreciated most about him was that he was really approachable. Having a conversation with him was really easy"

personable he was. The truth is, he could've felt some competition from me being around. After all, we were both competing for the same sponsorship money and attention from the Guard.

A lot of times in those situations – when teams from different forms of racing have the same sponsor – the drivers try to one-up each other to get more of a piece of the pie. Dan never made it a competition. He always made it feel like we were on the same team, just two guys who had the same goal. He made me feel like his teammate, and I really, truly appreciated that. ∎

HARD & FAST FRIENDSHIPS

One thing that is clear is that Dan Wheldon made a lot of friends in his racing career. Over the next few pages are some people whose work with him transcended just racetracks. They'd travel, climb, chat, help each other out... Or they just provided somewhere to relax with a grilled cheese sandwich

by MICHAEL VOORHEES

- PHOTOGRAPHER

DAN CONNECTION
IndyCar lifestyle photographer and friend

Photographer Michael Voorhees remembers with great affection his friend Dan Wheldon; the humblest guy who just loved having his photo taken

Danny and I came to the IRL at a similar time and right away we gravitated toward one another. Alongside the race photography, from 2004 to 2006, I was also hired to shoot lifestyle photos of all the drivers. It just so happened that 2005 was an awesome year for

Dan, winning the Indy 500 and the championship. For me, it was one of the greatest seasons in the history of the league with any of the drivers; and I was there to document it all.

I feel so lucky to have met Dan when his career was on the rise. We had a lot of fun during those years, traveling and hanging out together. We built up a really unique friendship that was based on a mutual admiration and trust. Dan recognized the value of what we were doing and put a lot of effort into it, as did I. We were a good match; we just trusted each other completely. I've worked with hundreds of athletes from sports around the world, and I can count on one hand the times I've had that kind of special connection.

Whatever we did, Dan was always fully involved and switched on. We would come up with ideas and concepts together and shoot a

The St. Cin family provided a source of escape from the buzz of the racing world

whole library of film. Dan loved having his photo taken, and loved to see the end results, too. He was like David Beckham to me. A beautiful man, both inside and out; and he always projected that into the pictures we created. It was a joy to be part of his career and to watch him develop from a bright, wide-eyed kid into a mature, amazing champion.

When IndyCar wanted a feature on drivers in their hometowns, doing stuff away from the track, I flew over to London with Dan. He was a very, very proud Englishman, so it was such an honor that he wanted to share his country with me. I think that trip kicked off our friendship and we really bonded. We had a fantastic time, lots of fun and laughs. I also drank a lot of beer! We went to the Autosport Awards together and it was fun to watch him interacting with the likes of his old karting rival, Jenson Button. It was great to see what a star he was.

I miss Danny a lot. I think about him all the time still.

The kid was my hero.

"He was a very, very proud Englishman, so it was such an honor that he wanted to share his country with me"

Taking in the sights, London, December 2005. DW was guide to his home city for a media shoot for IndyCar

by JENN ST. CIN

■ NEIGHBOR

DAN CONNECTION
Family friend

After long trips away, Dan would always head straight to family friend Jenn St. Cin's house to relax, escape and avoid using his kitchen

I got to know Dan and Susie before they had their first child, Sebastian. I'm not sure why, but our families just came together; we became part of each other's family really. We were pretty much inseparable. I was there when both Sebastian and Oliver were born. We just had a really close relationship.

Dan traveled a lot and, when he came home, it was always straight to our house. I think he knew he could relax and escape from things with us; he always felt comfortable here. Some of the best memories I have are of us all going to the Ritz Carlton in Orlando, just to get away. We had so much fun because nobody knew him there. I can remember all of us lying around the pool in lounge chairs, Dan fast asleep!

We didn't talk about racing much. He would confide in us at times about changes, although he didn't really need

us because he was so smart. He always figured it out.

People think it's a myth that he never used his kitchen, but he genuinely didn't! It was hilarious. He never, ever used the kitchen; but he loved home cooking. He would get home from being on the road, come straight to our house and say, "Jenn, I'm hungry, what are you fixing me?" He would sit right up on my kitchen counter while I cooked for him. One night I must have made six or seven grilled cheese sandwiches and he ate them all!

He loved coming around to our house. Being in the kitchen or messing about. He was really mischievous though. Our pool is very close to the back of the house, so Dan would run and jump in, knowing it would get all the windows wet. Every time he came I was like, "Thanks, Dan, you've just made my life hell now. I've got to go clean all the windows again!"

We have so many great memories. Susie and I can tell stories till we cry from laughing so much. He was so funny and he is just so missed.

HARD & FAST FRIENDSHIPS

by MIKE JOHNSON

■ FINANCIAL ADVISOR

DAN CONNECTION
Financial advisor, 2007-2011

No challenge would go unnaccepted. Facing the 14,000ft climb at Longs Peak

Summits are there to be reached whether in sport or in life. For DW, they were to be done in style, too

Dan was a remarkable young man. He lived life the way we wish we could all live it.

There was never a dull moment in Dan Wheldon's life. He was a compassionate and endearing young man who was highly motivated, driven and knew what he wanted.

I was first introduced to Dan by his sports manager, Adrian Sussmann, who asked if I could help with some financial matters. I said, of course, and we got along well right from the beginning. I started working with him strictly as a financial advisor but it quickly became more than helping him with financial issues, it became much more of a friendship, not only with me, but with my family which grew stronger and stronger right up until he died.

I wouldn't have said he was a good "businessman" when I first met him. That was left mostly to Adrian, who, of course, is extremely good at that. Back then, Dan wasn't married and was pretty wild. He would think nothing of spending thousands of dollars in a nightclub. In those days, he didn't really have much of an idea about money.

I said I'd work with him, but only on the condition that he would get serious with investing money and start thinking about his future. He became very focused on saving money and being more responsible and careful. When Dan focused on something then he was all in. He could be hard on Adrian at times and he was hard on me. Oftentimes he wanted to see this or that and he'd want it done his way. But I liked that, and I think Adrian did too to a large extent.

Dan spent a lot of time with us in Colorado. One day he said he wanted to climb a "fourteener", which is a 14,000ft peak. One of the more challenging 14,000ft peaks is Longs Peak, just outside of Boulder. It's an all-day trek, very demanding, and he was also coming from sea level. It's a 15-mile round trip, and you are over 14,000 feet when you get to the top. The air is thin at the summit and altitude sickness is a common problem. It's an amazing challenge but he insisted on doing it.

by DeMATTI

■ FAMILY FRIEND

DAN CONNECTION
BFF and Number One fan

When Rob DeMatti took a young kid from England under his wing, he never imagined the challenges Dan would set for him to earn race credentials

I was one of the first people Dan met when he came from the U.K. to race in USF2000. At the time, my buddy Brad Stoller and John Newberg, who worked for Jon Baytos at DW's new team Primus Racing would all hang out together. When Baytos signed Dan, he was like, "Guys, I've got it. I've got this great kid coming from England but he doesn't know anyone, so you need to take care of him."

We were a bunch of kids ourselves but we took Dan under our wing. He didn't have much when he got here, so we shared everything. We had some good old times back then and Dan never

DeMatti was in the box seat for his friend's first Indy 500 win, and signed proof

I told him I'd done it several times and I wasn't doing it again. I tried to talk him out of it. I said, "That's all I need, Ganassi on my ass because I let you do this..." He could have easily done something to jeopardize his racing, but this was a challenge he wanted to do.

We assembled a team of my nephew and other folks. Obviously he had no climbing equipment at all. We took him to REI, one of the big outdoor sports stores in the States so he could buy some equipment. He walked up to the salesperson in the store, and said, "I'm climbing Longs Peak, I'm going to need everything, and I'd like for it to be Armani. Do you carry Armani?"

That was Dan. If he was going to climb this mountain, he wanted to look as good as he could. We said, "No Dan, they don't carry Armani... This is a hiking store." That's the way he was, first class or he didn't do it.

But he did it; he made it to the top.

"I'm climbing Longs Peak, I'm going to need everything, and I'd like for it to be Armani. Do you carry Armani?"

forgot that. The minute he secured his full-time IndyCar ride with Andretti Green Racing, he told me to pack a bag and come watch him race. It's funny because although I was older, he was always the bigger brother. He was always there for me and made sure that I was part of everything.

I could go on and on about the great times I had with Dan, but some of the most memorable involved IndyCar hard cards – passes that get you access to any race.

Dan would never just *give* me a hard card; he would always make me earn it. From seriously stacked tequila and Jim Beam shots to being caned with bamboo, our hard card contests were always outrageous and never involved being sober!

On one occasion, Dan and I raced the St. Pete 5k for my hard card. But the deal was, he made me drink a six-pack of beer before the race, so that was pretty funny. I really trained for that race, and I'm still convinced he cheated, but he did beat me. So, no hard card for me that year....

Another time he made me drink shots of Patron [tequila] before

a 2-year-old's birthday party, then spend 20 minutes sitting in a bouncy house with the kids bouncing all around me. That was tough, but I got my hard card! Those were some good times.

I was well known for photo-bombing Dan after races. Whenever he won, you would always see me in the camera shot. Of course, a lot of the time, people back home in St. Pete would be watching just to see me on TV. There's an absolutely classic, full-page photo in the 2009 Indy 500 program. It's a close-up of Dan when he raced the National Guard car, but it's got me in the background, too. I was with Dan when he was signing autographs that year. He would make people turn to that page, then say, "Look who it is!" The fans would all rightly point out it was Dan Wheldon and he'd add, "Yeah, but look who's in the background." They'd look at me, then back at the picture and be like, "Hey, that's you!" So Dan and I literally sat there signing autographs together for an hour.

Dan was just fun all the time. I can't say this about a lot of people but I really never saw the guy in a bad mood. He was always joking, laughing; just a good old guy.

HARD & FAST FRIENDSHIPS

by PJ CHESSON

■ INDYCAR RACER

DAN CONNECTION
Friend and racer

**Sharing vital clues at the track and chasing speed by day...
Then fun times, laughter and trouble by night**

My relationship with Dan was more away from the track, and pretty wild. Every time I was with that guy, it was fun. We were laughing all the time, usually when we were being "over served" in a bar somewhere. I think I brought out the wild side in Dan, and he liked that. I imagine he was able to find something in everybody he really enjoyed. I think in me it was that wild side. In somebody else, he'd find a different quality and he would collect a little bit from everybody, and that was who he was. He became that person, almost like the great all-round guy. People loved him for that.

Having said that, I do have one memory from a racing perspective that really stands out for me, and it's from when we were racing at the Indianapolis 500 in 2006.

Dan knew I was in a real piece-of-junk car. The whole garage area

> ## "I love you, but if you tell anybody what I tell you, I'm never going to talk to you again...."

really knew that. This was when Dan was champion, an Indy 500 winner at the top of his game. He was really on a tear.

He was very secretive about his setups, but during the month he came over to me and said, "Man, you know I'm going to help you right now because I love you, but if you tell anybody what I tell you, I'm never going to talk to you again...."

He walked me over to the fuel pumps where they fill the cars up, where nobody else was standing around and started: "Here's what you need to do." He basically gave me a setup, with downforce numbers – it was different because we didn't have the same shocks and stuff, and we talked about that – but he put me in the ballpark, and he said that nobody else in the garage area was going to have anything like that.

We still had Carb Day and practice days. I asked for the setup, and my engineer looked at it and simply said, "No way..." I couldn't tell him why I wanted to try this because Dan would kill me!

JIM HAINES/IMS; DAN STRECK/LAT

He was right in contention that year, and led about three-quarters of the race. I was the only other car on the grid that year with a setup similar to what he had.

By the way, that car was a great car. Sadly, I got hit by another guy and crashed out on the first lap, but that had nothing to do with the car. And, Dan should have won that day too.

He really cared a lot; he was a super guy. He was so kind and so generous to anyone he came across, especially his friends.

Messing about in pit lane, but serious when it came to helping out a pal

DARRELL INGHAM/GETTY IMGAGES

by DAVE FURST

■ TV SPORTS DIRECTOR

DAN CONNECTION
Friend and sportscaster/reporter
at RTV6 Indianapolis

Professional relationship? Who needs that? With Dan and me, *everything* was personal, and that was just fine with both of us

Sure, we talked about the sport. His heroes. Rules. Regulations. Who's good. Who's competitive. Who sucks. It was all fair game. But it *always* quickly turned personal. Girlfriends. Ex-girlfriends. Who's dating whom? Who went out with whom?

Some of the material bordered risqué. But it was true to the idea that *nothing* was out of bounds. In fact, if there were a gossip column in IndyCar, he and I could've written it. Ghostwritten, of course. We would've changed the names to protect the innocent.

It got to the point where I'd do his bidding. Set him up on a date? Done. Grab him some of his famous English breakfast tea on the way to the track? Done. Naturally, he'd return the favor if I needed something, as well.

So would his young publicist, Susie. One morning before Carb

Day at the Indianapolis Motor Speedway, I had arrived at the No. 10 pit double-fisted: his English breakfast tea in one hand, my latte in the other. After shooting the bull for 15 minutes, he climbed in the car and I attempted to hop over the wall. He handled his part more gracefully than I did. I got tripped up – notepad going one direction, coffee in the other. The person who caught me was Susie – a sign of things to come with all-things Wheldon-related.

While in Japan, he taught me the meaning of "Kanpai!" *Cheers!* Lots of it. In fact, sake has never tasted the same since.

He made a point of unveiling his special Indy 500 helmets in our May interviews. That's when fans – Dan never failed to spend time with – were introduced to each year's Lionheart identity.

I'll never forget walking up pit road at Homestead one year for the first practice of the season opener. Dan is in the car, helmet on, and ready to roll. I hadn't seen him in weeks. He waved me over and asked me to lean into the car. "What's up, brotha?" he said, in the way only Dan could say it. Perfect. Let the season begin.

But, of all the moments we had, I always remember the TV interview we did at Indianapolis Motor Speedway as he was in the car, sitting on pit road, talking on the team's two-way radio. He confided in me that, "Nowhere else do I feel at home more than when I'm inside the cockpit of a racecar."

Poignant and personal, that's always been Dan to me. ■

MADE FOR TV

TV came calling when Dan Wheldon found himself without a ride, and found a talent who wasn't ready to quit the day job

by ROBIN MILLER

■ WRITER AND BROADCASTER

DAN CONNECTION
TV commentary partner, 2011

In 2010, while working for SPEED, I mentioned on television – and in print – that Dan Wheldon was in danger of becoming an endangered species because he was still really good on ovals and not so hot on road/street courses anymore.

It was a statement of fact because IndyCar was adding more and more road and street circuits, and ovals were vanishing from the schedule. It pissed him off, and he let me know about it after one race when he was on the podium and wondered why I would want to interview "an endangered species."

Of course, when 2011 dawned, Wheldon found himself without a full-time ride and only running Indianapolis for Bryan Herta. We did a little interview at his press conference in St. Pete and he was cordial, not frosty, and I wished him well at IMS.

Fast forward to standing on the yard of bricks at the Speedway following his stunning victory. He was holding his son Sebastian, grinning ear-to-ear and I was preparing to interview him for SPEED when he said: "Hey, Miller, pretty good for an endangered species." He didn't say it in a mean-spirited way, just a little jab to let me know he hadn't forgotten, but his interview was gracious and classy.

A couple weeks later on our conference call for NBC Sports Network, we learned Danny Boy was going to be in the booth. As ideas were being tossed around he made a suggestion:

"Why not have Robin go up and down the grid before the race like they do in Formula 1? Hell, I'll do it with him."

So, the Grid Run was launched at Texas and it was an instant hit because Wheldon was a natural with the microphone, and the drivers responded in kind. He started at one end of the grid (the

front) and I started from the rear. We covered a lot of ground and it was good, fun, spontaneous television.

But his commentary during the race was even better. He was animated, honest, funny and introspective as hell. That personality came right through the screen, and a TV star was literally born that summer but, of course, he wanted no part of being a television guy for at least another decade – he was a racer.

During the middle of August I got a good-natured call from Wheldon during a break in testing the new Indy car at Mid-Ohio. "Hey Miller, I love this new car and you are going to eat your words next year because I am going to kick ass on road courses."

And we all wish he'd gotten that chance. ■

STEVE SWOPE

"Hey Miller, I love this new car and you are going to eat your words next year because I am going to kick ass on road courses"

Using all the road and more, DW pushes it to the limit at Sonoma

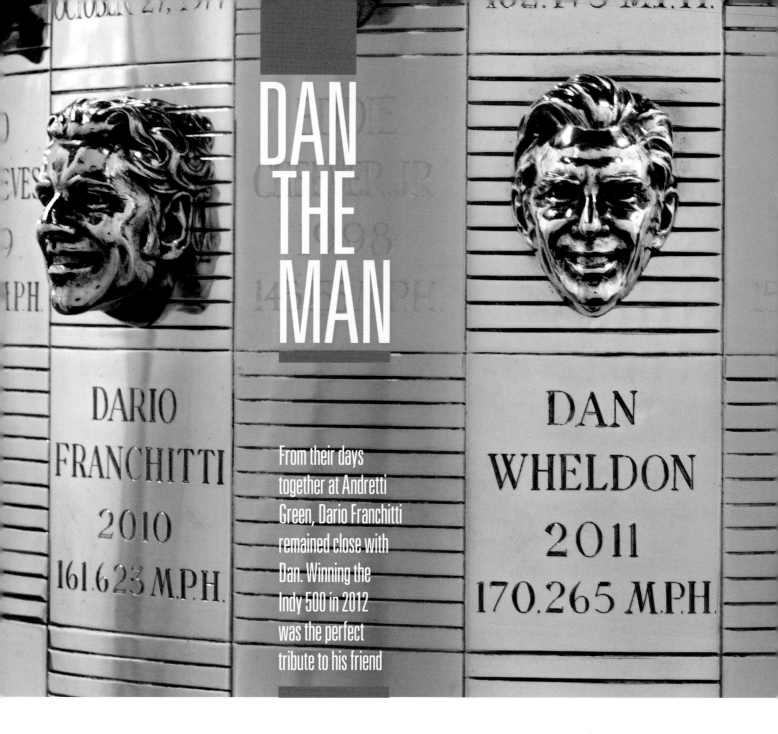

DAN THE MAN

DARIO
FRANCHITTI
2010
161.623 M.P.H.

From their days together at Andretti Green, Dario Franchitti remained close with Dan. Winning the Indy 500 in 2012 was the perfect tribute to his friend

DAN
WHELDON
2011
170.265 M.P.H.

There's no doubt that Dan learned a lot from us at Andretti Green up to 2005 and his first Indy win. It did go the other way as well. A lot of my love and passion for the Speedway, believe it or not, comes from him. He loved that place. He was 10 feet tall every time he walked through the gates. I remember in 2003 when I was in my back brace watching, he was in his first 500 and waxing on, "Oh Indy, Indy, Indy, Indy…" In '04, being there and watching the pure desire he had to win that race – it rubbed off on me completely. When he won it in '05 as my teammate, I saw what getting his face on the Borg Warner Trophy meant to him. I knew I wanted some of that. He loved racing there, and the people there loved him. They still do.

In my opinion, he was nearly the perfect young driver. Yes, he

certainly had an ego – we all had egos – but it didn't mean he couldn't learn, he was hungry to learn. He was smart in the questions he asked and he was never too smart, too big or successful to ask a question. He worked so hard at it, and he stayed hungry.

My God, he partied, too, I mean during those '04 and '05 years… If he'd not been getting the results on the track, somebody would've pulled him up. The fact was, he was doing the job on the track so there was no issue, but….

There's a story of him after winning his first 500, he was doing a radio interview the morning after. It had been a late night and he'd had little, if any, sleep. The announcer said, "Now we're going to go over to the winner of yesterday's Indy 500, Dan Wheldon…" Silence. They're like… "Dan? Dan? Are you there…?" He was fast asleep!

DARIO FRANCHITTI 2012 167.734 M.P.H

by DARIO FRANCHITTI

THREE-TIME INDY 500 WINNER, FOUR-TIME INDYCAR CHAMPION

DAN CONNECTION

Lifetime friends; teammates at Andretti Green Racing, 2003-2005

That again shows the difference between him in '05 and him in '11. In 2011 when we all went out, it was, "Yeah, party!" But Dan had one drink and went. It wasn't important to him anymore and that was the change in his life. He wanted to be with his family and kids.

With Ganassi in 2006, all of a sudden he's making money. In all the time we were at Andretti, he never bought dinner. I mean he won the 500 – think of the money – he won the championship, finished third at the 500 in '04...he wasn't hurting! Tony, me, Bryan we all bought our hefty portions of dinner. Dan? Never! In all those years, not once did he buy. He was, "Guys, guys, I don't make the kind of money you make! I'm just a young driver, I haven't got the money." Anyway, he signs a deal with Chip. We're all in New York for different things, and I get a phone call from Tony. DDub's in town and wants to buy us dinner. He does? Excellent! So we show up at this pizza place. I say pizza place, well, it's a bit swanky, but I thought if DDub's buying I know where we're going! Patrick Dempsey was in town, too, so he shows up. Tony, myself, and Bryan were there.

We go upstairs, and Dan's like, "Bottle of champagne, guys? Yeah, let's have some champagne." Whoosh – bottle gone. Four or five bottles of Dom Perignon later, we've burned our way through about five grand of DW's money. We were like, "How's he going to react?" So we just kept ordering more and more champagne. And, honestly, he was as good as his word. He said, "Guys you've treated me, you've bought me dinners for the past two or three years, I couldn't have done it without you." Put his credit card down and bought the lot. From that point on, you could hardly buy dinner.

He won the first race with Chip that year and the final at Chicago but still didn't win the championship, ending up tied for first with Hornish on points. This was the time when all of a sudden he couldn't drive on a road course. I used to follow him round and think, "What are you doing Dan?" I watched him, but I just didn't know what it was. I think he had a mental block.

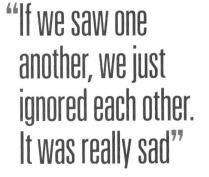

> "If we saw one another, we just ignored each other. It was really sad"

He was such a precise driver and a lot of the road courses we used to drive on were very bumpy, and he didn't like that. He couldn't let everything flow over the bumps and didn't know how to deal with it, which for Dan was very unusual. He got a crisis of confidence about it, and it just spiraled and got worse from there.

I do later remember him saying about the DW12, that he was feeling good on the road course. It was like "Look out boys, I've got the hang of this thing." That's about all we ever got out of him about

the DW12. He was sworn to secrecy. With Dan, when he was sworn to secrecy, there wasn't any gossiping. It was like, "Nah," and he never talked about it.

He was always super quick on the ovals and superspeedways, though, and Michigan in 2007 is when we really fell out, when we had that clash battling for the lead. I'd stalled earlier, come back out and gone from last to first. The car was very, very fast. Anyway, I got beside Dan and he was doing his job, making it very tough for me to get by. I was on the outside and he was sitting there, lap after lap. He started trying to side draft on the back straight. I moved away and he was following me, to keep the side draft. I stopped moving and he hit me. It was a stupid form of racing. We touched and next thing you know, I'm airborne. The thing takes off and I can hear the revs going du-du-du-du, hitting the limiter as the car is in the air, and my foot is still hard on the throttle.

It was a big old crash. I thought it was Dan's fault but he didn't come up and apologize. He didn't even come and discuss it, which I was really angry about. So, we got to the next race at Kentucky and I'd said in the press that I wasn't very happy with what Dan had done and the fact he hadn't come and apologized. I certainly wasn't reaching out to him, I was...mad.

So, we didn't speak. We're in the drivers meeting and he starts telling me that I was disrespectful in what I'd said in the press. I said,"F****** disrespectful? After what you f****** did?" Anyway, he takes off on his bike, so I chased after him, stopped him and grabbed him and gave him a real piece of my mind. This was a low point in our relationship, obviously!

We had no communication after that. If we saw one another, we just ignored each other. It was really sad. Then my brother Marino and our pal Brent Brush decided this was stupid. So, they got us together with a scheme where Marino took me out for a drink,

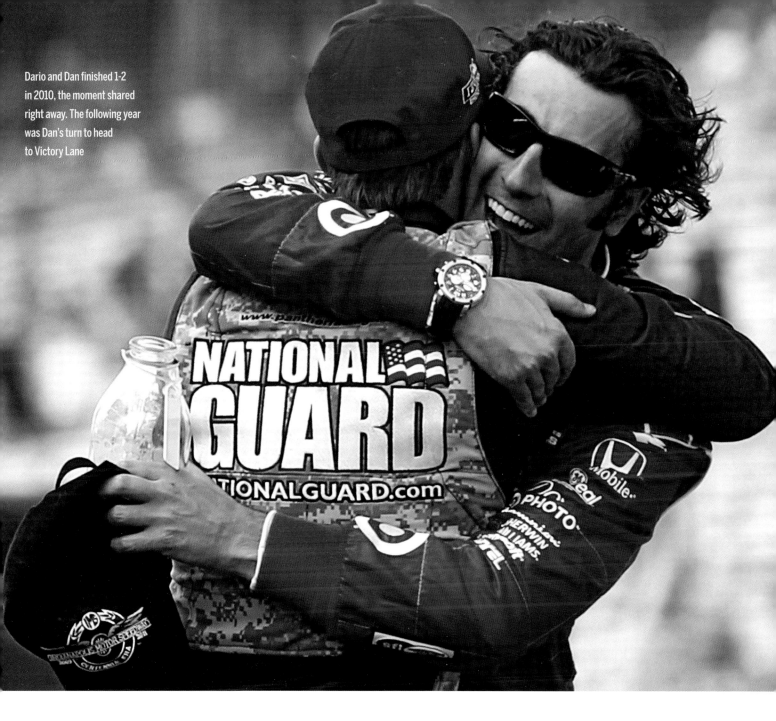

Dario and Dan finished 1-2 in 2010, the moment shared right away. The following year was Dan's turn to head to Victory Lane

Brushy "conveniently" taking Dan to the same place. Dan sees me sitting there; I see Dan and we didn't speak. The other two rush off to the bar, and return with a whole tray of Washington Apple shots. Brent says that we are all going to take a shot until Dan and I make up. Of course, we had a few drinks, we had a hug and that was it, we were fine again. I don't remember much else of that night, but Brushy tells me all the shots went.

By the end of that year, we were sort of teammates again at Ganassi as I'd signed for Chip driving in NASCAR for 2008. I did a couple of Nationwide races for Chip at the end of '07, so Dan and I had been starting to chat again. When we were racing we were never the type to pick up the phone and call each other every week; it wasn't ever that kind of "Hey what's happening?" type of thing.

Dan shows up at the NASCAR race at Homestead and I'm getting

ready for the race start — I was probably at the back of the grid anyway — and there's a commotion. It was like he'd been dropped from another planet, because there are all these NASCAR guys who are in jeans and whatever. Then this kind of "Metro Sexual" shows up with his tight outfit on and I thought, "That kind of looks like Dan," but not really, because he had these teeth; those huge chompers.

I'm looking at him coming toward me and all I could think to say to him was, "Did it hurt?" And he goes, "Yeah, it did kinda." The race starts and I'm just thinking of these teeth. I'm normally pretty good at focusing, but my head is just, "My God, what was he thinking?" I couldn't get it out of my head and I crashed... So Dan's teeth cost Chip a lot of money! Thinking about it, they cost Dan a lot of money, too!

Dan had been desperately unhappy at Panther. You could see

them just eroding his confidence. He was my opposition and my job was to beat him, but I hated seeing my friend like that. It was funny in that while I'd taken the seat he had been in, at that point he and I got on as well to the end of his life as we ever had.

At Indy in '09, Dan was running around in that Panther car and he looked like he was going to have an accident every single lap. The thing was evil, just evil. I went up to John Barnes and I said to him, "Whatever you're paying that guy, give him a bonus because anybody else would have stuck it in the wall at least 10 times." Yet he finished second both years.

The Indy 500, in 2010, where we finished first and second, what a race. Both he and I were on the same strategy, and we were both running out of fuel. It was a big game of poker. It was heart-stopping stuff, but to be able share that moment after. I mean obviously I'd

won so I was pretty happy, but to share that moment with him. He was so happy for me. Then the year after, when *he* won, I was able to do the same as he'd done for me the year before. It felt good.

The Panther thing just couldn't go on, and he was out in the cold. I remember saying – and he appreciated this – I don't understand how the hell we can have a series without Dan Wheldon in it, which I meant. It was just so stupid.

Oddly, at that time when he wasn't driving every week, I wasn't seeing him, so we spoke a bit on the phone. He wasn't ever really far from my thoughts. I was at Indy at some event during that time, I think it was an IndyCar Ministries thing, and one of the silent auction things was a picture of his '05 pace car. So I bought it for him, got it all packaged up and fired it off down to St. Pete's. I got the most beautiful note back.

Dario Franchitti's third Indy 500 win would transpire to be the final victory of his race career. Just as importantly it allowed the perfect way to honor his friend Dan Wheldon

It was so sad to see him doing the TV and grid run. Don't get me wrong; he was so good at it. Christ, he was a natural born broadcaster, and he had the gift of the gab. But that used to really irritate me and I said something about it, because he really shouldn't have been doing that, he should have been out there racing with us.

When he signed with Bryan for the 500 in 2011, I knew that if he could galvanize that whole thing, there's nobody who could make it happen better than him.

You could see exactly what he was doing all month. There was never any show, which was unusual for Dan, because Dan always wanted to be on top of the time sheets. Sure enough, he just had that confidence about him and that ability. And with Bryan, too – it was just brilliant, so nice to see.

You couldn't engineer a better script; that last corner, with JR. I mean that was poetic justice was it not? With everything that happened with Panther... I mean I feel bad for JR and the boys who worked there but you know what, that was just poetic. A big two fingers up....

It was so funny to see how changed he was and how he handled it differently. I hate to say it, but I think he expected the first 500 win. But what a different person he'd become out of the car this time. It was really cool to see him with Sebastian after.

During that month at Indy we had a great evening. A group text went around to Bryan, Dan, Tony, myself – "Right guys, let's do dinner. We're in Indy, we're all here together, we don't see enough of each other anymore...let's do dinner."

So, despite all our crazy schedules, we got organized and we went to Fogo de Chão and we told stories about the old times.

> ## "To have the three of us there finish 1-2-3 on that day...come on?"

Dan talked about his kids. That was one of the last times we were all together. It was so different because everything had moved on. Everything had changed but in so many ways it was the same. That was a really good night.

Dan was so much in our thoughts the next year. Any of the 500s are special as you can see by the pictures of us hugging for each other's wins in 2010 and '11. I wanted to win in 2012 and I wanted to win it so badly – I know Scott and Tony did too. You always want to win the 500, but there was a special reason for us that day.

I will tell you that 2012 Indy pre-race, when Jim Nabors started singing Back Home in Indiana I was in the car and just started bawling. I would always sing along – it was one of my things, I always loved that song. For some reason, it just hit me. Like "Jesus Christ, you've got a 500-mile race to run here you need to get focused."

It ended up all right but the emotion of that day started there. There were three hours of total focus, and then the emotion came back.

Then there were the white glasses; I mean the whole place went white with the people putting on the white glasses on lap 26 and 98. I still see people today who say, oh yeah, I've got my white glasses on as a tribute to Dan, and you realize what Dan meant to people.

To have the three of us there finish 1-2-3 on that day...come on? When you think about it, it was we three along with Dan's brothers carrying him at the funeral. It was something weird wasn't it? It didn't matter what order we finished in, because we would've all paid tribute to him that day.

Dan's and my successes in 2010 and 2011 mean we have our faces next to each other on the prized Borg Warner Trophy. That particular win for me, in 2012, means that with our buddy TK right there too, I'm now on either side of him on that famous trophy that has meant so much to us both – forever. ∎

CHOWEN PHOTOGRAPHY

BROTHERLY LOVE

A quality month of May leaves some tremendous memories

by HOLLY WHELDON LITTLE SISTER

THE 2011 INDY 500 will remain as one of my favorite times with Dan. Of course, winning the race was very special, but for me it was the whole event. I was 17 then, and Dan called me up and said, "Do you want to come to the U.S. for Indy?" I said I was already going to come for the race. But he said, "No, do you want to come for the full month?"

At the time I was caring for Mum, her Alzheimer's had taken hold and it was getting to the point where I was struggling, and we were looking into getting full-time care for her. I thought about what Dan was saying and, yes, I did actually want to experience it. So I said, "All right, let's do it."

I spent a couple of days in St. Petersburg with Dan, Susie and the boys and then we flew up to Indy. It was good to have the month because, obviously, I didn't see him very often; it was good to spend quality time with him and share that brother/sister love.

We stayed downtown and it was great to be on his schedule; to go around with him and experience it all. I went to all his appearances, watched him practice and was a part of it. Even the little things like carrying his bag – it sounds silly but I loved helping out in any way and just absorbing it all. If you're going to do it, do it all.

Everything seemed to go well all month. I remember being with him in the bus and just hanging out with him, Susie and the kids. It was different from what he was like in 2005 because then he had no kids or commitments. To see him in 2011, to really appreciate his 500 win with the two boys there, really getting what it meant to him, being in Victory Lane, and seeing how happy he was. All of it was fantastic to see and be a part of.

There are lots of things that stick in my mind from that month. About an hour before the race start, me, Susie, Dan, Elliott and Jason [Elliott's friend] were in the bus. Suddenly Dan says, "Right guys, do I go with white and blue boots or white and red?" We then had a full-on debate because he had an orange and white suit.... I thought it was really unusual, he was supposed to be in the green room for pre-race traditions and introductions in 20 minutes, or "zoning in" for the race, and he was still deciding what color boots to wear. That seems crazy even now.... We went for white and red.

Dan really wanted to win that race. With everything that was happening with Mum, the whole Panther thing and then JR [Hildebrand] crashing out at the final corner, it really felt like this is what we needed. This is the ideal finish to that part; that struggle.

Before the race, Dan told me there were two things he wanted. He wanted to win because he'd won in '05 and through that he had

Holly Wheldon with brother Dan:
"I really treasure those moments.
We had the best times together"

"He also wanted to win for his Mum. And, he did just that. You can see by the emotion on his face when he came in to Victory Lane"

DAN R BOYD/LAT

the Pace Car and a Baby Borg trophy. He wanted to get another win so Sebastian and Oliver could have a Pace Car and a trophy each. But he also wanted to win for his Mum. And, he did just that. You can see by the emotion on his face when he came in to Victory Lane, crying, and then him struggling to speak in the TV interview…. I have to say the milk tasted very good that day.

To celebrate after the race, we went out for dinner. It seemed very laid back. Obviously, after the win, Dan was doing media and stuff, so didn't get back to the hotel until late. We'd showered and we ended up in the Conrad having a really quiet dinner, with our brother, Elliott, Jason, Susie and a few others. A bunch of people were having drinks in the Conrad bar, but it wasn't the craziness that there was before. His priorities had changed. It definitely wasn't the way he was in '05. He was much calmer.

We did the Indy 500 banquet on Monday, then left to go to New York. Elliott had gone home by then. We had a great time doing all his media; we did the Dave Letterman Show and toured New York City.

The Empire State Building was an amazing moment. There's the section where the public can go… And we were able to climb another ladder to go to the top, where there's no fence at all, which is crazy! Susie had Oliver at the time and she couldn't climb the ladder, so Dan and I went up with Steve Shunck who was with us from IndyCar,

MICHAEL VOORHEES

and the lady giving us the tour. I had sunglasses hanging from the neck of my T-shirt and the woman said, "I wouldn't lean over too far or they're going down there!" It was just amazing to be up there and to share those special moments with him.

Las Vegas was supposed to be the same; Dan said I should go so we could spend time together. I flew to St. Pete to see Susie and the boys as Dan had left early for a media day in Los Angeles. He was out there with Brent [Brush] – Brent will hate me for this – and Susie and I called them up, asking what they were doing in sunny L.A. They said they were in bed together watching The Kardashians on TV! And we're like, "Oh, OK..."

Susie and I flew to Vegas with Jill, their nanny, and the kids. I'd

> ## "The Empire State Building was an amazing moment. We were able to climb another ladder to go to the top, where there's no fence at all, which is crazy!"

never been before and thought it was just the coolest city. I was 18 by then, but still I couldn't gamble. We had this awesome room – MGM had given Dan this suite and it was massive. There was this huge table in it and we all sat there every night for two or three hours just talking. The night before the race, Dan and Susie went to a dinner and I was in the room with his PA Emily Jones, when he texts me saying, "We got tattoos." I thought, yeah, whatever, but he was, "No, we really got tattoos." I was sure he was just messing with me because we both knew that Dad was really against tattoos.

When they came back, it was their proudest moment; the best thing he'd ever done. "Dan, it's just a tattoo, come on!" We knew when he told Dad he'd go crazy. Elliott, Jason and PJ [Chesson] had been out that night, too. PJ had told two girls that Elliott and Jason were lion tamers! We all sat around the table, chatting for hours.

Dan wouldn't stop going on about it and he was so excited to show everyone. I'd said that I really wanted to get one but didn't know what I wanted to get. It's kind of that mad 18-year-old moment where it sounded like a good idea. We called Dad and told him about the tattoos. Then he and Dad were talking about the race, but Dan kept going back to talking about their tattoos.

Hildebrand crashes at Turn 4 and DW makes the pass to the flag to win, 2011. Below: Holly Wheldon, "I love that photo of Dan's helmet for Las Vegas"

MICHAEL LEVITT/LAT

ANNE PROFFIT

Then the next day happened. It was a horrible, horrible day.

None of us spoke really after; and none of us slept that night. We were in that large room, poor Scott [Dixon] had come over, too, and was lying on the wooden floor with a blanket. I'd awakened the next day and, because there were so many people in the room, I just wanted to get out. I needed space; needed out.

I texted Brent about meeting for breakfast and, when I went downstairs, there was a bunch of media there, so I put my hoodie up, grabbed the first taxi, met Brent and went to Palms, where Dan and Susie had gotten their tattoos. I didn't really think about getting one then, and it was closed as well. We had breakfast at Palms and talked. As we were leaving, I noticed the tattoo place was open and I thought, you know what? I'm going to do it.

It was mid-morning and the plane back to St. Pete was leaving at 1pm. But I couldn't have cared less if I missed it.

We went in and I told them that my brother came in with his wife two nights ago but, unfortunately, he'd passed away yesterday. The guy was upset and remembered Dan coming in, but he wasn't the guy who actually did their tattoos. I explained that I just wanted to get a tattoo, with his initials and the year. We drew out a sketch

Holly with dad Clive after Dan's first Indy 500 win in 2005; the Empire State guide points out landmarks

and Brent was asking, "Are you really going to do this?" People kept calling to find out where we were and telling me I needed to hurry up.

There it was, my first tattoo. It hurt a little, but the guy was really sweet and being the same shop that Dan got his, makes it extra special. I love looking at it.

I had another one done in June 2012, around his birthday, on my thigh. I love the style of writing that the Lionheart is in on Dan's helmets, but that one hurt so much! Everything I have tattoo-wise has to do with Dan. Wrist, leg and then I had a small heart on my wrist too, which Susie and I did at the end of 2015. She and I have a really good relationship. It took a while to build from her just being my sister-in-law, but we have such a good bond now. We talk every day, which is really good for both of us. We kind of have the relationship I had with Dan; jokey, fun and we just get each other. The heart tattoo was just a mad moment on the last day I visited before Christmas. "Let's go get tattoos," and so we did. And, it's quite fitting that we did.

It's funny, recently a very good friend of mine said that is exactly what Dan did with Susie, and so, in a way, I was doing the same now. I had never actually thought of it like that.

There aren't enough words to describe how proud I am of Dan.

It just overwhelms me. It was nice to see him be a dad, taking on that responsibility, and he really enjoyed it. I feel for Oliver because he was very young, so he didn't get the chance to spend much time with his dad, but it was really sweet to see Dan's relationship with Sebastian. He was trying to get Sebastian into a kart. I remember we went to an outdoor karting place and Dan sat Sebastian on his lap and drove around the track. Sebastian's smile was as big as anything. You could see the connection they had, it was so sweet, and that Dan was so proud of him. It would have been amazing to see Dan be at a track with him; watching him and seeing him develop.

I really treasure those moments. We had great times together. But, as a family, we really had the best times. As siblings we were so close. Just going to visit and spending time with him, or the 3am phone calls, we used to have them, three or four times a week. I loved speaking to him for two hours. At times I'd be like, "Oh my God, let me go back to sleep!" but now I appreciate them so much. I still have old text messages on my phone that I read now and again.

I'm very proud of what Dan achieved in life, his two little boys and his wife. Like I said, there aren't enough words. It goes a lot deeper.

He always will be my little legend. ■

MILKING THE MOMENT

The fruit of a hard-working and trusting friendship came on May 29 2011 with a dramatic and popular Indy 500 win

by **BRYAN HERTA**

■ **FOUR-TIME INDYCAR WINNER**

DAN CONNECTION
Andretti Green Racing teammate, 2003-2005;
Indianapolis 500-winning team owner, 2011

The moment I've met people for the first time isn't something I usually remember, but I remember everything about the first time I met Dan Wheldon. It was at Indianapolis Motor Speedway in 2003, and it was in the Andretti Green Racing garages. Dan had been brought in as the team's most recent driver. He was the new kid on the team. Honda had just moved from Champ Car to the Indy Racing League, and they needed someone to pound out tons of test miles all winter long.

I don't think our teammates, Dario Franchitti and Tony Kanaan, had a lot of interest in doing that, so Dan came in and did that for the team. He arrived that season and was expected to just race sparingly while testing. But Dario's dubious motorcycling skills led him to crash his bike in Scotland after the second race of the season, so Michael Andretti called me and said, "Hey, we're going to need somebody to sub for Dario."

At the time, it was only supposed to have been a couple of races. Michael did a deal for Robby Gordon to drive Dario's car in the Indianapolis 500, and they asked me to come in and do some testing during the month of May at other tracks. I flew into Indy and came to the garages. I knew Tony and Robby very well, but I didn't know Dan, so we had to be introduced.

Here was this kid who was just full of bravado. He was confident in himself and what he was doing. He made an immediate impression on me. You'll hear other people say this: There was something about Dan. When you talked to him or interacted with him, he made a real connection with you. It didn't matter who you were. If you were a fan who met him for 20 seconds or if you were one of his good friends, he made a connection with you.

It was real and genuine. He could make you feel like you had just made a real connection with a person. That was my initial experience with him. He was very animated and sure of himself, but he was also very real.

I actually did a little bit of testing at Indy in 2003, but then I'd go off and test at places like Kentucky Speedway while the rest of the guys were preparing for Indy. I was back for qualifying weekend, and Dan had been really fast as a rookie all month long. He put down a solid qualifying run – he was fifth – but he was pissed afterward. He wanted to be on the pole.

thinking. Maybe I'd allowed too much complacency to enter into my thinking. In that 30-second exchange, he had made an impression on me. As much as Dario, Tony and I get credit for teaching Dan, I learned more from him than he learned from me. I remember that exchange like it happened yesterday.

From there, we got to know each other better. Dario came back at Pikes Pike, but then doctors told him his back hadn't healed well enough, and he was out for the rest of the year.

Dan and I raced together the rest of the season, and Dan finished the year strong – fourth at Chicago, fourth at Fontana and third at Texas. Keep in mind that this was his first experience on big ovals, but he was fearless and fast.

I'd been in Indy-car racing for some time, and I honestly thought my career was done when Michael moved the team to the Indy Racing League. But racing that year with Dan brought me back. The only way I can describe what happened to me during that stage of my career was a second lease on life. I don't mean to demean cancer survivors by making this comparison, but it was very much like surviving a serious illness and being granted more time. It was a second career that I never expected.

I approached it better and differently than I had in the past, and Dan had a lot to do with my approach. It was all about doing my best, but having fun while doing it. Dan and Tony and I – and Dario came

MAIN: DAN R BOYD/LAT; BELOW: ANN MILLER CARR

LEFT: JUN SATO/GETTY

I thought, "Here's an opportunity for me as the veteran of the group to spread some wisdom." I went over to sit with him and said, "It's a long race, Dan. You've got a great starting spot. You don't need to risk anything right now. Just focus on the race. You're starting fifth. That's great."

I'll never forget what happened next. He turned to me and said, "That might be good enough for you, brother, but it ain't for me." He wasn't being caustic. It was his mentality. He expected to be at the front, especially at Indianapolis. From the first day he got there, he expected that from himself.

It really struck me, and it changed my attitude and way of

"As much as Dario, Tony and myself get credit for teaching Dan, I learned more from him than he learned from me"

Main: Wheldon led a couple of hundred yards of the 500 miles – the final ones.
From left: DW and Herta go back years, and milestone IndyCar wins for Honda

LEFT: STEVE SNODDY/IMS   DAN R BOYD/LAT

back in 2004 to form a four-car team – all decided that we were going to have the most fun and do the most damage we could. We did exactly that.

We did it all in those days. We'd fly in private jets to New York just to hang out for dinner. We kicked ass on track, and we made the most of our time away from the track. It was an incredible time in my life, and I'll always be grateful to Dan for bringing that out of me. I don't think it could've happened with any other group of guys. It was the chemistry among the four of us, and Dan was a huge part of making that chemistry work.

Dan was the little brother in the equation. He was the rookie,

the kid we teased. I was the old guy. I was doing a lot of the engine development work for Honda at the time, so the boys fondly referred to me as EB, which stood for "Engine Bitch." I don't think I've ever told anybody else what EB actually stood for, but that is what they called me: EB.

We had a lot of fun teasing each other, and Dan was always a great target. Because he was young and because he was the rookie, we constantly teased and pranked him. But we also did it because he gave the best reactions. He would get so fired up when we punked him, which only made us punk him more.

We did a lot of little things to him. He was so particular about

Let the celebrations begin! Crossing the famous bricks and taking the checker opened a world of emotions and media attention

SHAWN GRITZMACHER/IMS RIGHT: PAUL WEBB/LAT

how his things were organized in his locker, so Tony would casually walk over and yank all the clothes in Dan's locker onto the floor. Dan would then fold everything precisely and put it back in its place.

I remember one time when the car was out on pit lane ready to go at Indy, and Kim Green was yelling at Dan to get out there and drive, but Dan wouldn't leave the garage until he had his locker sorted back the way he wanted. We had messed it up, and he wouldn't get out on track until everything was back in order. We got into a bit of trouble for that one.

One time I created this grand scheme. I knew there were a couple of people on the team who would blab to Dan, so told them that I had

a plan to play a prank on him. I told them I had a key to Dan's house and when he left town I was going to hire a moving company to come in and move all of his furniture and replace it with lawn chairs. I knew they'd tell Dan, and they did.

I told them the plan in the morning, and they went straight to Dan with it. Near the end of the day, Dan came up to me with a big smile on his face and said, "Hey, Hertabeast" – that was his nickname for me – "I gotcha. Just wanted you to know that I changed all the locks on my house. You're not getting in."

I just smiled, looked straight back at him and said, "Hey, Dan. I never had a key."

That's where the brotherhood was born. We realized that this was a time in our lives that was limited. We didn't know how long it would last, but we knew the four of us weren't going to be racing together forever. It wouldn't be exactly like that again for any of us. We just set out to do as much as we could in that time. It was perfect.

People still come up to me and talk to me about the silly things we did. We threw pies in each other's faces during interviews. We did some goofy stuff, but the fun transcended everything. It trickled down to the team. The mechanics would prank each other. It became an entertaining environment.

None of it was hurtful or mean-spirited. It was all very playful. It was almost like, if we didn't mess with you, it meant we didn't like you. It created a sense within the team that I believe was a major part of our success at the time. We felt invincible. It was amazing.

Time went on, and I got to see Dan make a metamorphosis from a kid with all this bravado who was never really as confident underneath it all – certainly not as much as he wanted people to believe – into a mature, accomplished, skilled racer and human being. In the beginning, he was worried about whether he was good enough and whether he would accomplish the things he wanted to accomplish. He almost overcompensated and came over the top with self-confidence.

But as success came for Dan, he changed. He started dating

Susie, they got married, and he became a family man. He made this crazy, incredible metamorphosis. Dan the person, by the end, was an amazing guy who made a positive impact on the people he met.

It wasn't just the two Indy 500 wins and the 2005 IndyCar Series championship title and 14 other wins that made the impact. His personality is what people are most intrigued by, even now. His ability to connect with people was remarkable. It's something I relearned through him – how you connect with fans and how you treat fans.

It was never enough for Dan to just sign a blank autograph. He always looked you in the eye and asked you how you were doing. He would crack a joke or say something clever. In a short period of time, he would do something that made that person feel like they really knew Dan Wheldon. They didn't just get an autograph. They got a little piece of him with it.

That's why the reaction when he died was what it was. Unfortunately, in racing, we live with tragedy. I don't imagine that there will come a time when it won't be part of our sport. But when Dan died, it was different. It was different for competitors and fans, but it was also different for me. Dan was the first close friend I'd lost to racing.

I don't think I'd ever seen somebody who was so beloved and didn't realize it at the time. Now, as we sit here today, Dario, Tony, Scott Dixon and I – we've all talked about this – have all made a commitment to ourselves and to Dan. We've all mourned him. We've been through the sad stuff. He wouldn't want us to dwell on that. He would want us to be happy and positive, and remember all the good times, and share it all.

Dan loved being loved. He loved racing. He loved his fans. He loved popularity. He would love all this attention. We said it at the memorial service they had in Indianapolis afterward. We joked that it was a shame Dan wasn't there because he would've loved the party. He truly would have enjoyed it.

On some level, we all feel a sense of duty to Dan to keep telling his story, to keep reminding people about him, to recognize his legacy and who he was and what he did in his lifetime. Not only would he have loved that, but also it's important. Dan's an integral part of the overall history of racing and specifically the history of IndyCar racing and the Indianapolis 500.

A hundred years from now, people will walk into the IMS Hall of Fame and Museum and see that No. 98 car. People might not know a lot about Dan then, but hopefully they'll know a little bit of the important parts. I want people to know more than the fact that he won the race twice. There's a lot more to his story than what he accomplished on racetracks.

I can still hear Dan's voice in my head. What I imagine him saying to me right now is, "Better make me look good, Hertabeast." Literally, that's what he would say, and I would reply, "It's hard not to, my friend." ∎

"We all feel a sense of duty to Dan to keep telling his story, to keep reminding people about him, to recognize his legacy"

DAN WHELDON'S SECOND Indy 500 win was a triumph far exceeding expectation, and the enormity of it caught up with him as he, and family, began their celebratory lap. Heading down pit lane to the cheers of the crowd, they met two media members, John Oreovicz and Ann Miller Carr, as well as friend and former teammate Dario Franchitti. Oreo takes up the story with the players, including sister Holly Wheldon and editor Andy Hallberg

TEARS FOR SOUVENIRS

One moment, freeze frame, captured by two people sums up the emotion of DW's second Indy 500 win

OREO: After the race, I was in pit lane seeking interviews when Dan, his wife Susie, Bryan Herta and Dan's sister Holly were about to start the victory lap in the Pace Car. Dario stopped him, intending to pull some kind of prank. But when Dario saw the tears of real emotion streaming down Dan's face, he couldn't bring himself to do anything. I was lucky enough to capture that moment between friends with a picture. Dario says that grainy iPhone shot may well be his favorite memory of Dan.

DF: I was going to car jack him! Then I saw him crying and I couldn't do it to him because he was really emotional. I was so happy that I was able to put aside my disappointment that day and be happy for my friend. We'd been through a lot by that point, and so had he. I love that picture.

AH: It's a great photo. But I also saw the woman I later found out

was Ann Miller Carr to the left of the shot in the salmon shirt with her camera, and I immediately thought: "I want get hold of the picture that she's taking...."

DF: I know her. She goes every year.

DF & HW: [as they see Ann's picture, above right, for the first time] Oh, my God....

　　[Long, long pause]

DF: Wow...

HW: Look at the emotion on his face....

DF: God, he was so happy that day.

AMC: As *Indianapolis Star* staff members shot the melee in Victory Lane, I'd been dispatched to find and shoot Dario (who finished 12th). I found out he was still in his pit. Dario saw Dan coming and started running to the car – I was in close pursuit

"I wanted to give him a hug and tell him that I was proud of him, because he'd been through a lot"

because I knew something was going to happen. I was the only photographer around...or so I thought, as it turned out writer John O. was there with his phone!

HW: I remember being in the car and driving down the pits and seeing Dario coming toward us. There were so many people in that car, Bryan was holding on to me because I was going to fall. I knew you wanted to dive, Dario, but then you saw his emotion.

AMC: I didn't know John was around when I was shooting those shots. I guess I was just concentrating, wasn't I? But those shots of Dan and Dario are some of my favorites, and I've been shooting auto racing as a freelance stringer for 38 years – most recently for the *Indianapolis Star*. But the *Star* never used the shots.

DF: What I was going to do changed in a hurry because I had thought to car jack the little bugger, to pull him out. And then I saw him; and it just wasn't the time. I wanted to give him a hug and tell him that I was proud of him, because he'd been through a lot.

HW: This is one of my favorite photos of you guys.

DF: Yeah, exactly. To capture moments like that is very special.

HW: Those shots are just incredible. ∎

179

Dan, congratulations on winning the Indy 500,

I know so many emotions must be going through your mind. What did you think when you came around Turn Four and saw Hildebrand in the wall?

I was just trying to go as hard as I could. I knew it was the last lap and they said that a lot of those guys were struggling on fuel. I just kept pushing you know...

I just want to say thank you obviously to my wife for her support through being a part-timer right now. It's a fantastic achievement. To the fans for being here. For Bryan Herta and everybody at Bryan Herta Autosport, that have just given me such a dream ride.

There are so many other people I want to thank. I want to thank Honda; they've always been behind me 110 percent. There's no organization like Honda. William Rast, I mean totally my style. It's a great sponsor for me and I feel like a *fashionista*. I'm gonna be wearing jeans tomorrow night, I know I'm supposed to dress smart, but I'm gonna be wearing my William Rast jeans. Curb Records, Big Machine Records, Forsythe Solutions, Firestone...

"It's been absolutely phenomenal. I love Indianapolis. I love the people. I love everything about it; the tradition, the history. I just don't know what to say anymore"

Take us back to the moment you actually saw Hildebrand in the wall and you knew you were going to win the Indy 500.

I just felt a lot of relief! Obviously I knew he was ok because I could see him moving. But it's an incredible feeling. I've been runner up for two years before this and I never gave up. I mean Kanaan nearly put me in the wall going in to Three which was very, very interesting but there's a lot of great storylines today.

I want to say hi to my family back home (very emotional), my mother... and you know, the Alzheimer's Association for giving me the opportunity to represent them. It's just an incredible day.

I'm taking my kids to Disney baby; I'm taking my kids to Disney!

KING OF THE CASTLE

Winning the Indy 500 means media commitments galore. In 2011, that included a photo shoot on a throne made of bricks

I have no idea why we thought building a throne of bricks inside the Indianapolis Motor Speedway media center would be a good idea, but I'm glad we heaved, sweated and cussed the plan into reality.

The end result was a memorable *RACER* magazine cover, with 2011 Indy 500 winner Dan Wheldon playing the role of "King of The Brickyard" to perfection. But, man, what a slog...

Having located a local brick and tile company, *RACER* editor David Malsher and I headed over the afternoon before Carb Day, chose a brick that (kind of, if you squinted) looked like the ones on the Speedway's start-finish line, loaded 300 into our rental SUV (apologies for the mess, Avis) and headed back to the track.

Problem was, the space for our photo shoot was on the second floor, meaning we had to "liberate" a wheeled dumpster from a passing cleaner, load them onboard, drag it onto the elevator, then unload the bricks once again – all 1,500lbs of them.

After a couple hours of toil, we were pretty pleased with the throne we'd built – arm and foot rests, a bit of an ornamental thing going on at the back – so we threw a sheet over it and crossed our fingers that the floor wouldn't collapse.

The finish of the race was a classic, with rookie JR Hildebrand putting his car into the wall in sight of the finish, and Dan grabbing a last-gasp, but highly popular win for Bryan Herta's underdog team. We had our story, so now we just needed the visuals to go with it.

As usual,. *RACER*'s shoot was scheduled for early the next morning, before the winner heads out for various TV interviews and the traditional shots on the yard of bricks. Oftentimes, the

by LAURENCE FOSTER

■ EDITOR-IN-CHIEF RACER MAGAZINE

DAN CONNECTION
Personal throne builder

driver shows up nursing an almighty hangover with eyes the color of a blood orange, but Dan was fresh as a daisy. Dinner with his wife Susie and young sons Sebastian and Oliver had been followed by an early night, which was exactly how he wanted it. His contentment was obvious, and – thankfully – so was his enthusiasm for the throne shoot.

Race suit on, Dan went through the various permutations for ace photographer Michael Levitt – wreath, bottle of milk, casual, serious – all while recounting the previous day's wild finish and pulling up his latest phone pics of his two boys enjoying the celebrations.

When Levitt declared himself happy with the shots and Dan got up to head to his next appointment, I asked him to autograph a copy of the official results sheet to go on *RACER*'s office wall. Before signing and adding "#98," he paused to read it. "I'm just checking that I did actually win," he chuckled. "See you soon, guys." ■

Footnote

1) Disposing of 300 bricks proved something of a challenge. We threw most of them into the dumpsters behind the pit lane grandstands, but a few rogue bricks remained in the media center. They were still there three years later. (Apologies for the mess, IMS...)

2) Dan liked a fairly snug-fitting race suit, and it was only when we came to work on the images for the cover and inside feature story that we realized his bare ankles were showing in the shots we wanted to use. Cue some nifty work from our office Photoshop savant, Ree Tucker, and you'd never have known...

GLORY DAYS

A festival of fun, stars, cars and recognition for a country's Indy 500 winner

By STEVE SHUNCK

- MR FIX IT

DAN CONNECTION
2011 victory media tour chaperone

The 2011 Goodwood Festival of Speed was truly a continuation of Dan Wheldon's Indianapolis 500 victory celebration. Just arriving at the wonderful event hosted by Lord Charles March in the beautiful surroundings of Goodwood House and its leafy estate in South West England, we knew some special days and experiences lay ahead. A little over an hour before he was scheduled to make his first run, Dan was already in his element – which only made the early morning arrival more fast and furious. It was exactly the way he liked things.

It was his first public appearance in Europe after that special win the previous month. Dan gladly posed for photos with adoring fans, signed autographs and flashed his million dollar smile as he walked though the massive crowd on a picture-perfect morning to meet with the most elite fraternity in racing – his fellow Indy 500 winners.

At the invitation of Lord March, the festival embraced the centennial anniversary of the Indianapolis 500, and 14 past Indy winners had made the trip to the UK to share the event with passionate fans, many who were being exposed to the joys of Indy cars for the first time.

Right down to the playing of "Back Home Again in Indiana", a specially made row of bricks at the startline, marching bands and yellow-shirted security guards, it felt like the Indianapolis Motor Speedway had relocated to rural England, almost in Dan's backyard where he grew up.

JEFF BLOXHAM/LAT

DW loved the history of the Indy 500 and was full of questions for the older, established winners who happily welcomed him into their exclusive club as they visited his homeland

When told he was scheduled to drive the gorgeous 1980 Indy 500 winning Pennzoil Chaparral on his first run of the day, Dan – like a kid at Christmas – immediately tracked down its winning driver, Johnny Rutherford.

He was full of questions for his three-time Indy winner friend, and wanted to hear stories and get as much information as he could about the car, just to connect with history and make his driving experience more memorable. Rutherford recounted that special month in May and the Memorial Day win...Dan listened, bright-eyed and nodding, soaking in every word Johnny spoke.

When he finally lowered himself into one of the most revolutionary cars ever to have been seen at the Speedway, Dan slowly ran his hand all around the steering wheel to further connect with the car, just as Rutherford had done on his historic day in 1980. Dan was the new breed of Indy winner – although he understood the importance of the Indy 500 and its tradition.

> ## "Hey, where do I plug the radio in? What? There's no radio? Man, how did these guys race back then...?"

From his new seat, he joked with the crew, waving his helmet headphone jack in the air. "Hey where do I plug the radio in? What? There's no radio? Man, how did these guys race back then...?" One more smile, modern William Rast-decaled helmet on, and a moment to savor firing up the engine and driving one of the most iconic and innovative cars to take the checkered flag at the Speedway.

While others at the festival were on the famous hillclimb to set times, Dan was there to enjoy it, and share his stage with his home nation's fans, waving as he drove by – something he'd not been able to do since leaving "home" for America in 1999. In later runs aboard a more recent Ganassi winner, there were some burnouts, but the Chaparral was treated with the respect it deserved. It was a winner, something Dan himself was, too, for the second time just a month earlier.

He embraced it all as he made his way up to the top of Lord March's driveway to rejoin his elite gang of fellow 500 winners. ∎

ROUTE TO INDY

On his way to IndyCar success, Dan Wheldon raced — and won — at all levels of the American junior categories

by JEREMY SHAW

- WRITER AND BROADCASTER

DAN CONNECTION
Sounding board/advisor in junior American career

Dan Wheldon was never one to stray too far from his roots. Even after winning an IndyCar championship and two Indianapolis 500s, he remained humble and always willing to pass along snippets of advice or encouragement to anyone who asked.

I first met Dan in 1999 after he came to the realization that his chances of making it to Formula 1 were increasingly slim and instead set his sights on a career in North America. As with so many other talented Europeans over the past three decades, it turned out to be a shrewd move. He won the USF2000 championship as a rookie, and then graduated rapidly through Toyota Atlantic and Indy Lights, winning twice at each level before making his IndyCar debut in 2002. He wasted no time in making his presence felt at the elite level either.

In 2011, my better half, Tamy Valkosky, an accomplished public relations specialist, switched from representing race teams on a full-time basis to Andersen Promotions, which had taken control of the Cooper Tires USF2000 Championship Powered by Mazda and was in the throes of developing the highly acclaimed Mazda Road to Indy. She also found the time to work with Dan and

Bryan Herta Autosport at the Indianapolis 500. It turned out to be a fruitful alliance, and two aspects of Dan's unlikely victory stand firm in my memory. The first came later in the evening. While Dan and the team celebrated in style with the team sponsors and other luminaries, Tamy remained hard at work in the team's garage, helping to spread the word about the win and helping to plan Dan's "victory tour." So, I headed out to procure some dinner, and soon returned to the garage with a McDonald's takeout. Sometimes this sport isn't quite as glamorous as it appears!

That point was drummed home again the following morning when we returned to the racetrack well before sunrise. Right on time, there was Dan, bright-eyed and bushy-tailed, ready to commence a rigorous series of TV interviews, each and every one of which he conducted with as much enthusiasm as the first. Impressive.

Later in the summer, when the opportunity arose for a media day on the Indianapolis Motor Speedway Grand Prix circuit to publicize the Mazda Road to Indy, we asked Dan if he would like to test-drive cars representing all three steps of the driver-development ladder – USF2000, Star Mazda, as it was then, and Indy Lights. His response was instantaneous and enthusiastic: "Hell, yeah!"

The day itself was cool and dry, and Wheldon could hardly wait to get started. His first run was aboard an Andretti Autosport USF2000 Van Diemen-Mazda with which Spencer Pigot finished second in the championship. Wheldon initially suggested he would complete just a couple of laps to warm up the car, then venture out

When the 2011 Indy 500 winner took up the offer to sample the junior category cars, the media took note; behind the wheel of the Star Mazda racer (right)

From the first step on the rung, USF2000 (left) up to Indy Lights (right), the test driver of the day had a lot of fun

again to gain a proper feel for the nimble little open-wheeler. Ten laps later he was still pounding around, gradually building speed, halted only when the team feared he might run out of fuel.

"I wanted to carry on but they threw the red flag so I thought I had better come on in," he explained excitedly with his familiar toothy smile. "It was a lot of fun. When I first came to the U.S., I started off in USF2000. That series is the way my IndyCar career started, and it was great to be back. I always felt they were a really good training ground for moving up the ladder system."

After spending some time debriefing with the team and attending media, Wheldon hopped aboard Team Pelfrey's Star Mazda car which, coincidentally, also had finished second in its respective championship chase in the hands of Californian Connor De Phillippi.

"You can tell you've moved up a rung of the ladder because you've got the sequential, 6-speed transmission and traction control," reported Wheldon, who turned competitive times despite a compromised seating position. "I wasn't probably giving the car its best because my knees were touching the (steering) wheel, but it seems sophisticated for an entry-level car, which is great. It's not honestly a huge step up from a 2.0-liter car (but) it is definitely a

> ## "He was still pounding around, halted only when the team feared he might run out of fuel"

step up – you've got the different dimensions, and you can do a lot more in the car. The rotary engine has a thin power band you really have to stay within, so you've got to make sure that you attack the corners; but, by the same token, you can't just really load on the brakes, you've got to try and carry that momentum. I think it's the perfect middle ground between USF2000 and Indy Lights."

Wheldon's level of excitement was ramped up further after sampling Norwegian Anders Krohn's Belardi Auto Racing Dallara Indy Lights car, despite its potential being masked by non-optimized gear ratios.

"I like that a lot... It gives you tons of confidence to drive fast, but now you can start to feel the weight like the Indy car. It's very nice to drive. It's very confidence inspiring. It's got that kind of brute, grunt power, I like to call it, like the old Indy Lights we used to drive, but it's got that weight with it, too. I think that's why you're seeing a lot of successful Indy Lights drivers doing well, because it is relevant."

Afterward, Wheldon hung out to joke and share stories with those present, including the cars' regular drivers. His enthusiasm was infectious, and the palpable joy he derived from returning to his roots – just as he did on a regular basis by attending major karting events around the country – was refreshing. He was a class act. ∎

ALL FOR ONE

Sam Schmidt's relationship with Dan Wheldon was all too brief

By SAM SCHMIDT

- RACE-WINNING INDYCAR SERIES TEAM OWNER

DAN CONNECTION
Bryan Herta Autosport Partner team, 2011

My first experience with Dan was as an IndyCar team owner in 2001. Indy Lights was being formed for 2002 and, since I'd been hurt in 2000, we really only ran full-time in IndyCar in 2001 with Davey Hamilton and 2002 with Richie Hearn. We were constantly looking for new talent, whether it was for Indy Lights or IndyCar, so I watched closely when he finished second in the Indy Lights championship in 2001.

The first thing that struck me was that he was quite the entertainer and quite the personality even back then. He was talented as a driver, obviously, but he was a huge character, too. He also did something I thought was incredibly smart. So many times you see younger drivers with talent who work their tails off but don't have a great deal of personal funding. They get to the point where they're about to graduate from Lights to IndyCar, and they throw everything they have at the Indianapolis 500. The logic is that if they make a name for themselves at Indy, their careers will be set. It's a bit unrealistic because of the level of competition at Indy and the competitive nature of the race. Everybody spends a lot of money at Indy, and everybody wants to win it. The truth is, as a rookie in a one-off at Indy, winning or even placing well enough to draw attention is next to impossible.

Dan was really smart. He took the money that would've been used on a 2002 Indy program. He bought two races with Panther

Racing – Chicagoland and Texas – in which he knew he could excel in that format with the team. Immediately I knew this was a guy who was smart enough to size up his own situation – whether that be funding or talent or whatever – and put himself in the best possible position to do well, make a good impression, and then leverage those results. He did well enough at those two races to align himself with Michael Andretti for 2003. The rest is history.

Dan stepped into Michael's program when Andretti had decent funding from Honda and a competitive advantage. Dan was a sponsor's dream. Klein Tools and Jim Beam didn't leave the sport because of a lack of attention they received through Dan, that's for sure. At that time, he also firmly embedded himself with Honda, and that was further reinforced when he won for them at Motegi in 2004 – Honda's first IndyCar win at its own facility.

When I come across kids in the Mazda Road to Indy program, their first question is, "How can I possibly become a paid driver in IndyCar if my parents don't have $20 million?" I use Dan as the example of someone who didn't have a ton of money but was very methodical about every step. Dan maximized everything he had.

During the time that Dan first established himself in the IndyCar Series, our team was only doing Indy Lights and a one-off at the Indy 500 every year, so there wasn't much personal interaction between Dan and myself. But when we decided to come back to IndyCar full-time in 2011, we really wanted Dan to drive for us. At the time, we had a full season commitment from Alex Tagliani, and we were trying to grow that to two cars in 2012. One thing led to another in 2011, and Dan ended up joining us for Indy through a technical partnership with Bryan Herta Autosport.

We knew we had a fast package that year at Indy in our collaboration with Bryan's team. Bryan had a long-term

Car owner Sam Schmidt and family celebrate a remarkable race success at Indy having already taken pole with driver of the #99 car (left), Alex Tagliani

"I took it all in at the time, just admiring what he was doing for us and how much he put into it"

relationship with Honda – and was a former teammate of Dan's – so he had that connection with him. Honestly, I couldn't believe he was available for the job as a one-off. Alex and Townsend Bell would drive the Schmidt cars, and Dan would drive the Herta car, but we were essentially a single team, since we were sharing everything. We did all the engineering and prep work together. Our guys prepared the No. 98 chassis and leased it to Bryan.

It was the first time I really got to spend time with Dan and get to know him after hours. I'm really disappointed that I wasn't around for the crazy days of his career in the mid-2000s, but I heard all the stories. I missed some good parties, and I know I would've enjoyed them as much as everyone else did.

The month of May was phenomenal. All three guys were fantastic throughout the month. It seems like every day they were all in the top five on the time sheets. We had a great deal of momentum and optimism, even going up against the big dogs. That created a confident setting. It also spun out a few of the competitors in the paddock, because they couldn't figure out why we were so fast. It wasn't just a fluke when Alex won the pole position and Dan and Townsend qualified on the second row. We had been fast every day leading up to that.

On the track, throughout the month, Dan Wheldon shined like I couldn't believe. It was a great team effort, but a lot of that could be attributed to Dan. He had a senior, veteran attitude of nurturing and assisting. He was never so competitive that he wouldn't work with everyone as a team. It was a one-off; he had every right to not show everyone all of his cards, but he did. It benefited the entire team throughout the month.

Dan was very gracious. I took it all in at the time, just admiring what he was doing for us and how much he put into it. He was always so polite and nice to every fan – especially kids. If you got an autograph from Dan Wheldon, you felt like you really knew him. He made you feel included and involved in what he was doing. You don't always see that at this level when people have been doing it

for that long. Dan never forgot how hard he worked to get to where he was, and he was working hard to get back to where he had been.

I didn't expect any of that from Dan. I was hoping for it – hoping he would step in and be fully engaged and into it – but I didn't know him well enough to expect it. But he was beyond my wildest dreams. He contributed to the Sam Schmidt Paralysis Foundation, he was fully involved in sponsorship activities, he did media events and fan appearances – he did everything in a complete, professional way that I only could have dreamed he would.

On race day, he reminded me of the way Arie Luyendyk was when I was his teammate in 1999. He was methodical all day long. He constantly evolved with the car and adapted to situations around him. He didn't care if he led a single lap until the last one. I can't tell you how much patience that takes. I never had that as a driver. I blew an engine and crashed twice in my three Indy 500s because I didn't have that patience. If my car was fast, I was going to the front *now*. That was my problem. Dan wasn't that way.

All month long, he was concerned with qualifying well and then being in position to win at the end. He did a fantastic job at both. Anybody who has raced at Indy will tell you that from your first laps there, it either fits you like a glove and you can't wait to get back there next year, or you hate it. Dan loved the place. He knew what to do there in every situation.

That unique situation I spoke of earlier – being successful

> ## "I almost quit IndyCar racing on the spot. I returned because I knew it's what Dan would have wanted"

as a one-off at Indy – Dan did it. Because of it, he found full-time employment for 2012. Unfortunately, we never could have imagined what would happen a few months later.

Las Vegas is hard for me to talk about. Fifteen years after my accident, I'm still a firm believer that things happen for a reason. I am witness every day to people our foundation is helping. Through that and continuing with racing and being able to watch my kids grow up, I'm aware of the reasons my situation happened and why I'm in this wheelchair. But I constantly think back to 2011 and can't for the life of me come up with a reason for it.

We actually had a bad weekend leading up to the race, but Dan never got down or frustrated. We took the same chassis we used to win the pole at Indy to Las Vegas. We meticulously labeled every part, and that's how Dan's car was built up. He wasn't fast at all in

Left: Schmidt stablemate and poleman Alex Tagliani congratulates winner DW; the crew worked tirelessly for their driver all weekend at Las Vegas (below)

PAUL WEBB/LAT;RUSSELL LaBOUNTY/LAT

practice. In fact, he was way back in the pack. We were pulling our hair out all weekend. Dan was flat-out but couldn't go any faster.

We changed a bunch of stuff leading up to qualifying, but we still qualified 29th out of 34 cars. With Dan's constant encouragement, we decided the night before the race to just tear it down and take everything back to the tub. We didn't know what we'd done wrong, but the guys stayed at the track for the better part of the night and took the car entirely apart and put it back together again. It was all hands on deck. We had to start last for the promotion – last to first to win a $5 million bonus – so we thought, "If this car wakes up like it did at Indy and becomes a rocket, then by all means, go to the front." But I told Dan that if it was anything like it was in practice, don't risk anything. Just hang at the back and have a good day.

But by lap five, he'd passed 10 cars. He came on the radio hooting and yelling. "This thing is fantastic," he said. "I don't know what you did to it, but the speed is back. I can go anywhere and do anything. I can drive around any of these guys." He was in his element and having a blast.

There's no rhyme or reason to what happened that day. There's nothing I can figure out about why something like that happens. There's no silver lining. I've searched for it, but I can't find it. It was devastating to everyone involved with the team. It was devastating to everyone who knew Dan. But mostly it was devastating to Susie and Dan's family.

I almost quit IndyCar racing right there on the spot. It had been 10 years since Davey Hamilton had his accident in one of my cars, and then this. I don't ever want to have that feeling again. It was two or three weeks later that my wife Sheila said. "At the end of the day, what would Dan have wanted you to do?" The answer is he'd want me to pick it up and get back out there. I returned because I knew it's what Dan would've wanted.

Dan was an electric personality. He never had a bad day in the time I knew him. It's been said before, but I'll repeat it: There won't be another Dan Wheldon. He was the complete package. He had talent, intelligence, skill, speed and a full understanding of the business of racing.

He also had a great love of and commitment to his family. I knew the Dan Wheldon everyone said had evolved and grown into a more mature family man. We had many very quiet conversations about our families, and there was no doubt in my mind that his focus and commitment was on them.

I'm a better person for having known Dan, even if it was only for a brief time. I believe everyone else who knew him feels the same way, and rightfully so. ■

PARADISE LOST

With pranks, unrepeatable nicknames and good times aplenty, Aussie Brett Murray remembers Dan as a real "ripper bloke"

DW was all set for V8 Supercar action in 2011 at Surfers Paradise, where he'd raced IndyCar in 2008

By BRETT "CRUSHER" MURRAY

■ AUSTRALIAN MEDIA ENTREPRENUER/
OWNER PIRTEK TEAM MURRAY

DAN CONNECTION
Ideas man and promoter of Gold Coast Races

I knew of Dan when he did Indy Lights with PacWest, in 2002, as he joined the team the year after I left to return to Australia. I had an emotional connection with him in that his 2005 win was called by Andretti Green's team manager John Anderson – the guy who recruited me to the States at the end of 1999. "Ando" was a great mate of mine, and he'd been robbed of an Indy 500 win with the Paul Tracy deal in '02, so I reached out to DW the night of his 2005 win, and thanked him for winning the race for Ando.

With that, I really got to know him socially and developed a proper friendship with him. We just hit it off and had this great relationship. I guess because he's English and I'm Australian we had a similar sense of humor in a lot of ways. We used to take the piss out of him mercilessly about his teeth, but you know, nothing was ever an issue. I think we both had a great respect for each other.

We'd call each other names that really *can't* be printed here. That's just how we were though. If we texted or called, that's what we called each other. I've still got the last message he sent me. He even signed my 2011 Indy 500 program that way...and told me to get him a V8 Supercar ride at Surfers. Which, we made happen.

Dan was supposed to be racing the Gold Coast 600 Surfers Paradise V8 Supercar race the week after Las Vegas with James Courtney for HRT, one of the most famous teams in Australia.

The next part of the story is the part we don't like to talk about. That was certainly one of the worst weeks of my life. We sort of battled through, I guess. The worst thing was we didn't have a chance to grieve really because everything was happening.

We put all our efforts into making it the best event we could, at the same time remembering and respecting Dan and his family. We had little tributes done, special helmets and stickers made and the trophy for the highest ranked International driver at the event was named after Dan. When we got to the Sunday night after the race, it was like uncorking the bottle. All the emotions came out as we tipped our hats to him.

When Dario [Franchitti] won Indy the next year, that really meant something. That day was just amazing; seeing the entire crowd wearing the white glasses in tribute to Dan. I can tell you that night was one huge celebration with all the clan from Scotland.

I'd just gotten to bed the following morning when Dario rang to see if I wanted to get my photo taken with him. So, I jumped straight out of bed and went down to the track. They were packing up when I got there, but Dario made them put everything back.

That photo of Dario and me in the white-rimmed glasses with the Borg Warner trophy is one of the most special photos I've ever been involved in. ■

> "When Dario [Franchitti] won Indy the following year. That day was just amazing; seeing the entire crowd wearing the white glasses in tribute to Dan"

From left: Darren Turner stepped in to partner James Courtney; the Dan Wheldon trophy for best international driver; White glasses back with the Borg Warner Trophy, Indianapolis, 2012

The international turn out for the inaugural Dan Wheldon Memorial Kart Race at a freezing Daytona Milton Keynes track close to where Dan grew up showed the respect among his peers. Alongside the family are such as IndyCar stars Dario Franchitti, James Hinchcliffe, former karting rival Anthony Davidson, ex-CART racer Nic Minassian and many more

DANNY BOY

Having met as mayhem-causing race school instructors, a a memorial kart race was the best way to honor his buddy

Jenson Button with Mowlem; Former Formula 1 racer Martin Brundle joined in

by JOHNNY MOWLEM

■ SPORTSCAR RACER

DAN CONNECTION
Racing school instructors 1996-1999, organizer of first Dan Wheldon Memorial Kart challenge, 2011

To me, he was "Danny" – it took me until only recently to call him Dan. Little Danny came to the Brands Hatch Racing School as an instructor when he was 17. I was one of the senior instructors, and I'd been around a while, about seven years.

Immediately, I got along very well with him, and took him under my wing. In those days, you had a lot more leeway as an instructor, and you could more or less do what you wanted. It was like the lunatics running the asylum! "Danny" came into that as a quite impressionable 17-year-old. There was me, Mark Webber, Gary Ayles, Nic Minassian and loads of other guys just beginning to break into the professional racing driver ranks, all basically doing what the hell we wanted. Health and safety hadn't shackled us the way the racing schools are nowadays.

We'd do the initial trial with the customer and then, afterward, we'd show them lines, slowly, then show them a lap at full speed, curbs, sliding, all of it. Dan and I used to have some epic races in the

school BMWs, trying to knock each other's mirrors off, probably scaring the hell out of the pupils.... One time I stopped in pit lane, and he ran into the back of me so hard the air bag went off.

Dan loved it all, but while he learned how to have a good time, he also wanted to know how to progress. Even then he was focused. I'm sure he was looking at us, thinking: "This is the life I want to lead, being a professional racecar driver."

It was the mid- to late-'90s, and we worked together for 15-20 days a month for a good couple of years. Dan was becoming a professional and earning his own money instructing, and we used to speak about his plans a lot. I was racing for Jackie Stewart and Paul Stewart Racing at the time, so I guess he saw me as someone going down the road he was trying to go down. He'd ask a ton of questions about how to move forward in racing. He was nine years younger than me, but nine years at that age is a lot.

We did talk about America. I knew he didn't have money behind him like some of the kids did – that's why he was earning money at Brands. I told him if he started doing well, the one thing I'd found in America was they don't ask, "How much money have you got?" They ask, "How much money do you want to be paid?" Things have changed now, but back then that's how it was.

He did start winning, with the USF2000 championship in his first year. Some of his races supported mine in sports cars that year, and he'd come to our truck and hang out. We'd laugh at how cool this

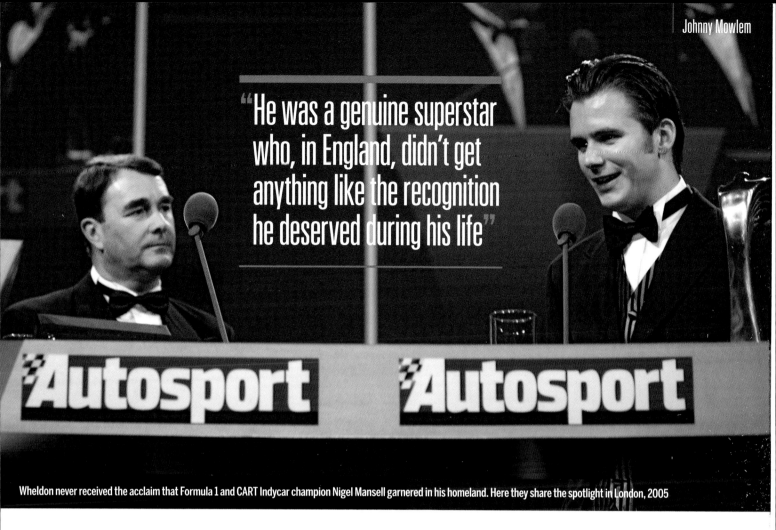

" He was a genuine superstar who, in England, didn't get anything like the recognition he deserved during his life "

Wheldon never received the acclaim that Formula 1 and CART Indycar champion Nigel Mansell garnered in his homeland. Here they share the spotlight in London, 2005

was both racing in America, and both doing well. It was so good to see what happened there as he kept moving up, and kept winning!

We didn't see each other as often once he reached IndyCar, but whenever we did see each other it was like turning back time.

One particular time was the Autosport Awards in London, England, in 2005. We hung out together the entire evening, and he was just like little 18-year-old Danny...and we had so much fun! I will never forget that.

He had just had his monster year, winning the Indy 500 and the championship. He was rightly being lauded, up on the stage with Britain's national hero Nigel Mansell, and there were rumors of Dan going to F1, where Mansell had become a world superstar. Dan's career was really taking off, going through the roof – it should only have been a matter of time before he had that "Mansell-mania"-type recognition and fame at home.

That is what annoyed me later; the outpouring of emotion in the UK national press after he died. Not so much that he was getting coverage, but my overwhelming feeling was, "Why the hell didn't you do this before?" He was a genuine superstar who, in England, didn't get anything like the recognition he deserved during his life. It was very unfortunate that I was commentating live for television during that Vegas race, and afterward I had TV and radio stations calling me up for interviews. All I could think was, "Why weren't you making this fuss when he won the Indy 500 a few months ago?!"

But it wasn't the right time for me to voice that opinion or give it an airing. It wouldn't have been nice for the family either.

That's one of the reasons I did the kart event in Milton Keynes that December, just a few miles from where he grew up. I wanted it to be a happy occasion for his family. I did most of the organizing while I was out in Zuhai, China, racing for Lotus and I was probably concentrating more on the karting than I was on my racing! I was on the phone to Jenson Button, Anthony Davidson, people like that, making sure they came. It was nice, because they turned up, and no one gave a damn about the racing, it was purely about just being there and remembering Dan.

I introduced paying cash to dock laps off of people or paying for getting laps back yourself, or to black-flag people. I got four or five people together, and all of us made donations to make absolutely certain that Clive Wheldon's team won the race!

The feedback I got from that night makes it honestly one of the best things I've ever done. But I wasn't doing it for me. I was doing it for Dan – Danny – and, more importantly, Clive, Holly and the family. That's what it was about. I don't think it could have gone any better, it was like the perfect evening.

Add in the fact that we raised the better part of $30,000 for Alzheimer's research. I know Danny would have been really happy about that because of his mother's situation at the time.

The only shame was that we had to run it at all. A crying shame. ∎

HARD ACT TO FOLLOW

Taking the cherished seat of a friend and an IndyCar racing legend was a tough task

By JAMES HINCHCLIFFE

■ INDYCAR RACE WINNER

DAN CONNECTION
Family friend and selected to take over car #27

I first met Dan through Dario [Franchitti] when I was racing Indy Lights back in 2009. I naturally knew who he was and followed his career up to that point. That's one of the sad things about it all; we had a pretty fun night at the championship banquet at the end of the 2010 season and, in 2011, we had really started to hang out a bit more. We really only had a couple of races, the 500 and Kentucky before we were in Vegas together.

But throughout 2011, we were a little bit closer. Even though he wasn't racing, he was still present at the racetrack. Everybody was always picking his brain about the development of the new car, and he was at the track doing his TV commentary. He was great at that – he was such a natural. It was something you could tell he really enjoyed. When you put a guy who loves racing as much as Dan did in front of a microphone to talk about racing, it's an easy, natural

thing to do. It came across so well on television. He had a lot of good insights, just the right amount to make it sound like he knew what he was talking about, but in such an uncomplicated way that a layman would understand.

After Las Vegas, it was widely reported that the deal was done and that Dan was to have gone back to Andretti. I can honestly say that when Newman Haas shut their doors at the beginning of December that year, I didn't think for one second I would have even been on a long list, never mind a short list, to take over the #27.

When I got the call from J.F. Thormann at Andretti, I was taken aback to be honest. The thought of being considered to fill in for a guy like Dan was incredible. It was something that did weigh pretty heavily on me. As we got further along, I genuinely wanted to, and did, reach out to the family because it was something I took very seriously. Dan's were awfully big, very nice, pretty white shoes to fill! I wanted to make sure everybody was going to be OK with it.

That was the start of a very good and close relationship with the family, especially Holly. She's become like a little sister to me. She was there when I had my first race at St. Pete in front of his family in that car, in Dan's car, which is what I always considered it was when I was driving there.

PHIL ABBOTT/LAT. OPPOSITE PAGE: CHRIS JONES & CHRIS OWENS/IMS, MICHAEL LEVITT & MARIA GRADY/LAT

Opposite: Taking a moment on the St. Pete podium after the first win; karting with Susie and gang; on parade with Holly; showing the "Way"

Obviously, a year down the road, being able to score my first win, and do it at St. Pete, too, made all of those things just so very special. That's an emotional event for anybody, any time, but being there with Dan's whole family, there's no doubt it was a little extra special. I took a quiet moment at Turn 10 on the cool-down lap to look up at his sign on the street there.

I have to thank him; I've got to believe that I maybe had a bit of help that day because there were a bunch of things that fell right for me that day. It may have been coincidence or it may not have been...you never know.

Holly rode in the 500 Parade with me in 2012. It was definitely tough for everybody being back at the Speedway, with Dan, the defending champion, not being there to defend it. It was a bit surreal, and it brought it all back.

As I said, that first race in 2012 was emotional, but you've got to get on with the job. I got to Indy and it all kind of hit again. I remember going out for qualifying and we ended up P1 with the #27 and, again, I was sitting there and thinking, "That was an awfully convenient gust of wind down the back straight..." Maybe he was trying to help me out the best he could.

In December 2011, the guys in the UK organized the first DW kart race there. Man, that was very cold! But, it was one of those almost therapeutic moments where all these people from all over the world Dan had known and had touched were able to come together. A lot of us knew of each other just from being in the sport, but never actually met. It really was a "celebration of life" event rather than grieving a death. I definitely wish it could have been a couple of degrees warmer but it was a great opportunity for us to get out there and be competitive in a friendly environment.

Since then, Susie's been such a superstar in organizing the annual karting event in Indianapolis, too. It's incredible getting to see the boys grow. Seeing Sebastian getting into karting and pacing the field for us is just so cool. You look at them and you do see little pieces of Dan every time. It's a beautiful thing. On one hand, it's obviously tragic that these kids are growing up without their father but, on the other hand, he very much lives on in both of them. ■

> "Dan's were awfully big, very nice, pretty white shoes to fill!"

SIGN LANGUAGE

Helio Castroneves won the first race of 2012 on the streets on St Pete, one of which was named after the city's hero

Not everyone knows this, but the touching of the Dan Wheldon Way street sign after winning the Grand Prix of St. Petersburg in 2012 wasn't my idea. A safety worker suggested it.

Everybody knows when I win races I climb the fence. I don't know why I stopped in Turn 10 after taking the checkered flag – normally I would've stopped in Turn 1 at the biggest grandstand. But there is another big grandstand in Turn 10, and after that race I stopped there instead.

As I got out of the car, one of the safety workers came running over to me. There were still cars coming around the track on the cool-down lap, so he wanted to make sure I wasn't in danger. This safety guy looked at me and pointed to the street sign. As soon as I saw him point, I was like, "No way."

It was a way to pay tribute and respect to someone we all loved. It was a way to recognize who Dan was. I didn't plan it or think it through. It was just spontaneous. Afterward, I realized that it was a suitable representation for the way all the drivers felt that weekend. I felt like I was representing all of us.

It was destiny that I stopped there and destiny that the safety worker pointed out the sign, but the tribute came from all of us. ∎

Youngsters with winning dreams. Justin Wilson looks on as Dan Wheldon recieves a pre-kart race presentation at a home event in the UK. Years later, the two would still be rivals and winners on the track, and good friends away from it. Sadly, both were taken from us too soon

MAKING SENSE OF IT ALL

The Wheldon and Wilson families have been linked in racing for years — and continue to be connected

DW and JW: The long and the short of it; Holly and Stefan, siblings united; Justin with Susie and Sebastian after Dan's passing

by STEFAN WILSON

- INDYCAR RACER

DAN CONNECTION
Brother of DW's kart and
IndyCar rival, Justin Wilson

knew of Dan because of the history he had racing with my brother, Justin, when they were kids. In 2009, I came to the States; I was there for the whole month of May, spectating and having meetings.

I was staying with friends in Indianapolis, an engineer and his family who used to work with Justin in F3000. That year my friend was at Panther with Dan, so I got to meet him when he came over to the house and so on.

I got to know Dan a little better when we spent some time together at the Indy 500 after party and, while he didn't really know me, he was already up to his jokes.

He had basically been trying to set me up with this girl all month and there was a lot of friendly teasing and banter... First time I meet him and he's already pranking me and joking around. I was looking up to him as an Indy 500 winner, and I didn't expect him to know who I was or to interact with me. That tells you a lot about Dan – he was naturally comfortable with people.

I'm sure that Dan and Justin did talk about their karting days, but all I recall was them talking about what was going on at that moment. They were usually talking about the last race, or the next race, or just having a chat, which was usually pretty funny.

Losing Justin was probably the hardest day of my life, and losing Dan was probably the second. In 2011, I was running the full season in Indy Lights with Andretti Autosport. I was in Las Vegas, and I was obviously devastated when we lost Dan.

I remember seeing him the night before. We'd had qualifying, and we were at the Palms hotel for an Andretti function. The team had a connection there, and they had a bar to themselves for a sponsor event. I was on my way out. When the elevator I was about to get on arrived, Dan and Susie stepped out. We exchanged some words, I don't remember what, and I didn't think much of it at the time, but that's the last time I saw him. It was a tragedy. With it being the last race of the season, you end up thinking about it all winter. He was on our minds a lot.

Looking back now, we didn't reach out as much as we should

have to the Wheldon family when they lost Dan. It was because we almost felt a little guilty. There was such a big connection between Dan and Justin, both born in '78, both raced in karting together and both were racing in IndyCar. So, I think we almost felt survivor's guilt that we lost Dan and Justin was still here... Now, though, we are sharing the same situation.

I know my dad spoke with Clive a little when we lost Justin. Obviously, they knew each other from when Dan and Justin were cadets and juniors in karts. I knew Holly was Dan's sister, but I first met her at Justin's funeral, although only to talk briefly. I got to talk with her more when she came to Indy for the Dan Wheldon Memorial Kart Race shortly after. I was actually a little nervous because I didn't know what we were going to talk about. "How do we make sense of it all?" was all we seemed to be thinking.

It was easy to talk with her. We've obviously been through something very similar – losing older brothers we looked up to – so we can relate with one another.

The one thing that amazed us was how the people, not just in IndyCar, but the fans around the world reached out in both situations. Graham Rahal deserves a thank you for the auctions he was behind for both Dan's and Justin's families. I know all that started when he put his helmet up for auction back in 2011 for Susie and the kids, and it grew from there. I really owe a huge thank you to everyone who helped with the auctions. There were so many who worked behind the scenes to make them happen. They were able to get people from NASCAR, WEC, Formula 1 and more to recognize and acknowledge two top British drivers, and get them to donate items. They did the same to help Julia and the kids four years later.

We are incredibly thankful that so many people reached out and let us know how much people thought of Justin. Myself, my mum and dad, Julia and the kids, it means something to us, and it will mean something to the kids when they grow old enough to understand.

I know Susie and the Wheldon family are still touched by the response they had back then, and I'm sure they draw the same comfort from it. As I said before, there's a connection there between Justin and Dan, and also between our families. They will be thought of often and forever missed. ∎

> "It was easy to talk with Holly. We've obviously been through something very similar — losing older brothers we looked up to"

THE LAP OF HONOR

IN 2012, ONE YEAR AFTER their memorable victory in the 95th Indianapolis 500, Bryan Herta took his driver Dan Wheldon's winning car for a celebratory lap of the 2.5 mile speedway. An estimated 250,000 fans paid tribute, wearing the free white trademark cardboard sunglasses as a mark of respect to Dan. Herta said after, "It was emotional, but great to see the outpouring of support for Dan and his family. There are a lot of people still feeling his loss."

RON McQUEENEY/IMS

Husband, father to their two boys and best friend. Susie Wheldon lost so much more than the rest of the world. Here she remembers Dan Wheldon as "one extraordinary human being"

MY DAN

Susie holds the 2011 Indianapolis 500 Winner's Ring; tattoos forever, Las Vegas; Dan the family man, with youngest son, Oliver

THE BOTTOM LINE is that everybody knows Dan as this awesome racecar driver, and he definitely was successful and amazingly talented. Yet the boys and I got to see this incredible part of him that was out of the public's eye. He was just an extraordinary human being, whether he was a driving a racecar or not. The time we spent at home, away from the track, he really enjoyed and took to it.

People saw Dan as this larger-than-life personality, which he was, and that never changed. This "young playboy" who had fun and partied hard, which he did, was also the guy who knew when to get down to business. For him, being at home was equally as satisfying. Just being with his family, with the boys and me, or his family in England. Dan loved all of that.

Going to England for holidays and simply being there, waking up at three in the morning and coming downstairs to have a cup of tea. We used to do that with Holly and we'd all be sitting around because we'd be jetlagged. Those moments are the ones I love. I hope people see that other side of him, too. And, certainly, for our kids there'll be lots of stories, even outside of racing. I just feel incredibly blessed that I was able to share all of that with him.

We met through my first job out of college. I had graduated from a small school in Tennessee with a degree in journalism and marketing, and I didn't know what direction I wanted to go. I knew a couple of girls who worked for a company called Keystone Marketing, and they were looking for somebody. I desperately wanted to get my feet wet in the corporate world, so I was willing to do anything. I started out as an intern, based in North Carolina, and didn't realize that Winston-Salem is about an hour north of Charlotte, which is NASCAR country. I didn't know a lot about NASCAR either, just what I'd seen on TV. So, I was thrown into it and realized there was this whole world of motor racing and NASCAR. I wasn't sure whether I liked it; it was just kind of a job.

THIS PAGE: CHOWEN PHOTOGRAPHY; OPPOSITE: BENITO SANTOS

Eldest son Sebastian already eying up the ovals in his bedroom; a wife's kiss for the winner. Victory Lane, 2011

They ended up hiring me full time. I was doing more of an administrative job then but really wanted to get my teeth into some kind of PR job and use my degree. At the time, NASCAR didn't allow distilled spirits in their sport but Jim Beam, one of our clients, had wanted to be involved in racing. They settled on Andretti – they wanted to be part of Michael's retirement year, with him doing his last Indy 500 and then also taking on Dan as this young, fresh driver. Kim Green had brought him in to the Andretti Green organization at the time and had a lot of faith in him, and that really fit the brand as well.

So, that's how it started. I was given that job as PR manager for Jim Beam and basically was the liaison between the sponsor and the team. I was really wet behind the ears; kind of "fake it 'til you make it." I knew a little bit about racing, but that was NASCAR, certainly not open-wheel which was completely different. I didn't know who all the players were, so I really had to learn fast.

Dan is one of those people who always made you feel at ease, so he was a big part in making me feel like I was doing a good job and part of the team. At this point, obviously, we were friends and just had a working relationship. That first year, in 2003, we were friends for sure but it wasn't until probably 2004 that we started to work together more closely, and we developed a really strong friendship.

His wins in the Indy 500 were, of course, very special. I was with him for both those wins in a different way. I wasn't even working for him in 2005, I was still working for the agency, but I remember being in Victory Lane…well, I wasn't even in Victory Lane, I was kind of standing outside, behind the wire fencing!

In my role as PR and certainly as his PA, I was always behind the

> ## "His wins in the Indy 500 were, of course, very special. I was with him for both in a different way"

scenes and I really enjoyed that role. I liked making things happen but not necessarily in the spotlight – even after we got married. So, in 2005, I was just kind of doing my thing, making sure Jim Beam was part of it and everything. He looked over at me, reached out and grabbed me, and gave me the biggest hug. It was like, "Oh, my God, this is awesome! Thank you so much." He wanted me to be a part of that moment for him, which I thought was really cool because I was just the PR person. I realized how much he valued our friendship at that point. I was outside and he was inside Victory Lane with all the fanfare, and he wanted to share that moment with me.

That night he was just raging and partying. Jim Beam threw this huge party and there were so many people. I was the one who had to stay sober because he had to be back at the track at six o'clock the next morning; somebody needed to be responsible. I don't even know what time it was that we rolled back to the hotel. It had to be about 5 a.m., and he had to leave at 5:30. He just had time to shower, change, and get back to the speedway where they were doing all those media appearances. That's where he fell asleep, waiting for his radio interview to be patched in….

Dan finished out his contract at Andretti Green then signed with Chip. It was at that time he made the move down to Florida. He was the reigning Indy 500 winner and champion, so he was getting busy, and Dan, as anybody who knew him can tell you, was very organized, very meticulous. He hired me as his PA, to manage his day-to-day business, so that all he had to do was worry about going to the racetrack and racing. We had already developed a pretty strong bond before I started working for him but that definitely brought us closer together because we were traveling everywhere.

After New Year's Day 2006, we hit the ground running with work. We went to Japan to a big Honda press conference with a lot of other athletes. That was followed by a whirlwind of testing and media appearances, so we traveled together to all of those. He'd just finished building his house then, so I would work on his personal business as well. We spent a lot of time together, but it wasn't until around the middle of 2007 that we became an item. I worked for him for almost two years before we were together as a couple.

It's funny, at the end of 2007, we went to a couple of races, but were keeping it low key. Dan proposed to me that December. A day or two later we were at the open test at Homestead. He was still at Ganassi and I was chewing the fat with the guys on the team. They were asking what I was doing for the holidays. Nobody saw it coming when I said, "Oh, I got engaged". I'd never brought a guy to the track, they'd never seen me with anybody and all of a sudden I'm engaged. They asked who to, and when I said Dan they were like, "Oh, OK...wait, Dan? Dan Wheldon?" There were definitely some shocked people! A few had a suspicion and felt like we should end up together, or they were completely floored. It was the best-kept secret in racing!

The Indy 500 was just such a different experience in 2011. We were married by then, and Dan didn't have a full-time ride. He decided to go with Bryan [Herta] for the 500 and had faith in his team in only their second start at Indy. It really was the underdog, but Dan had so much self-belief. Even when he didn't have a contract that year, he never doubted his ability, and they fed off that as a team. His positivity and being able to communicate that, "Hey we have a shot at this, let's all get our heads into it because we do have a chance here." I think they started to believe that possibility.

For the 500, I had complete "Mommy brain"! I'd just had Oliver who was a couple of months old, and I had a two-year-old...you don't sleep. I was holed up in this basic hotel room, with one bed and a crib. It was super-stressful, yet I was trying to make it the least amount of stress for Dan because it was a huge month for him, and it's very taxing emotionally and physically. Dan actually said to one of our friends that he thought I was going to go home.

I was in my zone trying to take care of the kids and all that, but there are still moments that stick out. I remember being down in the pits watching the race and watching it all unfold. He'd qualified well and was running in the top 10 for the majority of the race. With five laps to go, he was fifth or sixth or whatever, and all of a sudden I see people peeling off and I'm thinking, "Oh, my God...." With two laps to go, I didn't even know where to go, like "What's going on here?", and he wasn't even leading the race.

Then everything that happened with JR Hildebrand, at the last turn, took a minute to register. And there's me, the one who had had to get him into Victory Lane all the times he'd won before in his career; and I was standing there like a complete idiot! "Where do I go, what do I do?" even though I'd done that routine so many times before myself.

The outcome was an amazing story. We didn't show up at the after party until much later. Everyone was there and I think Dan might have been there for about an hour, then it was, "OK let's go home, our kids are there," and we just wanted to have a quiet moment with our family. I can tell you he definitely wasn't hung over for pictures the next day that time!

It was really nice that I was able to share both of those wins with him. It's something that he was proud of, especially to have wins for both of the boys. That was something he really wanted.

Also, I'm sure that on some level it was kind of like a middle finger to everybody who might have thought he was out of a ride, and might not have another chance. But that's the thing with Dan; he always had a plan. He always knew what to do next and made the best of where he was and what he was doing.

Even in the quiet moments in our marriage, he was never down on himself or pissed off at anybody about not having a ride. He didn't say this sucks or this isn't fair, never somebody owes me this, or somebody owes me that

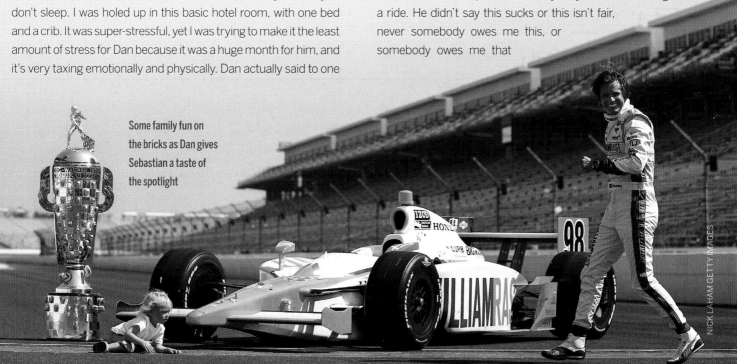

Some family fun on the bricks as Dan gives Sebastian a taste of the spotlight

Sebastian and Oliver get autograph tips from Scott Dixon; at the Victory Banquet

because I'm an Indy 500 champion. He made the decision, and nothing came to fruition before the season started in 2011. He was able to do a lot of great things he wouldn't have done if he'd been in the car, like commentating, which were really great experiences.

Of course, he'd rather have been in the car, but he was always positive and was never a complainer. He just made the best of what position he was in while he weighed it up and figured out what the next opportunities were.

Of course, one of those opportunities was with Andretti again for 2012. It's true that in Las Vegas there was just a really great feeling in the air. It was exciting to know he was going to be back at a top team, back with Michael where he'd won his first 500 and the IndyCar title. Dan was really busy that weekend with promotions and functions, and I had both the kids there, so there was a lot of juggling and events that we couldn't go to, just because the kids were young and they had to be in bed early.

One of the dinners Dan really wanted me to attend was at the Palms hotel to meet some of his sponsors for the next year. I said, "OK, I'll bring Oliver and it'll be fine."

We were supposed to sit down for dinner but Oliver was a little bit restless, so I was going to take him back to the hotel. Dan suggested just calling Jill [the boys' nanny] to come pick him up. I wasn't sure at first because I'd never left him with anyone before; but we did it. It was a really nice, intimate dinner and we were talking about everything. We stopped down by the Andretti sponsor reception, and I got to see a couple of people I hadn't seen for a long time, from back in the Andretti Green days. It was just a really nice feeling and vibe for the whole evening.

> "He loved life and taught me how to live each day to the fullest, with no regrets"

It was getting late, too. Dan said, "I can't stay long, the race is tomorrow." So, we're walking out and he had to use the restroom, which was right beside this tattoo place. Jokingly he said, "Why don't we get a tattoo?" I just laughed. I think he had wanted to do something with the boys' names or family or something for a while, but he'd never done it. I actually wandered in, just to have a look while he was in the bathroom.

He came straight in and said, "Right, what are we doing? Who's going first?" It wasn't like we even thought about it, or talked about it or decided, it was just like, here we are let's go ahead. I knew that I wanted to do something that was meaningful for both of us, so we decided to do our initials. It was just a really cool thing.

We went back to the hotel and Dan's brother Elliott, his friend Jason and Holly were there; we were all just talking and laughing. It was a really good night and a really good, amazing memory to look back on now.

When everything was happening, after Dan passed, obviously there are some things that I don't remember necessarily, just because you kind of go into shock. I was really just there trying to cope myself, and emotionally caring for my kids. I was still nursing Oliver at the time, so I was still trying to feed him without using the bottle. There was so much chaos going on around us and back at the hotel. When I think about it now, obviously, some time has passed, but it was really incredible how everybody came together and supported us. "What can we do?" It was great to see how everybody rallied around.

I run into people all the time who ask me, "Oh, Wheldon, is that...?" and they'll offer sympathy and support. It was definitely something that struck a chord, and not just with people in the racing community. It was a horrible tragedy, and how do you recover from that?

Dan touched so many people. He had an incredible ability to connect, and that was just one of the things that people admired and loved about him. They really did walk away and were like "Wow". He definitely figured out how to make everyone feel and know that they mattered; whether it was a fan, a yellow shirt at Indy or a VP at a Fortune 500 company.

I got so many letters and gifts from people, too. Fans reached out and wanted to share their story with me, maybe the last time they saw Dan or the first time they met him. A military member sent me his flag from where he was stationed overseas. He wanted me to have the flag they'd flown at half-mast and to know that they acknowledged Dan.

All these incredible stories came from people everywhere. I read every single one and I have them all filed away. That will be another great thing to share with the boys, as they get older.

I know Sebastian has memories. Both of them know Dan was a racecar driver and they are familiar with that world. I think Sebastian connects with Dan on that level, as he's karting now. He'll reference and ask, "Did Daddy do that? Did he win a lot of races?"

In as much as he can understand it, he can comprehend it. He actually even talks about how he wants to win the Indy 500 one day! I mean he's six, so I don't think he can grasp the magnitude of it and what it means to win that race, but certainly as he gets older he will.

Oliver won't have any of his own memories, he was only seven months when Dan passed. It's hard when I look at them sometimes just to think how much they're missing out on because Dan was such a great dad. He loved his boys so much. He was fun and full of energy, and I can see him running around with them and, obviously, being with Sebastian at the track. But they do have a lot of people who can fill in the gaps for them and tell them about Dan as they grow up, just as they have in this book.

I am so grateful for the love and support our family has received, and it is still ongoing. It is so important to me to keep Dan's legacy alive, not just for the fans and those in the racing community, but for our children. He accomplished so much in his career and at such an early age.

But for me, it is so much more than remembering him as a racing driver. He truly was an extraordinary human being. He loved life and taught me how to live each day to the fullest, with no regrets. To make the best of the opportunities you are given, but to always stay hungry. He taught me what it means to love someone unconditionally and made me want to be a better person, a better mother, and a better friend.

In spite of the fact that it is a tragedy Dan is no longer here, he left me with so many gifts I can share with Sebastian and Oliver. I see Dan in them everyday. And, for that, I am forever grateful. ■

CONTINUING THE LEGACY

AFTER EVERYTHING happened I didn't really know what I was going to do, but I wanted to do something. I knew it was important for Dan to continue the work he had started with the Alzheimer's Association and now as a tribute to his mother, too, who has since passed away. It was such an emotional thing for him being able to dedicate that win at Indy in 2011 to his Mom. So, for me to be able to carry on that work for him with the Dan Wheldon Memorial Pro-Am Karting Challenge is a labor of love. It really is.

New Castle Raceway and Mark Dismore Jr. have been incredibly gracious to host the event every year. The response has been amazing, too – I only have to pick up the phone and the drivers who participate every year are always quick to respond, "Yes, we'd love to do it." The sponsors that contribute are asking what they can do

and how they can help. It's turned into this really great event that not only supports Alzheimer's and the Dan Wheldon Foundation but also has become a great way to bring everybody together at the end of the season. It's good for the young karters, too. During the event I put on, there's RoboPong, which is big in the karting world, and something Dan participated in any time he could jump back in a kart. He won it, too! For these up and comers to be able to mingle with IndyCar and Indy 500 winners like Tony Kanaan and Scott Dixon and other pro racers, is special. I'm proud of that for sure, and so proud to carry on the legacy.

That familar, purposeful stride...

DANIEL WHELDON

DOB   June 22, 1978

BORN   Emberton, Milton Keynes, United Kingdom

KARTING CAREER

1988   Champion, RAC British Junior Kart
Championship
Champion, All England Championship

1989   Champion, RAC British Junior Kart
Championship
Champion, All England Championship

1990   Champion, RAC British Junior Kart
Championship
Champion, RAC British Senior Kart
Winter Series

1991   15th, RAC British Senior Kart
Championship (partial season)
2nd, Irish Kart Championship

1992   3rd, RAC British Kart Championship
Champion, Rye House Karting
Winter Series
Champion, Kimbolton Karting
Winter Series
Champion, Fulbeck Karting Winter Series

1993   Champion, RAC British Kart Championship
Champion, Rye House Karting
Winter Series
Champion, Kimbolton Karting
Winter Series
Champion, Fulbeck Karting Winter Series

1994   8th, British Formula A Kart Championship
Champion, Rye House Karting
Winter Series

1995   Winner, CIK FIA Senna World Cup
Kart, Japan
2nd, British STP SuperPrix
5th, British Formula A Kart Championship

THE WHELDON COLLECTION

RACING CAREER

1996   British Formula Vauxhall Junior Championship

CAR   Vauxhall Junior

TEAM   Jim Lee Racing

RESULT   Runner-up to champion Tim Mullen

RND	VENUE	RESULT
1	Donington Park	-
2	Brands Hatch (Indy)	1st
3	Thruxton	3rd
4	Thruxton	-
5	Silverstone	1st
6	Oulton Park	3rd
7	Snetterton	5th
8	Brands Hatch (GP)	5th
9	Knockhill	4th
10	Knockhill	2nd
11	Oulton Park (Fosters)	1st
12	Thruxton	4th
13	Donington Park	-
14	Donington Park	3rd
15	Brands Hatch (Indy)	-

(- denotes finished outside the top six or
was not classified)

JEFF BLOXHAM/LAT

1997   Slick 50 British Formula Ford Championship

CAR   Van Diemen RF97-Zetec

TEAM   Andy Welch Racing

RESULT   Joint fourth with Carl Breeze, behind
champion Jacky van der Ende, Ricardo
Sperafico and Richard Tarling

RND	VENUE	RESULT
1	Donington Park	1st
2	Silverstone	2nd
3	Brands Hatch (Indy)	-
4	Oulton Park (Fosters)	1st
5	Donington Park	-
6	Donington Park	-
7	Croft	2nd
8	Knockhill	-
9	Knockhill	4th
10	Snetterton	5th
11	Thruxton	-
12	Brands Hatch (GP)	4th
13	Silverstone	

(- denotes finished outside the top six or was not classified)

MICHAEL LEVITT/LAT

1998   Slick 50 Formula Ford Championship

TEAM   Duckhams Van Diemen

CAR   Van Diemen RF98-Zetec

RESULT   Third behind champion Jenson Button

RND	VENUE	RESULT
1	Thruxton	-
2	Silverstone	-
3	Donington Park	4th
4	Brands Hatch (Indy)	2nd
5	Oulton Park (Fosters)	-
6	Donington Park	-
7	Croft	1st
8	Snetterton	1st
9	Thruxton	2nd
10	Knockhill	-
11	Knockhill	5th
12	Brands Hatch (Indy)	-
13	Oulton Park (Fosters)	1st
14	Silverstone	1st
15	Silverstone	3rd

(- denotes finished outside the top six or was not classified)

1999   USF2000

TEAM   Jayhard/Primus Racing

CAR   Van Diemen RF-99 F2k

RESULT   Series Champion

RND	VENUE	RESULT
1	Phoenix	2nd
2	Charlotte	2nd
3	Charlotte	1st
4	Mosport	24th
5	Mosport	1st
6	Mid-Ohio	2nd
7	Road Atlanta	26th
8	Road Atlanta	24th
9	Circuit Trios-Rivieres	3rd
10	Mid-Ohio	1st
11	Mid-Ohio	2nd
12	Pikes Peak	1st
13	Sebring	1st
14	Sebring	1st

2000   Toyota Atlantic Championship

TEAM   PPI Motorsports

CAR   Swift 008.a-Toyota

RESULT   Runner-up to champion Buddy Rice

RND	VENUE	RESULT
1	Homestead Miami	1st
2	Homestead Miami	2nd
3	Long Beach	4th
4	Milwaukee	13th
5	Montreal	3rd
6	Cleveland	6th
7	Toronto	3rd
8	Trios-Rivieres	2nd
9	Road America	2nd
10	Monterey	1st
11	Gateway	7th
12	Houston	4th

2001   CART/PPG Dayton Indy Lights

TEAM   PacWest Lights

CAR   Lola T97/20-Buick

RESULT   Runner-up to Townsend Bell

RND	VENUE	RESULT
1	Monterrey (Mexico)	5th
2	Long Beach	2nd
3	Texas	10th
4	Milwaukee	3rd
5	Portland	10th
6	Kansas	3rd
7	Toronto	7th
8	Mid-Ohio	2nd
9	Gateway	1st
10	Road Atlanta	1st
11	Monterey	5th
12	Fontana	2nd

2002   Indy Racing League

TEAM   Panther Racing

CAR   Dallara IR-02-Chevrolet

RESULT   36th behind champion Sam Hornish Jr

(partial season)

RND	VENUE	RESULT
14	Chicago	10th
15	Texas	15th

TIM JOHNSON/LAT

2005 INDYCAR SERIES CHAMPION Dan Wheldon

2003 IndyCar Series

TEAM	Andretti Green Racing
CAR	Dallara IR-03-Honda
RESULT	11th behind champion Scott Dixon

(missed first two races)

RND	VENUE	RESULT
3	Motegi (Japan)	7th
4	Indianapolis 500	19th
5	Texas	20th
6	Pikes Peak	19th
7	Richmond	8th
8	Kansas	21st
9	Nashville	4th
10	Michigan	20th
11	Gateway	5th
12	Kentucky	8th
13	Nazareth	7th
14	Chicagoland	4th
15	Fontana	4th
16	Texas	3rd

2004 IndyCar Series

TEAM	Andretti Green Racing
CAR	Dallara IR-04-Honda
RESULT	2nd behind champion Tony Kanaan

RND	VENUE	RESULT
1	Homestead	3rd
2	Phoenix	3rd
3	Motegi	1st
4	Indianapolis 500	3rd
5	Texas	13th
6	Richmond	1st
7	Kansas	9th
8	Nashville	13th
9	Milwaukee	18th
10	Michigan	3rd
11	Kentucky	3rd
12	Pikes Peak	3rd
13	Nazareth	1st
14	Chicago	4th
15	Fontana	3rd
16	Texas	3rd

2005 IndyCar Series

TEAM	Andretti Green Racing
CAR	Dallara IR-05-Honda
RESULT	Series champion

RND	VENUE	RESULT
1	Homestead	1st
2	Phoenix	6th
3	St Petersburg	1st
4	Motegi	1st
5	Indianapolis 500	1st
6	Texas	6th
7	Richmond	5th
8	Kanas	2nd
9	Nashville	21st
10	Milwaukee	5th
11	Michigan	2nd
12	Kentucky	3rd
13	Pikes Peak	1st
14	Sonoma	18th
15	Chicago	1st
16	Watkins Glen	5th
17	Fontana	6th

2006 IndyCar Series

TEAM	Chip Ganassi Racing
CAR	Dallara IR-05-Honda
RESULT	2nd behind champion Sam Hornish Jr

RND	VENUE	RESULT
1	Homestead	1st
2	St Petersburg	16th
3	Motegi	2nd
4	Indianapolis 500	4th
5	Watkins Glen	15th
6	Texas	3rd
7	Richmond	9th
8	Kansas	2nd
9	Nashville	2nd
10	Milwaukee	10th
11	Michigan	3rd
12	Kentucky	4th
13	Sonoma	6th
14	Chicago	1st

2007 IndyCar Series

TEAM	Chip Ganassi Racing
CAR	Dallara IR-05-Honda
RESULT	4th behind series champion D. Franchitti

RND	VENUE	RESULT
1	Homestead	1st
2	St Petersburg	9th
3	Motegi	2nd
4	Kansas	1st
5	Indianapolis 500	22nd
6	Milwaukee	3rd
7	Texas	15th
8	Iowa	11th
9	Richmond	3rd
10	Watkins Glen	7th
11	Nashville	8th
12	Mid-Ohio	10th
13	Michigan	12th
14	Kentucky	17th
15	Sonoma	7th
16	Detroit	3rd
17	Chicago	13th

2008 IndyCar Series

TEAM	Chip Ganassi Racing
CAR	Dallara IR-05-Honda
RESULT	4th behind series champion Scott Dixon

RND	VENUE	RESULT
1	Homestead	3rd
2	St Petersburg	12th
3	Motegi	4th
4	Kansas	1st
5	Indianapolis	12th
6	Milwaukee	4th
7	Texas	4th
8	Iowa	1st
9	Richmond	4th
10	Watkins Glen	24th
11	Nashville	2nd
12	Mid-Ohio	17th
13	Edmonton	7th
14	Kentucky	5th
15	Sonoma	4th
16	Detroit	20th
17	Chicago	6th

Non-Championship Race

| TEAM | Panther Racing |
| CAR | Dallara IR-05-Honda |

RND	VENUE	RESULT
NA	Surfers Paradise	11th

2009 IndyCar Series

TEAM	Panther Racing
CAR	Dallara IR-05-Honda
RESULT	10th behind series champion D. Franchitti

RND	VENUE	RESULT
1	St Petersburg	14th
2	Long Beach	5th
3	Kansas	10th
4	Indianapolis 500	2nd
5	Milwaukee	10th
6	Texas	7th
7	Iowa	4th
8	Richmond	10th
9	Watkins Glen	10th
10	Toronto	14th
11	Edmonton	15th
12	Kentucky	11th
13	Mid-Ohio	16th
14	Sonoma	12th
15	Chicago	22nd
16	Motegi	8th
17	Homestead	21st

2010 IndyCar Series

TEAM	Panther Racing
CAR	Dallara IR-05-Honda
RESULT	9th behind series champion D. Franchitti

RND	VENUE	RESULT
1	Sao Paulo	5th
2	St Petersburg	20th
3	Alabama	11th
4	Long Beach	9th
5	Kansas	15th
6	Indianapolis 500	2nd
7	Texas	9th
8	Iowa	11th
9	Watkins Glen	6th
10	Toronto	10th
11	Edmonton	20th
12	Mid-Ohio	14th
13	Sonoma	25th
14	Chicago	2nd
15	Kentucky	3rd
16	Motegi	10th
17	Homestead	9th

2011 IndyCar Series

| TEAM | Bryan Herta Autosport |
| CAR | Dallara IR-05-Honda |

RND	VENUE	RESULT
5	Indianapolis 500	1st

| TEAM | Sam Schmidt Motorsports |
| CAR | Dallara IR-05-Honda |

RND	VENUE	RESULT
17	Kentucky	14th
(18	Las Vegas	Race cancelled)

OTHER RACES

2004 Milhas de Granja Viana

TEAM	Shell	
RND	VENUE	RESULT
N/A	Granja Viana Indoor Kart, Brazil	1st

2005 Daytona 24 Hour Race

TEAM	Howard Boss Motorsports	
CAR	Crawford Pontiac	
CLASS	DP	
TEAMMATES	Dario Franchitti, Marino Franchitti, Milka Duno	
RND	VENUE	RESULT
1	Daytona International Speedway	33rd DNF

2005 TaG/Yamaha 200 Lap Endurance Race

TEAM	Comet Kart Sales	
RND	VENUE	RESULT
N/A	New Castle Motorsports Park	1st

2005 Milhas de Granja Viana

RND	VENUE	RESULT
N/A	Granja Viana Indoor Kart, Brazil	1st

F PEIRCE WILLIAMS

2006 Daytona 24 Hour Race

TEAM	Chip Ganassi Racing	
CAR	Riley MkXI Lexus	
CLASS	DP	
TEAMMATES	Scott Dixon, Casey Mears	
RND	VENUE	RESULT
1	Daytona International Speedway	1st

2006 Robo-Pong 200 Kart Race

TEAM	Comet Kart Sales	
RND	VENUE	RESULT
N/A	New Castle Motorsports Park	35th

2006 Milhas de Granja Viana

RND	VENUE	RESULT
N/A	Granja Viana Indoor Kart, Brazil	2nd

2007 Daytona 24 Hour Race

TEAM	Chip Ganassi Racing	
CAR	Riley MkXI Lexus V8	
CLASS	DP	
TEAMMATES	Scott Dixon, Memo Rojas	
RND	VENUE	RESULT
1	Daytona International Speedway	41st

2007 Mazda Robo-Pong 200 Kart Race

TEAM	Comet Kart Sales	
RND	VENUE	RESULT
N/A	New Castle Motorsports Park	4th

2008 Daytona 24 Hour Race

TEAM	Chip Ganassi Racing	
CAR	Riley MkXI Lexus V8	
CLASS	DP	
TEAMMATES	Scott Dixon, Alex Lloyd, Salvador Duran	
RND	VENUE	RESULT
1	Daytona International Speedway	44th

2008 Robo-Pong 200 Kart Race

TEAM	Comet Kart Sales	
RND	VENUE	RESULT
N/A	New Castle Motorsports Park	15th

2008 All-Stars Karting Classic – Masters

TEAM	Arrows USA	
RND	VENUE	RESULT
N/A	Orange County Convention Center	13th

2008 SKUSA SuperNationals XII - TaG Senior

TEAM	Top Kart	
RND	VENUE	RESULT
N/A	Las Vegas	26th

2009 Mazda Robo-Pong 200

TEAM	Comet Kart Sales - Arrow	
RND	VENUE	RESULT
N/A	New Castle Motorsports Park	34th

2009 SKUSA SuperNationals XIII - TaG Senior

TEAM	Top Kart	
RND	VENUE	RESULT
N/A	Las Vegas	4th

2010 Robo-Pong 200

TEAM	Comet Kart Sales – Arrow	
RND	VENUE	RESULT
N/A	New Castle Motorsports Park	11th

2010 SKUSA SuperNationals XIV - TaG Senior

TEAM	KartSport North America – Arrow	
RND	VENUE	RESULT
N/A	Las Vegas	11th

REMEMBERING DAN WHELDON
LIONHEART
by Andy Hallbery & Jeff Olson

Editor	Andy Hallbery
Writer	Jeff Olson
Art Director	Steve Moore – eroomcreative.com
Managing Editor	Dyanne Gilliam
Assistant Editor	Johanna Husband
Cover Design	Sarah Henderson
Reprographics	Nathan Sargent
Project Manager	Holly Wheldon
Publisher	Susie Wheldon, Lionheart Books, LLC
Photography	**LAT** Michael Levitt, Phil Abbott, F Peirce Williams, Dan Streck, Dan R Boyd, Paul Webb, Walt Kuhn, Jeff Bloxham, Malcolm Griffiths, Michael Kim, Perry Nelson, Glenn Dunbar, Gregg Feistman, Mark Horsburgh, Peter Spinney, Lorenzo Bellanca, Tim Johnson
	Indianapolis Motor Speedway Ron McQueeney, Dana Garrett, Chris Jones, Dan Helrigel, Jim Haines, Shawn Gritzmacher, Steve Snoddy, John Cote, Leigh Spargur
	Motorsport.com Eric Gilbert, Jack Durbin, Ken Plotkin
	Getty Images Darrell Ingham, Robert Laberge, Nick Laham, Kevin Mazur, Rick Diamond, Christ Graythen, Jun Sato, Bob Harmayer
	Others Clive Wheldon, Benito Santos, Steve Swope, Steve Shunck, Michael Voorhees, Chowen Photography, Ann Miller Carr, Chris Walker, Jakob Ebrey, Jason Fowler, Joe Jacobson, Jenn St Cin, Michael Johnson, Rob DeMatti, John Oreovicz, Anne Proffit, Denis Davidson,
Thank you	American Honda Motor Company, T.E. McHale, Indianapolis Motor Speedway, Clive Wheldon, Dario Franchitti, Dan Layton, Tim Wright/LAT, Daniel Eaton & Mark Paul/Getty Images, Steve Shunck, Paul Pfanner, RACER magazine, Miguel Vega, Paul Laguette, Marshall Pruett, Paul Lawrence, Will Mann, Tom Rich, Mighty Fine Productions, Mark Plowman
Remembering	Justin Wilson, Ginny Ghee, Brenda McHale

Dan Wheldon at the Indy500

2007 Retired

2008 Finished 12th

2009 Finished 2nd

2010 Finished 2nd

2011 Finished 1st